THE COMPLETE GUIDE TO RFPS FOR LIBRARIES

D1707749

THE COMPLETE GUIDE TO RFPs FOR LIBRARIES

Frances C. Wilkinson and
Sever Bordeianu, Editors

Foreword by Katina Strauch

LIBRARIES
UNLIMITED™

An Imprint of ABC-CLIO, LLC
Santa Barbara, California • Denver, Colorado

Library of Congress Cataloging in Publication Control Number: 2018016326

ISBN: 978-1-4408-5939-7 (paperback)
      978-1-4408-5940-3 (eBook)

22   21   20   19   18   1   2   3   4   5

This book is also available as an ebook.

Libraries Unlimited
An Imprint of ABC-CLIO, LLC

ABC-CLIO, LLC
130 Cremona Drive, P.O. Box 1911
Santa Barbara, California 93116-1911
www.abc-clio.com

This book is printed on acid-free paper ∞
Manufactured in the United States of America

To our colleague, friend, and mentor: Linda K. Lewis. You were our
role model and we will always miss you.
—Fran and Sever

To Mariví. You are always an inspiration.
—Sever

CONTENTS

PART II: WRITING AND EVALUATING SPECIFIC TYPES OF RFPs

COLLECTIONS

WRITING AND EVALUATING SPECIFIC TYPES OF RFPs: INTEGRATED LIBRARY SYSTEMS

WRITING AND EVALUATING SPECIFIC TYPES OF RFPs: OTHER RFPs FOR LIBRARIES

PART III: VENDOR PERSPECTIVES AND ETHICS

Chapter 14: Vendors' Perspectives on Collections RFPs   227

Justin D. Clarke and Patricia M. Rodgers

Chapter 15: The Librarian–Vendor Relationship   239

Stephen Bosch

FOREWORD

A request for proposal (RFP) is a means by which a library or organization announces that funding is available for a particular project or program. Companies are invited to submit a proposal for the project's accomplishment. *The Complete Guide to RFPs for Libraries* is a wonderfully thorough look at the complete procurement process, including the philosophy behind RFPs, different types of requests, and the pros and cons in their preparation. The editors are meticulous in describing different types of RFPs through the contribution of chapter authors who are experts in their area of library or vendor operations and who have experience with the RFP process.

The book covers such essential questions as the following: What type of requests should be written (request for information [RFI], request for quotation [RFQ], or RFP) to meet the library's needs? What questions should be asked? How should responses be evaluated? How should the award be announced? Also, discussed are the RFP's aftermath, changing vendors, implementation, monitoring, evaluation, and follow-up.

The Complete Guide to RFPs for Libraries answers all those questions for academic, public, and school library collections, in various formats. For all of us, the important topics are covered thoroughly including descriptions, sample questions, and the evaluation process. The topics are comprehensive. They range from traditional—selecting approval plans for books and agents for serials, commercial binder services, and integrated library systems—to the sometimes overlooked or new areas including radio-frequency identification (RFID) systems, services for digitization projects, and emergency and disaster recovery services.

The final section provides the vendor perspectives and perceptions and is especially worthwhile, sharing the vendor's point of view on RFPs as well as the librarian–vendor relationship. Too often, librarians only see their point of view, and it is refreshing to give vendors a voice in the book. The section on ethics for librarians during the RFP process is also invaluable.

In a time when supposedly everything is "on the web" or "in Wikipedia," this monograph is an essential reference and go-to resource on the RFP bidding and solicitation process. Whether you are new to RFPs or an experienced hand, you will find something useful in this book.

—Katina Strauch
Charleston, South Carolina

PREFACE

In 1998, my colleague Connie Capers Thorson and I published a book titled *The RFP Process: Effective Management of the Acquisition of Library Materials* with Libraries Unlimited. Some chapters were written by us, while other chapters were written by either librarians or vendors with RFP expertise. Many aspects of libraries have changed in the past two decades, and RFPs are becoming more important and commonplace than ever. The profession has learned the value of the RFP process in procuring quality goods and services, and even libraries that are not obligated by statute to use the RFP process often choose that route. The RFP process is a tried and true method of evaluating vendors to provide the best product or service for the best price.

The first book focused primarily on developing academic library RFPs for a variety of approval plans dealing with a multitude of subjects such as fine arts, science, technology, and engineering, or geographic areas like Latin America, and included a chapter on Domestic and Foreign Serials. There was also a chapter that anticipated the dramatic changes that were starting to take place in the profession, which addressed the emerging market for "Library System Interfaces and Electronic Services from Book and Serials Vendors." It was around that time that serials vendors and some book vendors began their transformation into providers of online content while still continuing to provide the traditional services that libraries were accustomed to, such as subscriptions and claims for print journals. But basically, in 1998 most libraries would only issue an RFP for a book vendor, a serial vendor, or an integrated library system and maybe a binder.

Many of the issues that were emerging then have become commonplace. Today, libraries take for granted that a serial vendor will provide a full array of products, both print and full text electronic, that did not exist to the same extent in 1998. The pricing models have also evolved so that both vendors and librarians know what to expect. There are also areas that simply were not prominent enough in 1998 to warrant discussion, such as digitization and RFID systems, and libraries had just begun to develop emergency/disaster recovery plans.

The current book, with chapters coauthored and coedited with my colleague Sever Bordeianu, deals with products and services available to a modern academic, public, and school library. It is intended to be more extensive and as such addresses both traditional goods and services, such as approval plans for books and subscription services for serials, and new areas mentioned earlier. But the book attempts to accomplish more than that. It shows that it is possible to craft an RFP for such very diverse goods and services as integrated library systems, bindery services, and the abovementioned digitization, radio-frequency identification (RFID), and emergency/disaster recovery services using a set of basic principles. The vendors' perspectives are also represented as well as the critically important librarian–vendor relationship. The book's final chapter highlights the significance of ethics in business transactions and how ethical behavior ensures fairness for all parties involved.

On another level, the 1998 book and the current version are similar. There are chapters that address the theory, practice, and mechanics of RFPs and the detailed discussions of how to evaluate vendor responses. There are undoubtedly some emerging areas that the current book does not address, but the background on how to develop and implement an RFP will be useful for adapting the process to goods and services not covered in this book. Clearly, we feel that despite the intensity and time requirements of doing an RFP, it is a worthwhile effort, and it is the best insurance for acquiring essential, expensive products and services.

INTRODUCTION

The request for proposal (RFP) is a powerful tool that a library can use to purchase expensive goods or services. The RFP provides a structured framework for describing a need that has to be addressed, a product or service that can be purchased to address that need, communication with vendors, criteria for evaluating vendor offers, and a clear timeline to be followed by both the library and the vendor. While the structure of RFPs is reasonably well defined, their contents can be tailored to the specific product or service that the library is purchasing. A well-designed RFP will not only make the purchase decision more rational and objective, but it will also facilitate the implementation of the new services once the contract has been signed.

RFPs are common especially in government or state institutions, which are often required by law to follow the process when purchasing products or services that cost over a certain amount of money, for which there is not a sole source vendor. Private institutions and nonprofits, while not required to issue RFPs, can also benefit from the structure and organization of this powerful tool.

While there is enormous flexibility in how to design an RFP, there are some important elements that need to be included: appointment of an RFP committee, a good description of the library's need and the product or service it wishes to purchase, clearly defined evaluation criteria, a realistic timeline for each stage of the process, and clear and open communication between the library or its parent institution and all vendors. In addition, it has to be specified from the beginning who has the authority to approve and issue the contract.

This book will provide a complete guide for writing RFPs for the modern library. It covers a variety of essential products and services. Some are traditional products with which libraries have long experience, like approval plans, serials subscriptions, integrated library systems, or binders. Others are much newer such as digitization services or radio-frequency identification (RFID) systems. Some are less concrete, like the contracts for disaster recovery services. Yet the power of the RFP is that it can be adapted and used in any of these situations because the document is product neutral. It provides the framework for evaluating the products and services and issuing a contract.

Each chapter is written by a librarian or vendor with extensive experience writing, issuing, responding to, and evaluating RFPs. Part I of the book contains the introductory chapters that explain in detail the reasons for and the mechanics of RFPs. Part II is the librarians' perspective and contains chapters on procurement of most of the expensive goods and services that libraries buy today. Chapters 3–6 deal with RFPs for collections. Chapter 7 addresses consortia negotiations with publishers and recommends using a request for information or request for quotation instead of an RFP. Chapters 8–11 cover electronic services like ILSs, RFID systems, and digitization services. Two of the chapters contain appendices with sample RFP examples and other information. The last two chapters in Part II deal with disaster recovery and bindery, two unique areas that are of vital importance to libraries. Part III of the book contains the vendors' perspectives as well as librarian–vendor relationships. We librarians ask a lot of vendors, and their organizations have limitations just like ours—in personnel, budget, and time. Therefore, it is important to know the vendors' perspective of what it is like to respond to an RFP and why a well-written document with realistic expectations will lead to better results. A poorly written RFP could actually deter some vendors from responding, thus diminishing the library's options. Part III ends with a chapter that addresses ethics in business transactions and how ethical behavior ensures an even playing field for all parties involved. Finally, the book contains an extensive Glossary as well as a detailed Index.

While reading the book from cover to cover would be an instructive exercise, each chapter is complete on its own. Librarians can quickly turn to the chapter that covers the good or service they are considering buying to get a complete guide to how to proceed. The introductory chapters in Part I can also be consulted for a broader understanding on how to issue an RFP, but the individual chapters will provide the details for a specific good or service, from a professional who has actually been involved with a successful RFP.

During our careers, most of us will eventually be responsible for acquiring an expensive product or service for our library. One year, the library may need to get a new ILS; another year, the approval plan vendor may need to be renewed; and the next year, the library may need to contract for digitization services. All libraries should consider contracting with a disaster recovery service. This book provides a complete guide to purchasing these essentials, which enable libraries to function and provide the quality services that we do. We hope you find it helpful.

PART I

OVERVIEW OF
THE COMPETITIVE
PROCUREMENT PROCESS

1

RFP THEORY, PRACTICE, AND PLANNING

Frances C. Wilkinson and Sever Bordeianu

Whether you consider [an] RFP to be a panacea or a plague, participating in the RFP process, either as a librarian or a vendor, need not be a painful experience.

—Bob Schatz and Diane Graves

INTRODUCTION

All types of libraries—academic, public, school, and special libraries—need to purchase various goods and services, including collection materials such as books, journals, databases, and media as well as integrated library systems (ILSs), security systems, digitization services, disaster recovery services, commercial binding services, and so forth. Some libraries, especially private university and school libraries, and some special libraries, may be able to use an informal selection process consisting of little more than reading literature provided by vendors, holding conversations with vendor representatives, and then selecting the vendor that the librarian believes to be best suited. However, for most public institutions, a competitive procurement process is used. Increasingly, the request for proposal (RFP) is considered the most efficient and cost-effective way to select a vendor to provide library goods and services.

RFPs require leadership and time, but these collaborative processes are generally well worth the effort. Further, competitive procurement for state and city libraries is often required by law. "In the late 1970s and 1980s, a number of states amended their procurement codes to include activities engaged in by state agencies not historically subject to such oversight. This was done in an attempt to make competition more honest and fair, and to offer more opportunity for local businesses, particularly those designated as minority businesses, to compete" (Wilkinson and Thorson 1998, 3).

TYPES OF REQUESTS: THE RFP, RFQ, AND RFI

While the competitive procurement process is most often accomplished by employing an RFP process, other formal methods of vendor selection can be used, such as the request for quotation (RFQ) or the request for information (RFI), but they have limitations as stand-alone processes.

The RFQ, sometimes referred to as a "request for quote" or the "bid process," awards the library's account based on the lowest-price vendor bid. This process works well when purchasing specific goods, such as standard office supplies, a specific piece of computer hardware or software, or RFID products where there is little or no variance, but it does not work well when contracting for a service. While price—be it the service charge for serials and databases; discounts for books or commercial binding; or fees for ILSs, disaster recovery services, and so forth—is an important part of the decision, its value diminishes if service is poor. With the RFQ, all factors other than price are generally ignored, so services to libraries may be limited or unreliable, or both.

Unlike the RFQ, the RFI asks the vendor for information about its goods and services and usually does not ask for firm price quotes. The RFI can be a valuable tool to inform librarians' understanding of what different vendors can provide when a full RFP is not required. Also, RFIs can be very useful in the planning phase of an RFP, when librarians are deciding which elements are most important to include prior to writing an RFP. "The less formal nature of the RFI allows vendors to present information about themselves without investing an inordinate amount of time in the preparation of the document" (Wilkinson and Bordeianu 1997, 38). The RFI may prove especially useful when the library is not planning for on-site vendor visits as part of its decision-making process.

The RFP "represents a formalized process for documenting, justifying, and authorizing a procurement; allows for evaluating different solutions; and provides a means for establishing, monitoring and controlling the performance of the winning vendor" (Porter-Roth 1991, 26). In the RFP document, both required and desired elements are clearly stated, along with the steps that vendors must follow to submit a proposal for the library's account. Although the RFP considers many factors beyond pricing, the RFP process is often referred to in the vernacular as "going out for bid" or "the bid," but it should not be confused with the streamlined RFQ.

The RFP provides a concise, reasonably objective method to evaluate vendor proposals and to justify awarding the contract to one vendor over another, presumably avoiding decisions made based on emotional bias either for or against a particular vendor. Though time-consuming, the RFP is often the best method for the library to use because it is the only method that thoroughly considers both vendor service and price. If RFP committee members keep an open mind when evaluating vendor responses, the library will award its account based solely upon the vendor's ability to provide goods and services as ordered, on time, at the agreed-upon price, and to resolve problems occurring at any stage of the process as set forth in the vendor's proposal and confirmed by its references.

WHY LIBRARIES CONTRACT WITH COLLECTION MATERIALS VENDORS

Procurement codes generally allow libraries to purchase materials directly from a publisher, copyright holder, or a sole source; however, when multiple vendors offer the same goods and services, librarians use them because vendors save the library time and staff by providing a single point of service rather than requiring the library to deal with dozens or hundreds of individual publishers. A library vendor—sometimes called an agent, bookseller, dealer, jobber, or supplier—may be large or small, domestic or foreign, and may sell materials in one or more formats or languages. Such vendors may provide one-stop shopping for general materials or be highly specialized in an area such as art exhibition catalogs or gray literature.

Vendors have well-established connections with publishers, and they can place orders, claim missed print materials, provide invoicing to the library, and make payment to the publishers on behalf of the library. They also provide customized reports and recent and projected pricing trends as well as a full array of service and technological options, including databases with bibliographic information. With staffing reductions due to ever-shrinking library budgets, vendors often have more specialized knowledge of languages or formats such as Portuguese music than the library's staff. Materials vendors may also provide cataloging services, shelf-ready books, check-in for print serials, and negotiation of licenses for electronic resources. Ultimately, a partnership is formed between librarians and vendor representatives because librarians rely on vendors for library materials and services, while vendors rely on libraries for their continued existence.

How Librarian–Materials Vendors Relationships Have Evolved

Vendors have existed for many years, and they have been used extensively by librarians since the mid-20th century; however, vendors have existed for much longer than that. Through a complex series of mergers and buyouts and extremely creative and intricate means, some current vendors can trace their lineage back to the 1800s. The relationship between librarians and vendors has evolved over the past 50 years as the information age progressed; however, most core vendor services endure.

The late 1950s witnessed state and federal funding to libraries increase in support of education and technological development. Demand for books, journals, and emerging media increased, requiring new ways to create, reproduce, and disseminate these materials. At that time, the partnership between librarians and vendors mainly involved vendors supplying books and serials in printed format. By the late 1970s, runaway inflation and eroding buying power combined with an explosion of materials being produced to change purchasing patterns of libraries. Vendors were affected by all the events that influenced the library and publishing industries and were caught in the middle (Fisher 1993, 61–69). In the 1980s, two major events changed the library–vendor relationship even further. These included the escalating cost of serials and the introduction of automation into nearly all aspects of library operations. Librarians began to expect their vendors to advocate on their behalf against price increases with publishers and to be forerunners in automation (Presley 1993, 55–56).

The 1990s introduced a new consumerism, further altering the librarian–vendor partnership. Librarians began canceling serials in record numbers and conducting tougher price negotiations, as well as beginning to shift information access to new formats (Shirk 1993, 145). These trends continued in the 21st century as library budgets shrunk even more and electronic formats gradually became ubiquitous (see Chapter 4). Print cancelations and the transition to electronic formats led to reductions in the amount of binding (see Chapter 13). Rapid changes in technology resulted in increased demands for enhanced library systems. Further, many libraries became members of consortia, working with other libraries to procure more advantageous pricing arrangements for electronic packages of journals, often negotiating directly with publishers, eliminating the use of vendors and RFPs altogether (see Chapter 7).

WHY LIBRARIES CONTRACT WITH OTHER TYPES
OF VENDORS AND COMPANIES

While librarians most often use RFPs to identify the best vendor(s) to provide their collection materials, they also make frequent use of RFPs for other services including ILSs (see Chapters 8 and 9). Selecting a new ILS is not only a significant investment financially, but switching to a new ILS is a momentous investment of staff time and effort as well for both backroom support operations and discovery capabilities. As the ILS market consolidates, resulting in innovation slowing for some vendors, the use of RFPs is even more important to safeguard the library's investment as well as to provide a strong mechanism to not only secure best pricing and customer service but also negotiate new areas of innovation and support.

Librarians also use RFPs to make more informed decisions and obtain competitive pricing when contracting with vendors to provide a multitude of other goods and services, including security, inventory, and identification systems (see Chapter 10); digitization services for collections (see Chapter 11); disaster recovery services (see Chapter 12); commercial binding services (see Chapter 13); and many others. RFPs are used to select contractors for library buildings and renovations. They are also used to choose vendors or companies to provide furnishings, café concessions, servers, and computers as well as consultants for branding initiatives, strategic planning services, and training on various topics, or for virtually anything else a library needs.

OPPONENTS AND PROPONENTS OF THE RFP PROCESS

When commencing even the most cursory review of the literature, it becomes clear that both opponents and proponents of the RFP process abound; however, one area that most authors agree upon is that the RFP process is unquestionably both time-consuming and labor-intensive. As a result, many authors have pointed out pitfalls of the RFP process and warned librarians against its use, while others have ultimately sung its praises.

For librarians who are facing the process for the first time, "reactions may include confusion, fear, irritation, frustration, or even anger" (Wilkinson and Lewis, 2008, 1). This can be particularly true for librarians new to the RFP process and who are pleased with their current vendor. They may question why it is necessary to review their existing vendor's performance and services to determine if a new vendor can provide better service or pricing simply because of policy or law requiring competitive procurement.

For over three decades librarians have been warned about the downside to the RFP process. Wanninger (1990, 87) advises that "unless the library has the patience and pocketbook of the Defense Department and the stomach to put up with the expense . . . the Request for Proposal Process is a wicked waste of time and money." Clark and Winters (1990, 272) posit that "another disadvantage is that the law is inconsistently interpreted" and librarians are advised to lobby against the imposition of the process in their libraries. Whether writing about RFPs decades ago or today, most librarians and vendors caution that RFPs can be "badly conceived, constructed, and applied, resulting in few responses by vendors, and disappointments, lost time, and wasted resources for the library" (Matthews, Simon, and Williams 1987).

Over the past several decades, RFPs for most types of public institutions have become the norm either due to procurement codes or because librarians are discovering their genuine value. As a result, RFPs are used for procuring all types of goods and services and are increasingly seen as an important, necessary, and routine part of conducting library business. Anderson (2004, 21) acknowledges that even though the term RFP may produce an "involuntary shudder" in most librarians, the process can be worthwhile. Westfall (2011) describes how the RFP process was used at the University of Tennessee to save money by reducing service charges and standardizing invoicing processes. Waller (2003) describes why the RFP process is worth a librarian's time to conduct, pointing out two reasons that are sometimes overlooked: RFPs give the library the opportunity to examine its problems in greater detail that would normally occur and RFPs allow vendors to not only respond to stated requirements but also transcend them, adding more value to their proposal. Further, Calvert and Read (2006) conducted a focus group consisting of both librarians and vendors regarding use of the RFP for selecting a library management system/ILS and learned that both librarians and vendors found value in the RFP process, provided it was done well. Numerous other librarians and vendors agree that regardless of the RFP's shortcomings, there is no more thorough, objective method available.

PLANNING THE RFP PROCESS

Whether the library voluntarily embarks upon the RFP process or it is mandated by its parent institution or governing body, a clear, carefully constructed, and well-executed plan is essential to outline steps in the process and to keep it on track. The planning elements for RFPs described in this section can be applied to academic libraries, public libraries, and school district procurement centers and can readily be adapted to fit the needs of consortia (groups of libraries that engage in cooperative resource sharing and purchasing, including securing more advantageous pricing agreements or other negotiated items) when not negotiating directly with publishers.

Essential planning elements remain the same whether the library is embarking on an RFP to select a vendor to provide collection materials, ILSs, RFID systems, digitization services, disaster recovery services, commercial binders, or other library goods and services available in the marketplace.

Appointing the RFP Committee

The first step, after securing the support of the central administration to conduct the RFP, is to determine who should be involved in the RFP process and appointing them to the committee. Planning is time-consuming and requires well-considered input from all appropriate parties. "The library has to decide who should, or must, contribute to it" (Schatz and Graves 1996, 422). In very small libraries, one or two staff may conduct the process, but in larger libraries or consortia, a committee, task force, or working group is usually better, providing various viewpoints and balanced input to the process.

Depending on the type of proposal, the library's RFP committee should include experienced personnel who are knowledgeable in management of the area that the RFP covers (i.e., collections, ILSs, or other areas). In addition to including staff in the area(s) covered by the RFP, and depending on the institutional culture, staff from other units of the library such as technology and public and technical services areas should be involved, as well as someone who is authorized to represent the library administration.

Usually, a librarian with expertise in the area covered or in RFPs in general will chair the task force. Ideally, the chair should have expertise both in subject matter and in conducting RFPs. The chair should be aware that the committee may consist of individuals with expertise in various representative areas of the library, but all too often they are well-meaning novices when it comes to writing and evaluating an RFP and will need guidance and support throughout the process.

Committee Member Roles

Once the committee has been formed and a chair has been selected, the group will need to define the role of each member and who is responsible for what aspects of the process. "It is imperative that committee members understand clearly why they were appointed to the committee, what their role is within the committee, what the committee's role is in the award process, and the time frame in which they are expected to accomplish the tasks associated with that role" (Wilkinson and Thorson 1998, 8). Committee members must be clear about how their feedback will be gathered and evaluated. They must understand explicitly who is authorized to make the award based on the committee's evaluation of the proposal and its subsequent recommendation. Will this person be the library dean/director, the institution's purchasing officer, its governing board, or some other entity?

What Is the Library Procuring?

The committee must be clear about exactly what goods or services the library is interested in procuring. For example, if the library is procuring collection materials, is it looking for a vendor to provide print and/or electronic books through an approval plan? Or does it seek a vendor to handle domestic or foreign electronic and/or print serial subscriptions? Or is the library looking for a vendor that specializes in art exhibition catalogs or music scores?

Depending on which materials the library is procuring, the next step is for the committee to determine if it will write the RFP to allow only one vendor to receive the award or if it will allow the award to be divided among two or more vendors. The committee must consider carefully questions such as this to avoid potential unforeseen consequences. For example, in the case of collection materials, even librarians who are fearful of "putting all their eggs in one vendor's basket" may discover that "dividing an approval plan award makes little sense for domestic titles (e.g., separating out trade from university press titles, or dividing by subject areas). This type of separation creates a strong probability of receiving duplicate titles, especially in interdisciplinary subjects, and further the library is likely to receive a reduced discount corresponding to the lower number of books purchased from each vendor" (Wilkinson, Lewis, and Lubas 2015, 114). Also, in some cases the committee may consider dividing a serials subscription account, perhaps choosing to award its domestic serials to one vendor and its foreign serials to another vendor, thinking that a vendor can provide serials in its country of origin better than a U.S. vendor with offices abroad. Other librarians are just not comfortable trusting their account to one vendor because of concerns over vendor mergers or possible failure of the company. Still others believe that the advantages of having all their serial titles consolidated with one vendor, such as unified management reports on all titles and generally a lower service charge, outweigh these concerns (Wilkinson, Lewis, and Lubas 2015, 114).

If the RFP is written to select an ILS, the committee will need to ascertain if it will be using the vendor's knowledge base (KB) or if it might consider using a different, possibly more familiar KB product. If the RFP solicits a disaster recovery service, does the library expect one service to handle both small emergencies, such as relatively minor water leaks damaging only a few books, and full-blown disasters from fire, earthquake, or major flooding, impacting most or all areas of the library, or to use two, one for minor occurrences and one for major disasters? If the RFP calls for proposals for a commercial binder, will the materials sent be primarily books needing to be rebound or will some print serials be included? Does the library require preservation services, such as restoration or custom-fitted protective enclosures? Also, will the library require the binder's system to be compatible with the library's ILS binding module (if there is one), or will it require the vendor to provide a stand-alone option for transmitting binding information?

Once the committee clearly articulates what it is requesting a vendor to supply and whether the vendor's proposal must cover all or if it can cover a part of the goods and/or services needed by the library, the committee is ready to finalize the next step in the planning process, the timeline.

The Timeline

The timeline should be viewed as a dynamic document, open to modifications as needed. It displays the major activities involved in the RFP process, in order of their occurrence, with corresponding dates or date ranges during which those activities will be accomplished. The timeline should identify and fully describe each stage of the RFP, allowing sufficient time to complete each task. This key component of planning not only enables a successful outcome but also contributes to the sanity of committee members.

When possible, start the timeline a year before the new contract will begin because a generous time frame will allow for unexpected delays, which will inevitably occur at some point during the process. Allowing for ample time also provides for a smoother transition when transferring to a new vendor. For example, with collections, it is simpler to ask a new approval plan vendor to begin supplying books at the start of the (calendar or fiscal) year. Having an approval plan start at some other point in the year inevitably leads to duplicate and/or missed materials. Also, most serials subscriptions start at the beginning of the calendar year. Especially for collections, the library needs to allow time for the RFP to be written; vendors' responses to be composed, received, and evaluated; the contract to be awarded; and the new vendor to implement the account (Westfall, Clarke, and Langendorfer 2013, 190). When the RFP is for radio-frequency identification (RFID) products, digitization services, disaster recovery services, or commercial binding, the time frame for switching to a new vendor may be less critical. Nonetheless, the chair of the RFP committee should consult with their procurement or purchasing officer to see if new contracts are preferred to begin at a specific time of year.

Parts of the Timeline

The first step in the timeline generally includes either the RFP committee chair or the entire committee meeting with the institution's purchasing officer. Meeting with the officer early in the planning process can avoid delays later. The meeting provides an opportunity to begin building rapport between the parties. It generally also provides information regarding the boilerplate requirements of the purchasing officer and any other requirements or suggestions the officer wishes to share with the committee. "Typical requirements include a description of the library and its parent organization, the type of materials the contract covers, the dollar amount per annum of expenditure with a vendor for which a contract is required, . . . the beginning and end dates for the contract, the number of years the contract will cover, and the evaluation criteria" (Wilkinson and Thorson 1998, 9). The committee should be aware that, increasingly, institutions are requiring that contracts include a disclaimer stating that the dollar amount per annum is intended to provide the vendor with an estimated contract value but should not be considered a commitment to purchase that dollar amount if the library's budget changes.

The timeline should also include adequate time to identify vendors to receive the RFP (through directories, discussion lists, the institution's purchasing office, or other means) and to gather information from prospective vendors either by sending them an RFI or by arranging for them to visit the library. "Advantages to vendor visits include the opportunity for the library to meet with vendor representatives and through this personal contact get a sense of the vendor's way of conducting business, as well as to give the task force additional ideas of what elements it wants to include as either required or desired elements of the RFP. These visits also give the vendor a clearer perspective of the library to add in its proposal or to help in its decision not to respond to the RFP" (Wilkinson, Lewis, and Lubas 2015, 116). Although these vendor visits are generally done in the planning phase, the top vendors may be invited to visit the library during the final negotiation stage.

The next part of the timeline is writing the RFP document and sending it to the purchasing officer for preliminary review (see Chapter 2 and contributed chapters in Part II). Depending on the library's organizational culture, the committee may also send the draft RFP to the library's staff for comment prior to finalizing the document. This creates transparency in a process that is often tightly constrained by policy or law, provides for a larger perspective on what is needed or what should be required, and may facilitate buy-in from library staff when a vendor is eventually selected. This is especially important when switching vendors.

The quality of work performed at this early stage of the process sets the tone for the rest of the process. The committee must be vigilant because mistakes made early on can create serious problems later, especially in the evaluation phase. If the process is regulated by state or federal law, a single overlooked regulation may invalidate the entire RFP, wasting time and causing considerable frustration for everyone involved.

The next parts of the timeline are receipt of the vendor proposals, evaluation of these proposals, recommendations by the RFP committee to the library administration and the purchasing officer, and the award of the vendor contract or contracts. Adequate time must be given for each of these steps, especially evaluation of the vendor proposals. Awarding a multiyear contract to a vendor, especially if it is to a new vendor the library has no direct experience with, is a serious matter and should not be taken lightly or overly rushed.

The criteria that the committee will use when evaluating vendor proposals must be agreed upon in advance by the purchasing officer to avoid any appearance of bias or favoritism after the proposals are received. Usually, some amount of negotiation between the committee and the purchasing officer is needed regarding criteria for evaluating responses and making contract awards. Often the committee will create a scoring sheet, with a rubric for each section or category, that each member will complete either individually or during a meeting/discussion with the entire committee. This scoring sheet and rubric should be reviewed and approved by the purchasing officer. In some cases, the purchasing officer will provide a scoring form. Typically, the committee will find that the purchasing officer is concerned primarily with cost/pricing, so it is critical that the committee defines the set of minimum acceptable standards that must be met before any consideration of lowest cost can take place. Only the library is qualified to provide this information (Dowd 1991, 66).

CONCLUSION

Regardless of the type of library—academic, public, school, or special—and regardless of the type of goods or services they are procuring, there is universal agreement that the RFP process is time-consuming and labor-intensive for both librarians who engage in it and vendors who submit proposals in hopes of securing the library's contract; however, increasingly, all involved believe that it is worth the effort, especially when contracting for services. The RFP can create an impartial, unbiased, and fair vehicle for vendor selection. RFPs afford librarians the opportunity to get out of a purchasing rut and can provide a structure to learn—objectively and in detail—what different vendors have to offer. Further, the process promotes healthy competition among vendors and requires librarians to carefully consider and justify their decisions.

REFERENCES

Anderson, Rick. 2004. *Buying and Contracting for Resources and Services*. New York: Neal-Schuman.

Calvert, Philip, and Marion Read. 2006. "RFPs: A Necessary Evil or Indispensable Tool?" *The Electronic Library* 24 (5): 649–61. doi:10.1108/02640470610707259.

Clark, Stephen D., and Barbara A. Winters. 1990. "Bidness as Usual: The Responsible Procurement of Library Materials." *Library Acquisitions: Practice & Theory* 14 (3): 265–74. doi:10.1016/0364–6408(90)90027-R.

Dowd, Frank. 1991. "Awarding Acquisitions Contracts by Bid or the Perils and Rewards of Shopping by Mail." *Acquisitions Librarian* 5: 63–73.

Fisher, William. 1993. "A Brief History of Library-Vendor Relations since 1950." *Library Acquisitions: Practice and Theory* 17 (1): 61–69. doi:10.1016/0364–6408(93)90031-Z.

Matthews, Joseph R., Stephen R. Salmon, and Joan Frye Williams. 1987. "The RFP—Request for Punishment: Or a Tool for Selecting an Automated Library System." *Library Hi Tech* 5 (1): 15–21.

Porter-Roth, Bud. 1991. "How to Write a Request for Proposal: A Step-by-Step Outline for Analyzing Your Needs and Soliciting Bids." *Inform* 5 (4): 26–30.

Presley, Robert L. 1993. "Firing an Old Friend, Painful Decisions: The Ethics between Librarians and Vendors." *Library Acquisitions: Practice and Theory* 17 (1): 53–59. doi:10.1016/0364–6408(93)90030-A.

Schatz, Bob, and Diane J. Graves. 1996. "Request for Proposal or Run for Protection? Some Thoughts on RFPs from a Librarian and a Bookseller." *Library Acquisitions: Practice and Theory* 20: 421–28. doi:10.1016/S0364–6408(96)00069-5.

Shirk, Gary M. 1993. "Contract Acquisitions: Change, Technology, and the New Library/ Vendor Partnership." *Library Acquisitions: Practice and Theory* 17: 145–53. doi:10.10 16/0364–6408(93)90056-C.

Waller, Nicole. 2003. "What Is an RFP and Why Is It Worth Your Time?" *Library Technology Reports* 39: 7–11.

Wanninger, Patricia Dwyer. 1990. "The Sound and Fury of RFP." *Library Journal* 115: 87–89.

Westfall, Micheline Brown. 2011. "Using a Request for Proposal (RFP) to Select a Serials Vendor: The University of Tennessee Experience." *Serials Review* 37: 87–92. doi:10.1016/j.serrev.2011.01.005.

Westfall, Micheline, Justin Clarke, and Jeanne M. Langendorfer. 2013. "Selecting a Vendor: The Request for Proposal (RFP) from Library and Vendor Perspectives." *Serials Librarian* 64: 188–95. doi:10.1080/0361526X.2013.761031.

Wilkinson, Frances C., and Sever Bordeianu. 1997. "In Search of the Perfect Cover: Using the RFP Process to Select a Commercial Binder." *Serials Review* 23: 37–47.

Wilkinson, Frances C., and Linda K. Lewis. 2008. *Writing RFPs for Acquisitions: A Guide to the Request for Proposal.* Chicago: American Library Association, Association for Library Collections & Technical Services, Acquisitions Section.

Wilkinson, Frances C., Linda K. Lewis, and Rebecca L. Lubas. 2015. *The Complete Guide to Acquisitions Management.* 2nd ed. Santa Barbara, CA: Libraries Unlimited.

Wilkinson, Frances C., and Connie Capers Thorson. 1998. *The RFP Process: Effective Management of the Management of the Acquisitions of Library Materials.* Englewood, CO: Libraries Unlimited.

2

WRITING AND EVALUATING RFPs

Frances C. Wilkinson and Sever Bordeianu

Always do right; this will gratify some people and astonish the rest.
—*Mark Twain*

INTRODUCTION

The request for proposal (RFP) is a complex, multistep process, with well-defined stages, which need to be followed consistently. The RFP starts with a carefully considered, documented plan with a timeline that provides adequately for each stage of the process. Writing a thorough and well-thought-out RFP document is the most important element in the process. If the document is flawed, with instructions that are unclear and requirements that are not well defined, prospective vendors cannot adequately respond. Also, each requirement and question posed must be written using language that is unbiased, impartial, and nondiscriminatory. The committee charged with writing the RFP must ensure that the document, questions to vendor references, and evaluation forms are free from prejudicial language or leading questions that could unfairly favor one vendor over another.

After the months of planning for and writing the RFP have passed and the vendors' proposals are received, the RFP committee can finally evaluate them and recommend selection of a vendor or vendors to the library's administration and to the purchasing officer. If the RFP was well planned and executed by the committee, the evaluation criteria were clearly articulated, and the vendors responded sufficiently to the required and desired elements and questions, the evaluation process should not be too daunting. The RFP committee will receive its reward for all the hard work and time invested in the process by identifying a vendor(s) that they can partner with confidently.

PREPARING TO WRITE THE RFP

Early in the planning phase, the library's RFP committee, or at a minimum its chair, will meet with the procurement or purchasing officer. The RFP committee members and the purchasing officer will also discuss any policies or laws pertaining to the RFP process that the committee must adhere to, the roles of the committee and the purchasing officer, the proposed timeline, the format for the RFP document, the approach and procedures for evaluating the vendor proposals and contacting vendor references, and any other vital elements of the process.

In most cases the purchasing officer will furnish the boilerplate information about the institution, specifics about how the vendor should submit a proposal, the closing date for proposals, and so forth; however, the RFP committee should clearly understand what other types of support the purchasing officer offers. For example, will the purchasing officer attend all the library RFP committee meetings? Will the purchasing officer alone determine which vendors—based on the vendors' ability to provide the required goods or services—should receive the RFP, or will the committee have the opportunity to recommend vendors? How much time will vendors have to respond to the RFP? Should any questions that the vendor poses to the library committee be directed to the purchasing officer for response, or is the committee authorized to answer vendor questions? During the RFP process, what type of interactions between the vendor and the library are permissible? (See Chapter 17, Ethics for the RFP Process.)

WRITING THE RFP

The RFP will consist of several parts including instructions to vendors regarding proposal submission, the library's required and desired elements, vendor references, and the criteria that will be used to evaluate vendor responses. Whether the RFP seeks a vendor to provide collections materials, an integrated library system (ILS), or a service such as radio-frequency identification (RFID) products, digitization services, disaster recovery services, commercial binding, or something else, the RFP document must provide vendors with the information that they need to prepare their proposal. Contracts are typically awarded for several years, often with the possibility of multiyear extensions; therefore, when writing the RFP, the committee must consider not just what is needed today but what may be desired in the future. To accomplish this task, the committee should review the literature, be aware of developing technologies, and consider any anticipated changes in staffing and any other known factors such as plans to change its ILS during the contract period (Wilkinson, Lewis, and Lubas 2015, 116).

Instructions to Vendors

Ideally, instructions to vendors are provided jointly by RFP committee members and the purchasing office. These instructions communicate details to vendors responding to the RFP about pragmatic matters. The standard information and instructions include the proposal number; purchasing and library contact information; the due date and time by which vendors must submit their proposal; how the proposals should be received (generally electronically); any format requirements for the proposal; and instructions pertaining to alternative offers, cancelations, clarifications, failure to respond, late submissions, modifications, period of offer acceptance, public information, rejection of offers, any taxes (for services), and withdrawal of offers, as well as equal opportunity or affirmative action statements, a detailed statement of conflict of interest and debarment, and other information as determined by individual situations. The committee may also include background information about the library to aid the vendors in crafting their proposals to better meet the library's needs. Background information might include a description of the library's parent organization (university, community, school, or agency) or consortium, including its clientele, programs, and size and strength of collections; operating budget; staff size; and other appropriate information pertaining to the library such as information about its ILS, or in-house system, or in the case of very small libraries, that it has no integrated system (Wilkinson, Lewis, and Lubas 2015, 117).

Required and Desired Elements

Required elements in an RFP are the particulars that a vendor must provide to the library—they are nonnegotiable. The vendor must demonstrate that they can and will provide each and every one of the required items and services or the proposal is invalid. The RFP committee must exercise immense care in determining which elements it requires versus which it desires. Typically, the library limits the number of requirements in the RFP, including only those elements that the vendor must provide or be eliminated from consideration; however, its list of desired elements can be as long as needed to reflect the full range of what is preferred by the library. Nonetheless, the list should not be unrealistically demanding or biased toward a specific vendor.

When composing questions about either required or desired elements, remember that the vendor has to respond to each one in its proposal, and the committee has to evaluate each response to be able to justify its decision to its administration. The committee should be sure that its questions reflect only important considerations that are needed to make an informed decision rather than tangential curiosities. For example, if the RFP seeks a commercial binder, is the thickness of the corrugated cardboard box that books will be transported in an important factor? It is not uncommon for well-meaning, novice committee members to develop questions that may sound as if they are being thorough when in fact the questions will elicit information that is peripheral when determining the best vendor for the library's account.

RFPs can be structured in various ways. They can include a statement of requirements and a list of desired elements and ask the vendor to respond by addressing how they will or will not meet them. Many RFPs ask the vendor to respond to focused questions about each required or desired element. Answering these nuanced questions allows the vendors to focus their responses on aspects that are most important to the library.

RFPs generally include overarching criteria or categories under which the library's requirements and desires, along with the corresponding questions about each, are placed. Creating such categories not only provides structure to the document, but it also simplifies the eventual evaluation process because each category can be weighted and scored, rather than each question. The categories chosen by the committee may vary greatly by type of library, from committee to committee, and will depend on whether the RFP seeks to identify a vendor to supply collection materials, an ILS, or other goods and services. See Chapters 3–13 in Part II.

Although the specific criteria and/or categories will vary, there are some general categories that apply to nearly all RFPs, such as vendor management, which includes vendor background data and financial status, customer service, technology, which includes computer-based services, overall cost considerations, and vendor references.

Vendor Management

RFPs usually require the vendor to provide some management information and data. This can be accomplished by posing a series of questions to vendors that elicit information about the company's background and financial condition. These questions will vary by the type of library and the issues of greatest concern to the library staff and administration. Company data sought by the committee may include vendor history, vision, number of years in business, if the vendor is a subsidiary of a parent company, office/branch locations, number and kind of libraries the vendor serves, and characteristics that distinguish it from other vendors of its kind.

The financial condition of the vendor documents its financial state, demonstrating whether or not it is financially stable. This information has become imperative due to vendor acquisitions, mergers, and bankruptcy trends over the years, causing considerable turmoil in the industry. The library has a fiduciary duty to assure that its funds are spent wisely and will remain secure with its vendor of choice. The RFP can require the vendor to supply a statement of the financial health, such as an internal or external auditor's report to substantiate the vendor's financial solvency. In addition to or instead of an auditor's report, the RFP may ask for a statement of financial solvency or a letter of credit from the vendor's bank, or both. If the vendor is publicly traded, its financial information will be readily available to all. Some institutions may request a performance bond, banker's bond, or escrow account as "a kind of insurance to guarantee that terms will be met" (Wiegand 2005, 248).

In addition, the RFP may pose a series of questions to vendors to elicit information about vendor management issues. Again, these questions will vary by the type of library and the issues of greatest interest or concern. Some of the instructions and statements will be about requirements and must be labeled as such, while others will be designed to elicit information about how the vendor addresses the library's desired elements (Wilkinson, Lewis, and Lubas 2015, 118).

Customer Service

Another element that cuts across all types of RFPs, proffered by all types of libraries, is customer service. Customer service is of great importance, and its value should not be underestimated. The library's staff deserve to interact with knowledgeable, service-oriented vendor staff, who are readily available and who resolve problems accurately and promptly. Superior customer service creates satisfaction and loyalty, whereas substandard customer service will eventually cost the vendor the library's account.

Customer service is at the very core of the vendor–library relationship (see Part III for more information about the librarian–vendor relationship). Because of the importance of quality customer service, the RFP committee should craft its required and desired elements carefully to get the best understanding possible of how the vendor views its customer service role. For example, the committee may choose to require the vendor to adhere to performance standards such as specifying within how many minutes or hours the vendor will respond to queries from library employees, or it may ask for average turnaround times for various services.

For collection materials, vendor-based management reports are an important component of the vendor's overall service package. "These reports provide information about the library's current expenditures with the vendor or its historical expenditures and can be divided by elements such as country of origin or information contained in the library's original order (such as fund code). . . . Other reports cover fulfillment rate, fulfillment time, or the number of titles supplied in a given subject. . . . Both vendor and library system software is becoming increasingly flexible, making even highly customized reports easier to obtain and manipulate" (Wilkinson, Lewis, and Lubas 2015, 120).

Technology/Technical Specifications/Computer-Based Services

Technology services from vendors encompass a wider range of capabilities each year, and wants—limited only by librarians and users' imaginations—will continue to increase exponentially as technological capabilities and innovations expand. As Kerzweil (2001, 1) notes, "It is not the case that we will experience a hundred years of progress in the twenty-first century; rather we will witness on the order of twenty thousand years of progress." This rapid change in how technology allows librarians to better serve library users is simultaneously exhilarating and daunting. It requires extreme care and insight when composing questions in this category to predict what may be needed in the next several years.

Further, requirements and desired elements in the technology category, perhaps more than any other category in the RFP, will vary greatly depending on the goods or services being sought. Chapters 3–6 detail computer-based services for collection materials, Chapters 8 and 9 cover ILS needs, and Chapters 10–13 describe required and desired technical specifications for other procurement, including RFID products and digitization services, which make extensive use of technology, as well as disaster recovery services and commercial binders.

Overall Cost Considerations

Without question, price is an important factor in any RFP; however, when an RFP is preferred over a request for quotation (RFQ), price is usually not the most significant factor for librarians, though it may be for the purchasing office. The RFP committee will need to educate the purchasing officer about the value of other categories, such as customer service, when determining the weight placed on overall cost considerations.

Unless the RFP seeks proposals for a specific good such as printer cartridges, there will be many aspects to delineate in the overall cost considerations category. The committee will need to be very clear in its instructions to vendors about what is to be included in the pricing part of their proposal, and how it is to be structured. In some cases, it may be practical to include a worksheet for vendors to fill in various pricing details.

Obviously, how the vendor presents its cost information will vary considerably based on what it is bidding on: collection materials, ILSs, or other goods and services. For collection materials such as serials and databases, the vendor should provide a detailed list of all service charges and other fees for each of the years that the contract will be active; for approval plans the vendor will detail discounts offered. In addition, the vendor should indicate how they manage account prepays and credits to the account, any shipping charges, and so forth. For ILSs, the vendor may be asked to provide pricing for a bundle of services or price them à la carte. Typically, an ILS vendor will provide built-in price inflation at a set, reduced annual rate, for example, 4 percent. Also, include a question about terms for renewal or contract extension. Pricing models for other areas such as digitization or commercial binding differ substantially and are covered in Chapters 10–13.

Depending on the type of RFP, the committee may include general pricing questions such as:

- Is a penalty imposed for late payment of an invoice? If so, indicate the time period and amount of the penalty.
- Enumerate and describe in detail the costs associated with all value-added services that the vendor offers.
- Can rush services be provided? If so, what is the cost?
- What types of training does the vendor provide and what is the cost?

Vendor References

The vendor will be instructed to provide references, and carefully checking all the references is an essential step in the process. Most RFPs request three to five references consisting of libraries comparable in size and type to the library issuing the RFP. Ask that the vendor submit one reference from a library that recently transferred its account to the vendor. Contacting a reference that recently awarded its contract to the vendor will give the committee an indication of how well the vendor handles the account transfer process. Also, when the RFP asks for a vendor to provide collection materials, the committee should ask that one of the references use the same integrated ILS as the library. This will give the library insight about how well the vendor's systems interface with the library's system.

Prior to this step in the RFP process, the committee should prepare a list of questions to ask each reference. The task of calling or e-mailing references will usually be divided among the committee members. Often these reference calls are made with two or more committee members present to improve accuracy and avoid potential bias on the part of a single committee member. In some instances, especially when the committee is small, conducting conference calls to references, where all committee members can participate, or at least hear responses, can be useful and instructive.

EVALUATING VENDOR PROPOSALS

Evaluation of vendor proposals should begin as soon as the deadline for submission has passed and the purchasing officer releases the proposals to the committee; however, planning for the evaluation process will have been done either before or as the RFP was written. The evaluation criteria will have been clearly delineated in the RFP (as mentioned earlier), reflecting the value the library places on each section of the request. Again, many libraries give the most weight to customer service elements, and although price is important, usually libraries do not weigh it as heavily as customer service. Most librarians agree that it is not wise to "evaluate mainly on the basis of speed, price, and accuracy" (Alessi 1992, 118). RFP committee members must hold the library's real needs and priorities paramount at all times and not be swayed by enticing features or services offered by the vendor that the library does not need or will not use.

The first step in the evaluation process is for each committee member to read carefully each vendor's proposal and review any supplemental materials. If the vendor offers access to its electronic systems, committee members should closely review and experiment with the system's functionality and capabilities. Adequate time should be allocated in the evaluation schedule for this task so that it is not rushed, potentially causing some important aspect to be overlooked.

Evaluation Forms

Typically, committee reviewers will use a standardized form containing the various point-weighted criteria to evaluate vendor proposals. A form can promote objectivity and support more even application of agreed-upon criteria. Just as the categories included in the RFP will vary based on the goods and services the library seeks to procure, the weight given to each of the categories will also vary from library to library. The evaluation form and weighting systems may be prepared by the committee when the RFP was written or may be supplied by the purchasing officer.

When the committee chooses to use a form to evaluate vendor proposals, each member will evaluate each vendor proposal. There are many variations regarding how RFP committees go about evaluating vendor proposals. One simple system is to assign a percentage to each category (e.g., 40% to customer service or 10% to vendor management) with the total for all categories adding up to 100 percent for ease of calculation. The committee may have members initially evaluate each category independently and then hold a meeting where evaluators share the percentage score that they assigned to each category, explaining what criteria they used to arrive at their score, or the committee chair or purchasing officer may simply collect individual committee member scores and average them into a composite committee score.

Making the Recommendation

Once each committee member has completed their evaluation, taking into consideration all parts of the vendor's proposal, its references, and the vendor's on-site visit if there was one, evaluation forms have been tallied, and recommendations have been discussed, it is time to prepare the recommendation document. The recommendation document should open with a statement listing all the vendors who have submitted proposals and the criteria used for evaluating them. It should contain a statement naming the vendor(s) recommended to receive the contract, the reasons for the recommendations concisely stated, and the averaged evaluation score for each vendor along with the cost comparison. In addition, this document should discuss the considerations that led the task force members to their recommendations (Wilkinson, Lewis, and Lubas 2015, 127–28).

Depending on the library's organizational culture and procedures in the purchasing office, this document is typically reviewed and endorsed by the appropriate library administrator or library management group as well as the purchasing officer. Depending on the type of library—academic, public, school, or special library—the recommendation may need approval at a higher level, such as a chief executive officer, governing board, or other entity.

AWARDING THE CONTRACT

Once the recommendation is thoroughly vetted and approved, the purchasing office or other department in the parent organization officially awards the contract. Each vendor that has submitted a proposal must be notified of the award. In some cases, the RFP specifications and the vendor's proposal will constitute the contract; however, some institutions require and will produce a separate contract document. When required, preparation of this document is the responsibility of the purchasing department or legal counsel's office, rather than the library's.

If the Contract Is Questioned or Contested

Scrupulously following the RFP process from the initial phases through the evaluation and award stages of the contract assures that the outcome is unbiased and ethical. This attention to detail provides the library with an objective tool to respond to vendors who may have questions about the process or contest the award.

ONGOING EVALUATION OF VENDOR PERFORMANCE

Libraries routinely conduct evaluations of vendor performance. These reviews have been the norm in many libraries for years. A historical view of vendor evaluation methodologies and studies from 1955 to 1987 is found in an annotated bibliography prepared by the Acquisitions Subcommittee of the Library Committee of the Association for Higher Education of North Texas

(Vendor Study Group 1988, 17–28). Current articles and books abound on evaluating vendors who supply collection materials, including approval plans, firm orders, and serials subscriptions. Joseph R. Matthews's book, *The Evaluation and Measurement of Library Services* (Matthews 2007), includes information on technical services evaluations.

General sources such as Rachel Applegate's *Practical Evaluation Techniques for Librarians* (Applegate 2013) and *Getting Started with Evaluation* by Peter Hernon, Robert E. Dugan, and Joseph R. Matthews (Hernon, Dugan, and Matthews 2014) may also be helpful. Articles on evaluation of ILSs and other products and services for libraries are far less prevalent than evaluation of book and serials vendor, but the importance of libraries evaluating what they pay for is beginning to emerge as a component in some articles.

Evaluations range from simple one-factor studies to complex data analyses on multiple factors. Library staff will decide when the evaluation will begin, its duration, and what method of evaluation will be used. One size does not fit all. There seem to be as many variations on the theme of vendor performance evaluation as there are libraries conducting them, but ultimately, each library will need to tailor its evaluation to best fit its specific needs.

Why Libraries Evaluate Vendor Performance

Librarians are obligated to expend their budget prudently, and they have an obligation to confirm that vendors are living up to the spirit and specifications of their contract. Cargille (1999, 94) reminds us that "librarians are required both legally and professionally to safeguard the budgets over which they have control and to assure themselves that dollars are being spent wisely and efficiently." As Black (1994, 58) noted, "Accountability and value for [the] dollar are two issues frequently discussed" in vendor performance evaluations. Hirshon and Winters (1996, 140) confirm that "the library must ensure that the vendor meets all the mandatory conditions of the contract."

One acknowledged benefit of the lengthy, arduous RFP process is to obtain the best vendor services for the library at a fair price. This benefit is best realized through a vendor performance evaluation. An informal evaluation of the vendor can begin immediately after the contract is awarded. For example, engaging in good communication practices from the beginning sets the tone for the librarian–vendor relationship. Early detection and resolution of minor problems often prevent dissatisfaction later in the contract period. As soon as enough time has elapsed for sufficient data to be collected, a formal evaluation can commence. This evaluation will either confirm or call into question early perceptions library staff may have about the vendor. As Cargille (1999, 94) points out, "It is reasonable to check one's intuitive judgments occasionally with fact."

CONCLUSION

Academic, public, school, and special libraries use vendors that provide many types of goods and services. Vendors function as an extension of a library's staff, saving the library both time and money. Writing an RFP that reflects the library's needs and desires and thoroughly evaluating vendor proposals is labor-intensive and time-consuming, but it is also the most thorough and objective method available for libraries to select vendors.

The library's responsibility does not end when it selects the most suitable vendor. Librarians must verify that the vendor delivers the goods and/or ongoing services that it agreed to in its proposal. Further, librarians should ensure that the vendor is fulfilling its obligations by conducting vendor performance evaluations and by working with the vendor to correct any deficiencies. "It is through the combined efforts of library and vendor staff together, each striving to produce the best possible service, that we ultimately progress toward our respective goals" (McLaren 1999, 86).

REFERENCES

Alessi, Dana. 1992. "Vendor Selection, Vendor Collection, or Vendor Defection." *Journal of Library Administration* 16 (3): 117–30.

Applegate, Rachel. 2013. *Practical Evaluation Techniques for Librarians.* Santa Barbara, CA: Libraries Unlimited.

Black, Graham. 1994. "Why Do Evaluation?" *Library Acquisitions: Practice and Theory* 18 (1): 57–60.

Cargille, Karen E. 1999. "Vendor Evaluation." In *Understanding the Business of Library Acquisitions.* 2nd ed., edited by Karen A. Schmidt, 90–99. Chicago: American Library Association.

Hernon, Peter, Robert E. Dugan, and Joseph R. Matthews. 2014. *Getting Started with Evaluation.* Chicago: American Library Association.

Hirshon, Arnold, and Barbara A. Winters. 1996. *Outsourcing Library Technical Services: A How-to-Do-It Manual for Librarians.* New York: Neal-Schuman.

Kerzweil, Ray. 2001. "The Law of Accelerating Returns (Essay, March 7, 2001)." *Kerzweil Accelerating Intelligence.* http://www.kurzweilai.net/the-law-of-accelerating-returns.

Matthews, Joseph R. 2007. *The Evaluation and Measurement of Library Services.* Santa Barbara, CA: Libraries Unlimited.

McLaren, Mary K. 1999. "Vendor Selection: Service, Cost, and More Service!" In *Understanding the Business of Library Acquisitions.* 2nd ed., edited by Karen A. Schmidt, 75–89. Chicago: American Library Association.

Vendor Study Group. 1988. *AHE Vendor Director for Acquisitions Librarians.* Dallas, TX: Library Committee Association for Higher Education of North Texas, Acquisitions Subcommittee.

Wiegand, Sue. 2005. "Financial Issues: Changes in Serials Acquisitions in the 21st Century." *Serials Librarian* 2005: 241–51.

Wilkinson, Frances C., Linda K. Lewis, and Rebecca L. Lubas. 2015. *The Complete Guide to Acquisitions Management.* 2nd ed. Santa Barbara, CA: Libraries Unlimited.

PART II

WRITING AND EVALUATING SPECIFIC TYPES OF RFPS: COLLECTIONS

3

RFPs for Library Collections: Preparing, Writing, Evaluating, and Follow-Up

Lee Sochay

INTRODUCTION

The term "collection vendor" encompasses many different types of vendors that offer a product, in the form of content, a service, acquisition outsourcing, or portals for access, or both. Procuring these products or services may be a very simple process, such as purchasing a book directly from a vendor, or very complex, such as obtaining a multiyear deal for electronic resource content in which pricing structure and licensing will be negotiated. Depending on the complexity of the procurement and the number of possible vendors, a request for proposal (RFP) may be the best avenue for the acquisition. For the Michigan State University Libraries (MSU Libraries), a transfer of subscription procurement and management services was required as the company that previously performed these services went out of business. How would this task be accomplished? Should the titles just be transferred to an existing vendor? Should a different vendor be selected and just send the business their way? It was decided that the best approach would be to use an RFP.

REASONS FOR AN RFP

A need is identified. This need can arise from a new required service, an answer to new technology, a response to changes in the marketplace, a change in the mission or vision of the organization, or the need to improve the value of services or products due to budgetary constraints. Is an RFP required for the procurement? Tom Sant lists in his book, *Persuasive Business Proposals: Writing to Win More Customers, Clients, and Contracts*, the reasons to use an RFP.

For decision makers, what are some of the benefits of conducting an RFP to solve this need?

- Compare vendors, offers, or prices in order to make an informed decision.
- Clarify complex information.
- Make the buying process more "objective."
- Slow down the sales process.
- Solicit creative ideas, become educated, or get free consulting.[1]

By reviewing these benefits, a decision can be made about the necessity of using an RFP. Along with this list, there are other reasons that an RFP could be advantageous. It documents the procurement process and can justify or satisfy requirements of governing bodies such as university purchasing departments, library boards, and government departments. Also, the competitive nature of an RFP builds in competition. "Competition is the major technique used to hold costs down. As a procurement professional, your job is to get the best value for the lowest cost to your company."[2] This competition can drive down pricing while giving opportunities for vendors to offer their best solution for your need.

For the MSU Libraries, the decision to use an RFP came down to a few reasons. It brought in a competitive nature to the process enabling the opportunity to find the solution that offered the best value while fulfilling the need. It was important to make an informed decision as we were only familiar with a couple of the vendors that offered subscription management services. It clarified complex information as we wanted to document the buying process and how it would continue into the future. And, it made the buying process more objective as we wanted to find the solution that gave us the best opportunity to fulfill our needs from a qualified vendor, not just the vendor that we had used in the past.

THE VENDOR VIEWPOINT

Understanding the vendor viewpoint for the investment in the utilization of time and resources in an RFP response and the approach of that response can assist in the development of the RFP. In his book, *Persuasive Business Proposals: Writing to Win More Customers, Clients, and Contracts,* Tom Sant advises vendors that "the important point is that you should always do some prudent qualifying before committing yourself to the time and effort of writing a quality proposal. There is no use submitting your offer to someone who has no budget, no authority, or no real interest in working with you."[3] By understanding this point, it is important from the beginning that the library be able to state that a budget exists, a process has been approved to seek a solution for an identified need with the ability to release a purchase or a contract, and that each potential vendor will be treated equally in the process. It is important for vendors to know that there are funds that are dedicated for the project and the resolve of the library to see the project implemented. Vendors will be less likely to spend significant time and money to prepare a proposal if the funds or buying decision is unlikely to occur. A statement from the library director on the dedication of funds and resources to see the project through will put many vendors at ease. This can be a simple statement. Details such as how much budget is dedicated to the project should be left out. After all, the most competitive solution that works for the library and its stakeholders is the result that would be considered a success. And remember, a proposal is the intellectual property of the vendor. It is unethical to prepare an RFP if the only goal is to solicit ideas on how to solve a problem, and worse, to share it with a vendor's competitors. By keeping these points in mind while you are developing the RFP helps to ensure that you will get the best effort in the submitted proposals.

Sant further advises vendors: "The proposal positions what you have as a solution to a business problem, and helps you justify your price, even if it's slightly higher than your competitor, by showing that you will provide superior value."[4] "So if we can present the right content in the right order so that decision makers see we have the right solution, we will win and so will they."[5] Working with vendors that take this kind of approach can be very beneficial to the library. This takes the approach of working as partners to deliver the solution that answers the need while providing fair compensation to the vendor. "In the book, *Getting to Yes: Negotiating Agreement Without Giving In, Penguin* (1981), by Roger Fisher and William Ury (reissued in 1991 with Bruce Patton), the idea of negotiation on the merits, or principled negotiations, is presented. This strategy is also known as win-win. Fisher and Ury urge negotiators to 'change the game.' Basically, they describe a strategy that focuses on coming up with solutions that give mutual gain. Often that means developing an idea that is new in order to solve an issue between two parties."[6] It is a win-win scenario that will not only address the needs of the library but will also help in the library–vendor relationship to ensure a smooth implementation and good relations for future work that may be done.

So, how do you determine or evaluate the viewpoint of the vendor? This is part of the investigative process in the development of an RFP. Ask as many questions that you can think of and provide yourself with honest answers and accurate information. Questions such as "Are the answers addressing our needs?" "Are vendor information exchanges addressing the need or do they only provide product information?" "How quickly do vendors respond to inquiries?" can give an indication to the viewpoint and culture of the vendor. These questions can also help in the actual writing of the RFP. The desired characteristics for vendor relations and interaction can be specified or at least addressed in ways for the vendor to include in their proposal. The following example shows how this information was included in the MSU Libraries RFP.

CONSIDERATIONS AND QUALIFICATIONS FOR THE VENDOR

1. Costs, including staff time, for implementation, training, maintaining, and documenting new workflows and procedures to use your subscription procurement and management services.

   What is the pricing model for the services? When prices are set for specific client libraries, what are the factors, such as extent of collections? What has been the pattern of cost increase from year to year, and is it possible to negotiate multiyear pricing to increase our ability to predict costs?

2. Necessary auxiliary purchases

   Necessary auxiliary purchases should be disclosed as part of the response to the proposal. Any issues about interoperability between the web interface and our existing integrated library system (ILS) (III Sierra), or with associated software such as OpenURL link resolvers, should be stated clearly. Switching to different auxiliary software is not out of the question, but we want to understand the reasons, costs, and results of any such recommended change.

Respondent Qualifications

Provide the following information as part of your proposal:

1. Provide the company name, address, telephone number, fax number, website address, e-mail address, and point of contact for the company.
2. Provide a brief description of the activities and organizations your company participates in to ensure that you are up-to-date on current technology.
3. Provide the name, address, telephone number, fax number, and e-mail address for your company's help desk and technical support office.
4. Identify the online tools your company has available to assist customers.

5. Provide a minimum of three references. Reference information must include the following: contact name, company name, address, telephone number, fax number, e-mail address, and the dates services were provided. Use Schedule 1 References at the end of this RFP to provide this information.
6. Provide a list of clients who have discontinued utilizing your service within the past 12 months along with a reason for their departure. List should include contact name, company name, address, telephone number, fax number, and e-mail address.
7. A current copy of your terms and conditions must be included with your proposal.
8. An implementation schedule must be provided with your proposal to ensure the processing of all subscriptions, as listed in the renewal subscription attachment, to avoid lapses in coverage.

THE RFP AS PROJECT

"A project is a sequence of finite dependent activities whose successful completion results in the delivery of the expected business value that validated doing the project."[7] In this case, the execution of the RFP is the project. As a project, it has a start date and it has an end date. It has a development phase, an implementation phase, and an evaluation phase. All these elements contain the different finite tasks that need to be completed. Some of these tasks include preparation and planning, document development, releasing the RFP to the vendors, evaluation of the proposals, solution selection, handoff for implementation, and evaluation of the process. "The project is unique, but how we manage the project is not. Each procurement is unique, but how we get to the executed contract is not. It is a group of processes that create the map leading to successfully completing procurements."[8] You can learn from project management to manage the RFP process, and the rest of this chapter takes this approach to each of the phases of the RFP as a project.

Planning and Communication

"Planning is the most important aspect of getting your procurement completed. Your plan is the map that gets you from where you are now to a successfully executed contract."[9] As with any project, planning and communication will enhance the probability of success, even though there is no guarantee. Planning includes how to develop the RFP as well as thinking about how the RFP will be implemented and then finally evaluated. Planning also includes defining success for the RFP and for the subsequent project. "It is important to have a clear definition of success . . . at the beginning of the project."[10] This will enable the process to provide the best solution for the library.

Communication is also critical throughout the RFP process, from the simplest procurement to the most complex negotiation. The plan, main goal and expected outcomes, tasks, definition of success, and evaluation must have clear and concise communication with all the stakeholders. This will keep everyone on the same page and build in efficiency in the process. This also promotes buy-in, or an understanding of why the need must be addressed from the stakeholders for the project, with the confidence that it will be managed without major disruptions or at least the opportunity to plan for any disruptions. "Promotion also can be done within the library. Providing information on the new vendor and system can instill confidence in the acquisitions unit that orders can be placed, there is stability and reliability in gaining access to new resources, transferred titles will remain as is without losing resources and should be transparent to the end user."[11] For the MSU Libraries' RFP, this was accomplished through department meetings throughout the process. In reaching out in this manner, people were able to ask questions and make comments, feel a part of the process, and gain an understanding of the extra work that would be put on the RFP team. It was beneficial to have that understanding of the prioritization within the RFP team and within acquisitions as it alleviated stress and helped in planning and keeping normal workflows operating efficiently.

Preparation before the RFP

Before the organization decides to send out an RFP, it is allowable to make direct contact with vendors in order to gather information regarding their specific product or service. After the RFP is released, communication with vendors must be limited to specific contacts and through specific channels specified in the RFP. Until then, have vendors visit and demonstrate their product or service. A short-term trial can be an excellent way of learning how a product or service behaves in real applications.

If there is time and budget, visit other libraries that have implemented the product or service. This can provide great insight into how it works in real-world applications, and it provides a great opportunity to ask questions and obtain user feedback. Also, if the time frame allows, make use of conferences and visit vendors' booths, attend demonstrations, and ask questions.

Another good way of finding a solution to a need is to post questions on library listservs. There is a good chance that other libraries have the same need. You could find out how they managed the need, found a solution, and if that solution was successful. You might even find out a simpler solution that will not expend time and resources.

Remember to investigate the intangibles such as customer service, reliability, update frequency, and the vendor's financial strength. This will give insight into the core competencies of the vendor, the financial viability of the vendor, the performance of the vendor on similar projects, the corporate culture, and any corporate philanthropy. These all add to the information that can be utilized writing the RFP document and as selection criteria in evaluating proposals.

At the end of this information-gathering stage, redefine the purpose and scope based on what you learned based on what is attainable in the marketplace, list the desired features for the project as the basis for the functional specifications and requirements, and start to make a list of potential vendors that will be invited to submit a proposal.

RFP DEVELOPMENT

Carol Smallwood in her book, *Frugal Librarian: Thriving in Tough Economic Times*, lists four parts to the RFP. These parts are a good outline to follow to develop the RFP.

- Introduction. Tell interested parties what you are looking for in general.
- Job specifications. Spell out exactly what you need done.
- Date by which you expect responses. This should be based on when the current contract expires . . . and enough time for you to review all the proposals and make a decision.
- Disclaimer. For one reason or another, you do not accept any of the proposals from vendors. You must state up front that this possibility exists so that vendors are aware of it.[12]

As you get started on the RFP development, it is important to understand that there is a project that needs to be completed based on a favorable decision resulting from the evaluation of vendor proposals and an agreement in place. The RFP is the basis for this project. As such, the RFP should be written in a way that will walk you through the implementation process and set the foundation for project success. As such, also think about the evaluation and assessment methodology of the project from the very start of the development of the RFP.

The Introduction section of the RFP document sets the background for the project that the vendors are bidding on. It is here that a background of the institution can be given. For the MSU Libraries' RFP, a description of the library staff, the number and types of patrons that we serve, the existing software and systems that we use, and recent implementations that might impact a proposed solution are all part of the introductory narrative. It is here that the need is identified and the main goal and a list of benefits can be described. It is also here where the information such as vendor considerations for pricing models or any auxiliary purchases that are required is included. The parts of the MSU Libraries' RFP are shown next.

THE MSU LIBRARIES' ENVIRONMENT

The MSU campus community includes approximately [number of students, faculty, staff and support staff, and partner libraries]. In service to MSU's land grant mission, residents of the state of Michigan are also eligible to use [the print collection and to access most digital resources onsite]. The library collection consists of [X million] volumes with digital and online materials becoming a larger proportion of the materials budget.

Acquisitions, processing, and cataloging are managed using. . . . We use OCLC as our cataloging utility.

At this time, several systems assist library users to identify materials and gain access to the collection.

- The newly implemented . . . [systems and services for users]
- Second, the OPAC (from III) provides coverage of records . . .
- Third, the homegrown ERASMUS system (which can be seen at http://er.lib.msu.edu) serves as a "shadow catalog" . . . providing access to many kinds of online resources, and provides access to freely available online resources.
- Lastly, we use the Serials Solutions knowledgebase to update electronic holdings in the OPAC . . .

The job specifications will spell out what the product and/or services are required to do. They can also provide desired features and functions that will enhance the overall solution and bring value to the library. The scope of work and the functional and technical specifications define the goods or services that will solve the need and the goals that are identified in the RFP. "You must have a detailed, specific, complete description of the goods or services you are procuring. The more detailed and specific this scope of work (SOW) is the better your Request for Proposal (RFP) will be and the higher value your company will receive from your work."[13] The SOW and the functional and technical specifications are developed from the information that is gathered in the information-gathering phase.

The next section will define the logistics of the bidding process. This will include the date and time in which the proposals are due and in what format (print, electronic, or both) they must be submitted. Include the number of copies of the proposals that must be submitted. This is condensed from the MSU Libraries' RFP.

PROPOSAL DATES, TIME, AND LOCATION

All dates pertaining to the processing of the RFP are listed below. These dates include:

Written Question Submission: Determine Date.

Written Question Response: Determine Date, allow enough time to research questions.

Proposal Submission Date and Time: Proposals must be submitted by this time.

Proposals shall include a cover letter signed by an authorized representative, sealed and sent to the specified address by the Proposal Submission Date and Time listed above.

Note: The outside of the mailing package shall contain reference to "Proposal #XXXXX Subscription Procurement & Management Services for the MSU Libraries" clearly marked so due attention can be given to recording the date and time the package was received.

Number of Proposal Copies

Send two hard copies of your signed proposal to the address listed in this document by the due date and time of submission. Hard copies must be sent to comply with the requirements of the bid process.

The methods of communications for questions and answers or any addenda that will need to be released are all specified in this section. And, include a request for references. For the MSU Libraries RFP, the references that were included in the RFP were considered along with other libraries that had experience with the vendor. This provided a clear picture of working with a certain vendor.

The disclaimer includes the statement that you may not accept any of the proposals. But it can also clarify any rights that you reserve in the evaluation, negotiation, and selection of a proposed solution. The disclaimer for the MSU Libraries' RFP is shown next.

The MSU Libraries reserves the right to reject any and all proposals, wholly or in part, and to make awards, which, in the opinion of the MSU Libraries, are in its best interest. The MSU Libraries reserves the right to waive any irregularities in bidding and to contact bidders during the bid evaluation time period for clarification of information.

Evaluation will be based on the bidder's ability to meet the requirements and technical desirability as outlined throughout this document as well as price. Also, the MSU Libraries does not herein limit the methods or factors to be used for evaluation.

The MSU Libraries will determine the successful bidder in its sole discretion. The MSU Libraries reserves the right to further negotiate in its own best interest.

Other legal requirements could also be added in the disclaimer. These legal requirements include applicable antidiscrimination laws, how the contract could be terminated, and liability issues. By thinking of these things on the front end, you can contact the appropriate people or departments such as university legal counsel and purchasing departments for preapproval, so the RFP is not delayed due to these concerns and requirements.

As with any project, there will be a team to develop and implement the RFP. The size of the team will depend on the complexity of the RFP. The team needs to have the appropriate number of people who represent affected units in the library, understand the marketplace, understand the technical and logistical aspects of the products or services, know the financial constraints for the project, have the communication skills to manage interdepartmental updates and vendor questions, and incorporate any legal requirements. Too many people on a project may overcomplicate these tasks while too few may miss important aspects. But make sure the RFP team understands their overall purpose: to develop, evaluate, and recommend the best solution of the library's needs. "In procurement the product is the executed contract. So the product-oriented processes are the activities required to find competitors, do a competition, negotiate an agreement, draft the agreement, have it reviewed, and obtain final approval (signatures)."[14]

It is possible that there are templates for the RFP that a vendor can supply.

Do not use a supplier's RFP template. Although using a shortcut is tempting, a supplier's RFP is directed at getting the supplier everything that the supplier wants. A supplier's RFP does not address your company's needs at all. As a shortcut, you can take any type of valuable information from a supplier's template and include it in your own RFP, but be careful here—know exactly what that information means to your company as well as to the supplier.[15]

"A well-structured RFP will greatly increase the likelihood that the proposals submitted will be easier to evaluate and provide an apples-to-apples comparison for your team."[16] Not only will a well-structured RFP help in evaluating the solutions, but if the goal is to have a well-defined response, the requirements need to be clear and explicit. Detail is key to eliminate ambiguity in responses or responses that are dissimilar. The RFP needs to be designed and structured to provide a solution, not a checklist of features. This is the approach used for the Subscription Procurement and Management Services RFP. We needed an overall solution that addressed not only the functional requirements but also within the designated time frame, with usability and flexibility going into the future.

> It is important to specify clearly who is responsible for completing which tasks. If your vendor expects that the library will have specific steps completed prior to the system's implementation, then you need to see to it that they are accomplished. If you expect the vendor to do them, ensure that the vendor understands that and schedules appropriate time to complete them.[17]

These expectations need to be clearly defined in the RFP. Without these expectations defined, the basis for the proposals' SOW and the pricing will not be comparable or accurate. This may cause the evaluation of proposals to be impossible and, if selection is made, changes in the contract price either just before or worse during implementation. For example, the expectation was for the library to provide an updated title list as the basis for the proposals. This gave every one of the bidders an equal basis in which to base their pricing structure as well as their timeline and resources they would have to use to order these titles for the library.

The timetable is an important part of any project. This includes the time that it will take for any dependencies to be accomplished, the actual time of implementation, any contingency time added in, and time for training and promotion. In the case of the subscription management services, the training was limited to the staff in how to use the web interface. However, some training may need to be involved for selectors who may want to search the database of serial titles for journals that need to be added to the collection. Does the ordering process change with a new vendor? Are there new lead and lag times for when an order is placed to access the resource? By allowing the time for training and promotion, a positive attitude can be nurtured aiding in the success of the project. Bidders should be prompted within the RFP to provide training materials, webinars, and on-site sessions as part of their proposal.

So, now all this information has been gathered, demonstrations have been observed, questions have been asked, and discussion has been conducted among the members on the RFP team. "It is all the more important to take a step back in the middle of your implementation and analyze your progress."[18] Are the functional and technical specifications addressing the need? Is the timetable doable or does there need to be adjustments? Are the features just bells and whistles that overwhelm the intent of the RFP? Do you have the resources that can implement any proposed solution? Is there anyone else who needs to be included or needs to provide input into the RFP? Are there new technologies that have surfaced that need to be included in the RFP or that can solve the issue without going through an RFP? By answering these questions before releasing the RFP to bidders, time and effort can be saved, and a refocusing can take place on addressing the real need of the library.

MAIN GOAL AND OUTCOMES

In creating the evaluation goals and outcomes, Doran's S.M.A.R.T. criteria would be useful to keep in mind. These criteria could also serve as guidance to develop both realistic and useable evaluations.

- Specific—Be specific in targeting an objective.
- Measurable—Establish measurable indicators of progress.
- Assignable—Make the object assignable to one person for completion.
- Realistic—State what can realistically be done with available resources.
- Time-related—State when the objective can be achieved—that is, the duration.[19]

Then ask yourself the following questions: What is the goal of the project? Is it to save money? Is it to grow the breadth and depth of a particular subject area? Is it to add flexibility in the ordering process or in the types of formats that can be obtained to strengthen the collection? The resulting project should only have one specific main goal, and these are just a few examples of the questions to ask in the development of that goal. In the case at the MSU Libraries, the migration or transfer of Subscription Management Services would provide for an efficient management of serials subscriptions to ensure accessibility to the resources to the users of the library. It is also important to list the principle benefits that are expected from the project. The principal benefits listed in the MSU Libraries' RFP are as follows:

- Provide an overview of electronic and print holdings.
- Provide tracking of subscriptions to ensure delivery and accurate records.
- Simplify procedures and workflows for ordering subscriptions and payment of invoices.
- Provide acknowledgment of purchased new subscriptions and renewals.
- Claim missing or nonavailable titles.

These benefits support the main goal of the project of ensuring access to our serials subscriptions for our users, and they will assist you in mapping out the implementation and evaluation of your procurement project. "It is important to outline the expected outcomes of the project from the very beginning."[20] These are the measurables for the main goal, and these measurables need to be evaluated in a certain time frame. The electronic and print holdings need to be searchable by a certain date. Subscription tracking for renewals and cancelations needs to be in place before access is lost. Interfacing with the electronic resources management (ERM) module in the library catalog to provide efficiency in the workflows by a certain date can be observed. Acknowledgment of renewals and cancelations needs to be in place by a certain date to ensure accuracy in the collection. These principal benefits are all realistic and measurable and support the main goal of the project. By listing them as a part of the RFP, the implementation project will have a clear path and the best chance for success. Lastly, there may be outcomes that may not have been originally thought of that could be beneficial or harmful. There needs to be a reaction plan or procedure in place among the RFP team that can address unexpected issues in an efficient manner. The results may be a revision in the SOW or the need for a future project. For example, the subscription management service may address the immediate need of ensuring access to serials resources, but to address the risk of having a sole provider go out of business, another vendor can be considered in an overall procurement strategy.

Functional and Technical Specifications

The functional and technical specifications will be the result of the information gathering and the development of the main goal and benefits of the project. These should be specific and steer the bidders into providing a solution and not a checklist of features. Functional and technical specifications from the MSU Libraries' Subscription Procurement and Management Services RFP shown next are an example. See Tables 3.1 and 3.2.

FUNCTIONAL AND TECHNICAL SPECIFICATIONS

Proposals shall indicate your ability to provide the services listed next. Each item must be addressed. Even though there may be standard practices that address a particular item, we would like the bidder to expand their responses to provide a detailed description of a particular service, feature, or function.

Table 3.1 Vendor Overview

Item #	Requirements
1	Provide information on the current ownership and management structure.
2	Provide information of the financial stability and sustainability of your company.
3	Provide information on your share of the subscription agency market at this time and two years ago.
4	Provide information on the basis of your service charge and how it will be renewed annually.
5	Provide any recent relevant company news you wish to share.

Table 3.2 Service Requirements

Item #	Requirements
6	Describe the processes for creating a new order, renewing an order, canceling an order, and making a claim.
7	Electronic invoicing using the EDIFACT (.edi) format with invoices including MSUL reference numbers for each subscription title.
8	Different pricing models and ordering options must be selectable through the web interface.
9	Notifications of price increases in a timely manner.
10	Different subscription formats must be displayed through the web interface.
11	Provide acknowledgments of payments, cancelations, and transfers made to the publishers on our behalf.
12	The tracking, access, and transfers of licenses.
13	The tracking of publication schedules and the availability of different editions from foreign countries.
14	Provide information on the support staff structure for the subscription procurement and management services.
15	Explain your policy regarding the cancelation of the subscription procurement and management service.
16	The web interface must include, but is not limited to, help sections, FAQs, glossary of terms, languages, compliance with accessibility and usability standards, and an overview/dashboard screen.

17	Provide information on web browser requirements, online security and privacy protection, system redundancy/ backup, downtime due to system crashes and scheduled maintenance/upgrades, and the ability to work offline.
18	Provide information on the support staff structure for the web interface.
19	A coverage analysis of the titles and publishers on the attached renewal subscription list must be included.
20	The service must provide updates to bibliographic and historical information for publications in all formats such as platforms, URLs, titles, publishers, stand-alone journals, databases, and packages.
21	The tracking of e-content registrations.
22	The tracking and updating of orders placed, enabled electronic resources, progress of claims, delays in delivery, and title changes in a timely manner.
23	Budgeting and cost assessment tools, including but not limited to, the reporting of multiyear price comparisons of print and electronic resources.

Specific functions of the service are addressed, but words such as "provide information" or "describe" help to formulate the narrative for the solution to the need.

RELEASING THE RFP

The investigative work is done, and the RFP document is complete. It is now time to send the RFP to several vendors. There are several ways to find qualified vendors. Colleagues from other libraries are a great resource for recommendations. Online business directories or conference exhibiter indexes are great places to check. Professional organizations will usually list sponsors or organizational members online. These sites can give some insight into the dedication or activity a vendor has in the marketplace. "If you want bids from at least three vendors, it may be wise to contact five or six. Some will not respond or follow through with a bid."[21] For the MSU Libraries' RFP, four vendors were invited to bid, each acknowledged their interest to submit a bid, and each one received the RFP. Proposals were received from three of the four vendors with no response or explanation from the fourth.

The method in which the bidders are to submit their proposals must also be specified. This will guide each bidder in how to respond and prove uniformity in the formatting of all the proposals, and it will set the RFP as the sole basis for the proposals. This uniformity provides for a fair playing field among the vendors where the emphasis is on the solutions that they can provide. An example of the method of response is shown next.

The response to this RFP must be a written proposal in line with the specifications set forth in this document. The format shall reference section titles and numbers of each information request. Bidder responses to this RFP may become part of a final contract negotiated with the bidder.

Oral Information

The bidder shall not base the proposal on oral information from any employee of the MSU Libraries. In the case that errors or omissions are found in the proposal form or specifications, the bidder shall at once inform the MSU Libraries contact who will immediately publish the correction to all bidders given a request for proposal.

Question and Answer Period

Diana Lindstrom sums up the question and answer period quite nicely in her book, *Procurement Project Management Success: Achieving a Higher Level of Effectiveness.*

> To be fair and ethical, having effective management of communications with potential suppliers is very important. All communications with potential suppliers should go through the procurement lead. In a fair and ethical procurement, all potential suppliers have the right to know what information is being communicated to all of the other potential suppliers to minimize the opportunities for under-the-table deals between any employee of your company and a supplier. Ensuring that all potential suppliers know what is being communicated to all of the other potential suppliers will also stand up in court if a disgruntled potential supplier sues your company for illegal practices.[22]

A single point of contact is crucial during the question and answer period. In this way, there is a reliable path for questions to be asked and fairness is built into the process. All answers to questions need to be disseminated to the entire bidder list. This ensures fairness in the process and acknowledgment that a question has been received and answered. With multiple paths of contact, questions may be missed or answers may only go to one or some of the vendors possibly giving them an advantage.

"If any vendor notes something that you have missed, and you add it to the list of duties to be performed, then each competing firm must be notified in writing of the change, so all responses are based on the same terms. . . . Accepting a late proposal would not be fair to companies that worked hard to meet the deadline."[23] With accuracy and fairness, this will give you the best chance to get valuable proposals that offer the best solution to address the need. In the MSU Libraries' RFP, insurance that this was being followed meant requiring acknowledgment of all questions and responses as a part of the proposal.

Along with fairness and accuracy, this specified process adds protection for you. It reduces the risk of challenges to the final vendor selection and any legal consequences that may result. Again, vendors will invest time and resources in responding to an RFP, and it is in the best interest of everyone to keep the process documented, clear, straightforward, and fair. Examples for communication requirements during the question and answer period and the requirements for any addenda to the RFP are shown next.

COMMUNICATION REQUIREMENTS

Communications with the [name of library] shall be accomplished through the [name of] as designated in the section titled, "PROPOSAL DATES, TIME AND LOCATION." Any firms that deviate from this requirement are subject to disqualification.

The [name of library] desires a single point of communications be set up with each bidder. Bidders are requested to identify the person and his/her address, telephone number, fax number, and e-mail address.

Addenda to the Request for Proposal

In the event it becomes necessary to revise any part of this RFP, an addendum will be provided to all bidders who have indicated an intent to respond. Bidders are required to reference receipt of the addendum number in their bid response.

Warning: The [name of library] will not consider or examine late proposals. Additionally, only such supporting material as is included with the official proposal can be assured consideration during the evaluation process.

Question Submission and Response

Written questions will be received by the [name of library] regarding this RFP as follows:

Question Submission—Questions regarding the functional and/or technical specifications of the proposal shall be e-mailed to the [name of library] contact on this proposal. Questions shall reference the section numbers of the bid document unless the questions pertain to areas not covered by the functional and/or technical specifications.

Question Response—Written questions received will be responded to in written format. Each question with its response will be returned to allow all questions and responses to be shared. The questions with their responses will be e-mailed to the designated contact person on or before the specified Questions Response date.

EVALUATION OF THE PROPOSALS

"An outstanding proposal will recommend solutions, and not merely describe products or services."[24] The process for evaluating the proposal is developed in conjunction with the development of the RFP, at the beginning of the process. "By determining your criteria for vendor selection early in the process, it is easier to make a decision and then defend it if need be."[25]

Designing the proposal evaluation when the RFP is developed will enable you to write the RFP with realistic outcomes in mind, based on the investigative work that you have performed on market solutions to similar needs and vendor capabilities. First, this makes for a stronger written RFP document. Second, it supports a clear and definite RFP process as the vendors prepare their proposals. And third, it communicates to the RFP team and the appropriate stakeholders exactly what goal and expected outcomes are desired. Often, the SOW and the functional and technical specifications will set the foundation for the evaluation. Other intangible factors should be included in the evaluation such as customer service, core competencies of the vendor, financial stability, corporate philanthropy, and pricing stability. The important thing is to have this developed early in the process and implement it equally and consistently across all vendor proposals. This can be done using a weighted scoring system, in the form of a scoring matrix. An evaluation scoring matrix ensures that you will evaluate the proposals based on the solving of the need as well as complying with the functional and technical specifications. The proposal that scores highest on the matrix may not be the lowest priced. It is okay to select that proposal if the price is agreeable to the budget of the project. The scoring matrix will provide the justification to any governing purchasing entities, the library director, or any stakeholders as to why the lowest bid was not selected. For the MSU Libraries RFP, a weighted scoring spreadsheet was created, and each individual on the RFP team independently rated each proposal. The scoring matrix is shown next.

	PROCUREMENT AND MANAGEMENT SERVICES RFP SCORING MATRIX			
Item #	Requirements	#1	#2	#3
1	Provide information on the current ownership and management structure.			
2	Provide information of the financial stability and sustainability of your company.			
3	Provide information on your share of the subscription agency market at this time and two years ago.			
4	Provide information on the basis of your service charge and how it will be renewed annually.			
5	Provide any recent relevant company news you wish to share.			
6	Describe the processes for creating a new order, renewing an order, canceling an order, and making a claim.			
7	Electronic invoicing using the EDIFACT (.edi) format with invoices including MSUL reference numbers for each subscription title.			
8	Different pricing models and ordering options must be selectable through the web interface.			
9	Notifications of price increases in a timely manner.			
10	Different subscription formats must be displayed through the web interface.			
11	Provide acknowledgments of payments, cancelations, and transfers made to the publishers on our behalf.			
12	The tracking, access, and transfers of licenses.			
13	The tracking of publication schedules and the availability of different editions from foreign countries.			

(Continued)

Item #	Requirements	#1	#2	#3
14	Provide information on the support staff structure for the subscription procurement and management services.			
15	Explain your policy regarding the cancelation of the subscription procurement and management service.			
16	The web interface must include, but is not limited to, help sections, FAQs, glossary of terms, languages, compliance with accessibility and usability standards, and an overview/dashboard screen.			
17	Provide information on web browser requirements, online security and privacy protection, system redundancy/backup, downtime due to system crashes and scheduled maintenance/upgrades, and the ability to work offline.			
18	Provide information on the support staff structure for the web interface.			
19	A coverage analysis of the titles and publishers on the attached renewal subscription list must be included.			
20	The service must provide updates to bibliographic and historical information for publications in all formats such as platforms, URLs, titles, publishers, stand-alone journals, databases, and packages.			
21	The tracking of e-content registrations.			
22	The tracking and updating of orders placed, enabled electronic resources, progress of claims, delays in delivery, and title changes in a timely manner.			
23	Budgeting and cost assessment tools, including but not limited to, the reporting of multiyear price comparisons of print and electronic resources.			
	Totals			

The committee then came together to discuss and develop a master evaluation sheet in which the final decision was recommended.

Checking References

To help make the final decision and before signing any contracts, it is a good idea to call references to make sure your evaluation and recommendations are right for your library. Carol Smallwood in her book, *Frugal Librarian: Thriving in Tough Economic Times*, provides a good list of questions to ask the references.

- How long have you used this company?
- Is the service good or excellent?
- Do they respond well to requests for extra work?
- Would you rehire them?
- Do they change who services your location frequently?
- Have there been any problems of note?[26]

After this process, gather all the evaluation information and submit the final decision to the governing purchasing entity. There may be final checks on completing an agreement such as any terms and conditions that need review, any licensing requirements that need review, or any approvals that require signatures. But at this point, the work of the RFP team is completed. The purpose to provide a recommendation for a vendor product or service has been accomplished.

EVALUATE THE PROCESS

After completion, it is important to evaluate the process and determine what went right, what went wrong, and what could be improved, now and in the future. Robert Wysocki, in his book *Effective Project Management: Traditional, Agile, Extreme*, lists six distinct questions to examine as you evaluate a project. These can be applied to the RFP process as well.

The post-implementation audit is an evaluation of the project's goals and activity achievement as measured against the project plan, budget, time deadlines, quality of deliverables, specifications, and client satisfaction. . . . The following six important questions should be answered:

- Was the project goal achieved?
- Was the project work done on time, within budget, and according to specification?
- Was the client satisfied with the project results?
- Was business value realized? (Check the success criteria.)
- What lessons were learned about your project management methodology?
- What worked? What didn't?[27]

First, the goal of any project is to succeed in its defined goals and objectives. Did the RFP produce a vendor and a recommendation for a solution to the main goal? Does the proposed solution address the need as stated in the RFP? The second point evaluates the timeline for the release of the RFP, the receipt and evaluation of proposals, and whether or not it results in a signed contract. Was the RFP process turned around in a timely manner? Will the solution still be effective or did the process outlive the need? Was the time put in by the RFP team within reason so as not to cause inefficiencies in other workflows? Third, the client can be thought of as the stakeholders affected by the need as well as the governing entities of the library. Did the recommended solution get approved? Was the recommended solution satisfactory for the staff and for collection development? Is the library administration pleased with the efficiency and professionalism in the process? The fourth item is a longer-term evaluation as it includes examining the resulting project. Did the implemented project succeed in the defined goal and outcomes? Did the RFP process assist in the implementation and success of the project? Remember, the implementation of the proposed solution and the evaluation of that solution need to be built in to the RFP from the very beginning. Adjustments can be made along the way, and they should be. However, there is a stated goal. There were solutions proposed. There was a contract issued. The implementation of the project was designed based on the need, SOW, and the functional and technical specifications of the RFP. This will define the success of the overall project.

Next, you need to look for any lessons learned about the project management methodology that you can apply in the future. Is there something that you can do better? Are there better resources that we could have used? Are there different tools that would have helped you in the process? Did you have the right team assembled? Did you take the right approach to developing the RFP? Answering these evaluative questions honestly will help in any future RFPs that will be used to procure a product or service that will benefit the library.

Lastly, take the overall viewpoint and ask yourselves what worked and what did not work. This can examine everything from the development of the RFP and how information was gathered, the writing of the RFP and defining the main goal and expected outcomes, writing the SOW and defining the functional and technical specifications, the management and communication within the RFP process, and finally the evaluation of proposals and the final recommendation. This is an overall evaluative process to look for areas of improvement and processes that can be retained.

EVALUATION OF THE PROJECT

Assessment and evaluation are not tasks that you come up with at the end of your project. They are things that are thought of from the beginning and integrated into the whole process. There is a learning process from the beginning of development of the main goal and outcomes of the RFP through the implementation of the product or service. You really want to get an idea of the impact on all the stakeholders who are affected by the product or service.

CONCLUSION

A need is realized and communicated. A determination is made that a solution is available in the marketplace and it is complex enough where an RFP is the best way to obtain a valuable solution. A team is assembled to plan and develop the main goal, desired outcomes, and the functional and technical specifications. The RFP is developed into a formal and legal document. The process is specified and communicated to qualified vendors who are invited to propose a solution. Proposals are received and evaluated. Success comes with the selection of a proposed solution that is within budget and turned over to the appropriate staff for implementation. The RFP process can be used again and again for the purchase of a variety of products and services. By using the process, success can be achieved whether it is in improved subscription management services, providing greater depth or breadth in a subject area, automating collection development for improved efficiencies without sacrificing quality, or enhancing the discoverability of resources.

NOTES

1. Tom Sant, *Persuasive Business Proposals: Writing to Win More Customers, Clients, and Contracts* (New York: AMACOM, 2012), 6.

2. Diana Lindstrom, *Procurement Project Management Success: Achieving a Higher Level of Effectiveness* (Plantation, FL: J. Ross Publishing, 2014), 36.

3. Sant, *Persuasive Business Proposals*, 8.

4. Ibid., 5.

5. Ibid., 23.

6. Lindstrom, *Procurement Project Management Success*, 168–69.

7. Robert Wysocki, *Effective Project Management: Traditional, Agile, Extreme* (Somerset, NJ: John Wiley & Sons, Inc., 2013), 7.

8. Lindstrom, *Procurement Project Management Success*, 11.

9. Ibid., 47.

10. Kerzner, Harold R., *Project Recovery: Case Studies and Techniques for Overcoming Project Failure* (Somerset, NJ: John Wiley & Sons, Inc., 2014), 5.

11. Karen Knox, *Implementing Technology Solutions in Libraries: Techniques, Tools, and Tips from the Trenches* (Medford, NJ: Information Today, Inc., 2011), 61.

12. Carol Smallwood, *Frugal Librarian: Thriving in Tough Economic Times* (Chicago: ALA Editions, 2011), 178.

13. Lindstrom, *Procurement Project Management Success*, 42.

14. Ibid., 12.

15. Ibid., 212.

16. Knox, *Implementing Technology Solutions in Libraries*, 21.

17. Ibid., 41.

18. Ibid., 61.

19. George T. Doran, "There's a S.M.A.R.T. Way to Write Management Goals and Objectives," *Management Review* 70, no. 11 (1981): 35–36.

20. Knox, *Implementing Technology Solutions in Libraries*, 11.

21. Smallwood, *Frugal Librarian*, 179.

22. Lindstrom, *Procurement Project Management Success*, 133–34.

23. Smallwood, *Frugal Librarian*, 179.

24. Thomas Cappels, *Financially Focused Project Management* (Boca Raton, FL: J. Ross Publishing, 2003), 117.

25. Wysocki, *Effective Project Management*, 89.

26. Smallwood, *Frugal Librarian*, 180.

27. Wysocki, *Effective Project Management*, 305–6.

OTHER RECOMMENDED READING

Buser, Robin A., Bruce E. Massis, and Miriam Pollack. 2014. *Project Management for Libraries: A Practical Approach.* Jefferson, NC: McFarland.

4

RFPs for Academic Library Collections: Selecting a Serial Vendor

Susanne K. Clement and Christine N. Sraha

Serials are remarkably like people in that they are born, change names, marry, divorce, have offspring, and finally die. Serials also have been known to come back from the dead and resume living, often in a different format or with a different focus.

—Joseph A. Puccio[1]

INTRODUCTION

For most academic libraries, the contract with the serial vendor[2] represents the single-largest acquisitions expenditure. Journals and serials have long been the principal collection expenditure—even before the ubiquity of electronic resources. Many libraries now see their subscriptions approaching 80–90 percent of the overall collections budget, and serials continue to represent the largest share of this expenditure. The request for proposal (RFP) is the formal document to solicit information and bids for new contracts, and, depending on the laws regulating procurement at an institution, it may also be necessary to go out to bid at specified intervals to renew contracts with existing serial vendors. It takes careful consideration to develop serial RFP criteria that ensure the library will be getting the best services and offers. The process is often long and complex with expectations to have multiple companies vying to provide this service. Thus, the RFP process used to select one or more serial vendors needs to be conducted thoughtfully, methodically, and thoroughly.

For the purposes of this chapter, the serial vendor will refer to all ven-dors, subscription agents, or continuation dealers who supply periodicals to *libraries*.[3] Serial vendors have been around for a very long time—some since the 19th century—first trading with print journals and later also managing subscriptions and access of electronic journals to libraries. The serial vendor manages the myriad ways libraries acquire journals. Acting as an interme-diary between publishers and libraries, the serial vendor often consolidates thousands of library journal orders and manages communication between publishers and subscribing libraries.[4] Libraries send their periodical orders or renewals, together with payments, to the serial vendor, and the serial vendor consolidates subscriptions orders and payments to individual publishers on behalf of their client libraries. Likewise, the serial vendor also troubleshoots problems between the library and the publisher, from libraries not receiving subscribed issues, to ensuring that linking to content is working, to manag-ing the subscription payment from the libraries to the publishers. For a vast majority of libraries, it makes financial sense to use a serial vendor to manage serial subscriptions. Unless the library is very small or highly specialized, thus requiring only a few subscriptions, the cost of staffing needed to manage all direct contact with individual publishers would quickly exceed the serial vendor's service charges.

The number of serial vendors has shrunk significantly in the past few decades—the results of bankruptcies,[5] mergers, consolidations, and acquisi-tions. At one point, the now defunct Association of Subscription Agents[6] had more than 40 members internationally.[7] This means that today libraries have fewer vendors from which to choose and that libraries need to pay close at-tention to the financial stability of any serial vendor with which they choose to conduct business.[8]

THE RFP PROCESS AT YOUR INSTITUTION

Most public or governmental institutions (including libraries within these in-stitutions) are required to get goods, equipment, and services at the most benefi-cial cost possible, and that usually means going out for bid. However tempting as it might be to consider contracting with multiple vendors, each with accounts below the procurement requirements for soliciting bids, it is rarely a good idea. Besides being an acquisitions nightmare, smaller accounts tend to have higher service fees, and if the library has a large serial subscription list, there may no longer be enough serial vendors available to service all of the library's titles.

The RFP is the formal document to solicit bids for new contracts and some-times to renew contracts with existing serial vendors. It is imperative to be familiar with the processes used at your institution for it can make a very big difference whether the library is able to conduct the RFP process by itself or whether it has to work through the procurement office and the timelines and queues of that office. It is also important to know what entity has the authority to sign the final contract with the successful bidder: Is it the library, the unit to which the library reports, or some other entity? Most likely, depending on the cost of the contract, final approval may rest with the highest entity that governs the library and the institution. For example, at the University of New Mexico where a multimillion-dollar serial vendor RFP was finalized in 2016, the Board of Regents had to review the final recommendation and then vote to either accept or reject the recommendation.

One or More Libraries

The RFP could include serials subscriptions from several different organizationally and fiscally independent libraries, whether internal or external to the institution. If that is the case, first be familiar with all the procurement rules that govern all the participating libraries and next decide if the additional work of trying to manage an RFP process with many participants will be beneficial to the process and to the end result. There are advantages and disadvantages to collaboration with other libraries. One of the main advantages is that the total account will be larger, and generally larger accounts tend to get better pricing. The major disadvantage is that it requires more time to coordinate and communicate between participating libraries in preparing, reviewing, evaluating, scoring, and deciding the outcome of the RFP. As well, each library may have different needs that they are looking to fill from the serial vendor.

Do Your Homework

Before setting up a meeting with the procurement office, the first step in soliciting a serial vendor (or renewing the contract of a current vendor) is to read the procurement requirements and limitations of the institution or governing body that oversees the participating library/libraries. Most institutions have websites that provide information for vendors on how the procurement process works for the institution—including laws (for publicly funded institutions), policies, and procedures. It is useful to spend some time reviewing these documents to get a general idea of the process. Even if the library went through a bid process some years ago—whether for serials or some other product or service, review the documents on the procurement site. Laws change, as do policies and procedures. For publicly funded institutions, this is especially the case, as they have to comply with increasing requirements for transparency and thus more policies and procedures. Also, staffing changes—not only in the library but also in the procurement office—may result in the loss of institutional history.

The next step in the RFP process is to decide exactly which subscriptions the serial vendor will handle and what value-added services you would like the vendor to provide. Will the vendor only handle print serials? Will it include electronic serials? Will it include journal packages from individual publishers? Will the serial vendor work with one or more library consortia? Will it work with specialty vendors that work with unique serials such as those required by area studies? Will it include standing orders? Deciding all of these details before starting the process will save significant time—for the library and for the serial vendors responding to the RFP. Part of the RFP process is to provide the vendors with an accurate list of titles, so they can calculate their service fees.

In addition to the subscription services, the library can take advantage of other services and products such as usage statistics harvesting and consolidation, a link resolver, and other holdings management tools that may integrate with other library systems. These value-added services may be written into the serials vendor RFP and are increasingly becoming part of the standard serial vendor offerings.

Based on the projected serial expenditures for the titles, a vendor will manage (or a subset of your expenditures if you use multiple vendors) how likely is it that the procurement regulations require an RFP process and how likely is it that the library can *just* pick a serial vendor and sign a contract with that vendor. If the projected serial expenses are below the cost required to go out for bid, is there some other reason for wanting to use the RFP process to select a vendor? There could be many reasons for using the process to select a serial vendor—even for smaller accounts—such as getting better service or pricing by using a systematic and empirical process of evaluating offers.

It is possible, but not very likely (especially if you are with a public institution), that you can select a serial vendor through a noncompetitive sole-source procurement process. The National Association of State Procurement Officials (NAPSO) defines "sole source procurement" as

> any contract entered into without a competitive process, based on a justification that only one known source exists or that only one single supplier can fulfill the requirements. Although states generally do not permit non-competitive procurements by statute, exceptions are allowed where competition is not feasible.[9]

It might be possible to use the sole-source clause for a subset of highly specialized serial titles that traditionally have only been available through one vendor. However, proceed with caution—it is possible that additional vendors are now also servicing these specialized titles.

Finally, read the library's current serial vendor contract. What are the contract terms and service fees? When does it expire? Can it be renewed under the current contract, and if so, when and for how many years?

Meeting with Your Procurement Office

Once familiar with the procurement process and the terms and expiration date(s) of the current serial vendor contracts, schedule a meeting with the procurement officer. If this person is not familiar with procurement for libraries, expect to explain what a serial vendor is, what it does, and why it is necessary to contract with one or more vendors to manage the library's journal subscriptions. Ask the procurement officer to review all the terms of the current contract(s). If the library is very satisfied with the current vendor, find out if procurement policies will allow the library to renew a contract for another fixed number of years without going out for an RFP.

It is very useful to develop a good working relationship with the procurement officer. Besides reviewing the RFP process, the officer can evaluate whether renewing a current contract is an option or whether sole source is an option. During this meeting find out the timeline involved from the procurement office's perspective. Discuss in great detail the RFP processes and who will be responsible for the different components—from developing the structure and questions for the RFP to the mechanism for announcing and posting the RFP. Understand how vendors will respond to the RFP, and find out who and how to communicate with vendors during the RFP process. Be very clear on what constitutes the final decision-making process. Find out if there is any boilerplate language that must be part of the RFP. Most likely, there will be things that the library is allowed to do before the RFP is posted and other things that the library will not be allowed to do once the bid process has started and the RFP is under review.

It was not that many years ago, the RFP process was primarily a paper-based process where vendors submitted a single report that addressed the RFP questions. More recently, procurement offices—especially in public academic institutions—have moved to all-online systems that post RFPs and allow vendors to submit their responses online. It is therefore necessary to understand the structure of the online forms: Can the vendor submit a single report that responds to all questions in one narrative, or does the vendor have to respond to individual questions in separate sections? For instance, if a question can have a yes/no answer, will the vendor have an opportunity to make modification such as "No, but we . . ." or "Yes, this is how . . ."? Will there be a limit to the type of materials that a vendor can upload into the system, and can the online system accommodate a variety and quantity of file formats? Since most likely only the procurement office and not the library will be managing this process, understanding what can and cannot be done with the online form is extremely useful and will guide how RFP questions are structured and formulated.

Regardless of whether the library needs to use the RFP process or not, consider building a formal evaluation process of your vendors into the annual acquisitions workflow review. If using more than one vendor, ask the same questions about all vendors in the internal evaluation. Engaging everybody who works with serials in the library—not just staff in acquisitions but also reference and subject librarians—into this evaluation can provide a holistic picture of how well the serial vendor is performing. Is the library receiving or getting access to what it paid for or are there problems? If print subscriptions are not received regularly, has the serial vendor been able to troubleshoot? If access to electronic journals has become problematic, has the vendor responded in a timely manner or has the library had to contact them repeatedly about the same problem? Since many libraries use teams to manage serial subscriptions (print and electronic), keeping track of communication between the vendor and the library can sometime become difficult, and it is easy for problems to fall through the cracks. Rather than letting problems persist over time, the annual internal vendor evaluation can highlight whether problems are temporary or whether problems are systemic and thus necessitate changes. The evaluation also allows the library to systematically collect information about its service expectations of a serial vendor—something that is critical to know as the RFP is written and, more important, as the RFP evaluation matrix is developed.

Developing Your RFP Timeline

The RFP process is rarely quick, and it can easily take as much as one year from start to finish—from when the library starts working on the RFP to the date that the serial vendor contract must start (often at the start of the fiscal year). Just as it takes time for the library and its procurement office to prepare an RFP, post it, and then evaluate it, it also takes time for the vendors to respond to the RFP. Vendors typically need at least a month to respond to an RFP. Even though most vendors likely respond to multiple RFPs yearly, each one is unique and requires individual attention. Also, keep in mind that if the RFP is posted in the spring, the new contract will most likely not go into effect for more than a year. The final decision needs to be made in time for any vendor transfers to be completed before the annual subscription renewal deadlines that usually come around August or September.[10] The timeline can be shorter or longer, depending on local laws, policies, and procedures; the number of libraries that will be part of the RFP process; and who will have the authority to approve the successful bid.

Using a recently completed serial RFP at University of New Mexico as an example, we recommend developing the timeline by working backward. Start with the desired date of the new contract and then factor in time for all the steps necessary to develop, post, and evaluate the RFP to get a realistic sense when the library needs to start the RFP process to ensure a successful outcome (see Figure 4.1).

Start of New Serial Vendor Contract, Including Transition Time

Most likely the serial vendor contract will start at the beginning of a fiscal year (July 1 for most academic libraries). Starting at the beginning of a calendar year is less desirable due to the cyclical nature of when serial renewals have to be communicated to the serial vendor. The timeline should take into consideration any necessary transition time if the library will be changing

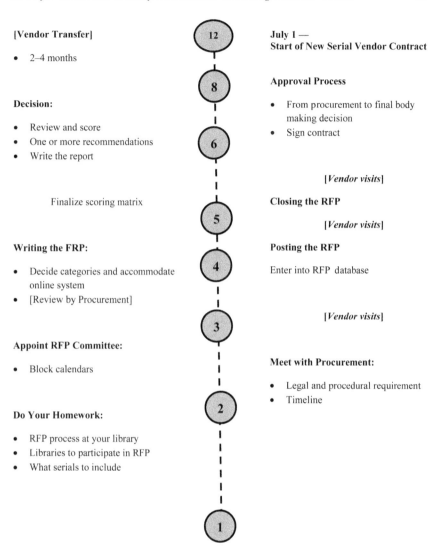

[Vendor Transfer]

- 2–4 months

Decision:

- Review and score
- One or more recommendations
- Write the report

Finalize scoring matrix

Writing the FRP:

- Decide categories and accommodate online system
- [Review by Procurement]

Appoint RFP Committee:

- Block calendars

Do Your Homework:

- RFP process at your library
- Libraries to participate in RFP
- What serials to include

July 1 —
Start of New Serial Vendor Contract

Approval Process

- From procurement to final body making decision
- Sign contract

[Vendor visits]

Closing the RFP

[Vendor visits]

Posting the RFP

Enter into RFP database

[Vendor visits]

Meet with Procurement:

- Legal and procedural requirement
- Timeline

= Approximate number of months from beginning to end

Figure 4.1 Serial Vendor RFP Timeline

serial vendors. The RFP should include questions about how vendors handle account transfers and the time involved. Depending on the size and complexity of the account, expect between two and four months to transfer subscriptions from one vendor to another.

Approval Process

The approval process can take longer than expected—especially if the highest authority for an institution has to grant that approval (the size of the contract often determines this). Knowing the future meeting schedule of that body is critical, especially if there are times when it does not meet on a regular basis (e.g., the summer or winter breaks). The procurement officer will be a great help in managing this part of the RFP process, and that office will also know how much time is needed from receiving the library's final recommendation to being able to present it to the final authority. Each institution is different, so getting this part of the timeline right is vital to the successful start of a new contract.

Decision—Reviewing, Scoring, and Writing the Report

Reviewing and scoring vendor proposals can easily take several weeks—again depending on the complexity of the account, the number of participating libraries, and the number of responding vendors. Set firm deadlines early in process for this important review. Documenting the work early and throughout the process can expedite the writing of the final report with the library's recommendation.

Vendor Visits

In the timeline, build in ample time for potential vendor visits. The meeting with the procurement officer will explain the level of flexibility regarding when the vendor visits can be scheduled.

Posting and Closing the RFP

During the meeting with the procurement officer, find out the amount of time they need to post the RFP. If all of the library's questions have to be transferred into an online RFP form, that office most likely will need a week or more to get this completed. The process can be speeded up by submitting sections to the office as they are completed rather than submitting them all at once. The procurement officer will also set the required amount of time that the RFP is open for response.

Writing the RFP

Allowing enough time to actually write the RFP is critical—again, allow sufficient time to deal with the complexity of account(s), number of participating libraries, and internal reviews. More details about writing the RFP questions are listed next.

Appoint the RFP Committee

Unless the library is fairly small, it is more productive to appoint an RFP committee than having everybody in the library involved in the process. So, who should be members of this committee? Certain positions are key, such as the heads of acquisitions, e-resources, and collections should be included. The head of technical services as well as the library's fiscal agent should also serve on the committee. In addition, consider including one or more staff members who deal with serials on a daily basis, such as staff who manage invoicing, receiving, and linking to electronic content.

Public services representatives might also be included in the committee. Since much of serial work today includes managing linking to electronic content, public services is an important voice in evaluating how well a serial vendor is responding to linking problems. Finally, if the RFP includes more than one library, each participating library should also have representation on the committee.

As with any committee, scheduling can quickly become a nightmare. At the University of New Mexico, we found it most beneficial to block committee members' calendars soon after they were appointed to the committee for time periods when we predicted high-volume RFP committee work—whether for developing questions for the RFP, for vendor visits, or for evaluating and scoring submissions.

In the interest of expediency and efficiency, one or two people should chair the committee. The chair(s) will manage the whole process, including communication between library partners and library administration(s), as well as between the committee and the procurement office. Most likely, the chairs will have been working on the RFP process for some time before the RFP committee is appointed. As soon as the committee has been appointed, schedule a meeting to get everybody oriented to the processes, timelines, and deadlines.

Meet with Procurement

It is not a bad idea to schedule an appointment with the procurement officer while still doing the homework. Depending on the workload in that department, it could take some time to get this meeting scheduled. This meeting will address the legal and procedural requirements followed by the institution.

Do Your Homework

What needs to be done is covered before starting the RFP process, but when building the timeline, it is important that the chair(s) have enough time to prepare for the process. This is when current contracts are reviewed, when potential collaborating partners are contacted, and when procurement is contacted to go over the legal requirements, institutional processes, and major timelines.

WRITING THE RFP

The literature has many good examples of the types of questions that should be part of the RFP. Wilkinson and Thorson, in "Domestic and Foreign Serials," provide a thorough discussion of the core categories that should be included in a serial RFP.[11] Micheline Brown Westfall has a short and succinct list of categories that her library used, and she noted, for example, that at her institution customer service issues would be rated higher than the service charge.[12] Debbie Schachter does not specifically address RFPs for serial vendors, but her article provides some very useful recommendations on how to write clearly and succinctly. She also recommends that after reviewing past documents from a previous RFP, it is better to create new documents as things change often more than expected.[13] Though the timeline proposed by Helen Clegg and Susan Montgomery is rather unrealistic for serial vendor selection, they have a clear outline of how questions can be structured and their "Five Tips for Good RFPs" are especially useful for novice RFP creators.[14]

Based on a recent serial RFP at the University of New Mexico, organizing our questions into the following broad categories was most useful (each category will be discussed in more detail next):

- Introduction—Tell the vendor about the library/libraries and what the contract will cover.
- Company background and financials—Have the vendor tell the company's story.
- Customer service—What services does the vendor provide and how does the vendor deal with problems (the vendor's or the library's)?
- Vendor-provided database—How does the vendor interact with its customers?
- Reports and analytics—What reports can be accessed by the library directly from the vendor database, and what additional services can the vendor provide?
- Service charges and fees—What is the cost of doing business with the vendor?
- References—What do the vendor's current customers say about the vendor?

There may be additional categories that are required or recommended by your institution, such as a category for commitment to sustainable practices.

Single or Split Contract

Early in the RFP process make sure that you have a discussion of the advantages and disadvantages to splitting your serial list between two or more vendors or to keeping all titles with just one vendor. It is less work for Acquisitions to keep all serial titles with just one vendor—all titles are together in one place, invoicing comes from just one place, only one vendor code is maintained, and only one company is contacted to deal with problems, new orders, renewals, and the like. The disadvantage to the library of using just one vendor is that most of the library's acquisitions budget is tied to one vendor. The fear of a vendor bankruptcy can have significant ramifications for libraries. The advantages to having two or more vendors is that you lower the risk to the acquisitions budget and that if one of the companies is not performing to expectations, it is easier to transfer titles between vendors as each will have a contract with the library. The disadvantage to the library of having your serial titles split between different vendors is that Acquisitions has to communicate with multiple vendors to deal with problems, invoicing, renewals, claims, and the like. Other disadvantages are that serials data will have to be gathered from multiple vendors when compiling reports, service fees may be higher, and the library's serial history will be in multiple places.

Some of the issues that have arisen recently in the literature and at conference presentations, reflect libraries' uneasiness with perceived vendor stability. The most recent bankruptcy of a serial vendor that left many academic libraries with millions of dollars in lost prepay subscriptions[15] has raised the question whether libraries even should engage in prepayment of subscriptions and, if they do make prepays, whether these should be insured.

RFP Categories

Introduction

The introduction allows the vendor to gauge if they are interested in submitting a bid. Responding to an RFP is very time-consuming for a vendor. Even though most vendor contracts are somewhat similar, the RFP process will differ between institutions, the composition of the accounts will differ, and thus each RFP needs to be individualized. In the introduction, describe the library or libraries that will be part of the contract and when the contract needs to start. Include the potential size of the account and, if it includes more than one library, how accounting will take place. Describe the type of serials and electronic products that will be included.

If multiple libraries are participating in the RFP, also include information about how the institution(s) may review and reward the successful bid(s). The vendor needs to know whether each participating library will make its own decision or whether there will only be one decision—binding on all participating libraries. The vendor also needs to know whether there is a possibility that the contract will only go to one vendor or if the contract might be split among several vendors. Further, the bidders need to know if there is a possibility that one participating library will select just one vendor and that the other participating libraries may select two or more vendors. Vendors need this level of specificity to develop their service fee structure. If the RFP instructions are vague on these issues, expect vague pricing—something that ultimately can sour the relationship with the successful vendor(s).

Company Background and Financials

Most likely the library personnel already know something about most of the serial vendors, but asking each company that responds to the RFP to provide company information is not only prudent but also very enlightening. How does the company represent itself? Where is it located? How many employees? Ask about the company's finances. Getting this information can be difficult—especially for privately held companies—but it is always interesting and informative to see how a company responds to these types of questions. Although it can be difficult to interpret company finances, as Lorraine Busby points out in her excellent article about the two most recent serial vendor bankruptcies, libraries should conduct as thorough a review as possible.[16]

In the company background section, find out the range of customers the vendor works with: Are any of these similar to the library's account? If a vendor primarily handles small public libraries with mostly popular serial titles, then it most likely is not the best choice for a very large academic library with a very large and complex serial list. What is the company's future strategic direction—will it be investing in infrastructure and staffing? These are all issues that will affect how well the company will perform during the years of the contract and how they will interact with their customers. If the library is used to using prepays for subscriptions, what assurances can the vendor provide that the library's subscriptions have indeed been paid to publishers?[17] Since most of the interaction with the vendor will be electronic, what kind of backup and disaster recovery processes does the company employ? There may well be other questions that you might want to ask about individual companies, but during the RFP process, it is necessary to ask the same questions of all companies.

Customer Service

This is one of the key sections in the RFP. It should describe in detail how the vendor will conduct business with the library. At a minimum it should address the following:

- Account management—Who will be the library's main contacts with the company, and how does the vendor service the various components of a contract?
- Communication—How does the company manage communication to and from the library; what are its service standards; how does it transmit announcements, news, and updates; and does it have a user group?

- Problems—How does the vendor address problems regardless of where the problem first occurred? How does the vendor address ordering and invoicing problems, and what processes are in place to ensure productive communication?
- Subscription management—What types of serials does the vendor manage and conversely what types does it not; what are the timelines for renewing, adding, or canceling subscriptions; how does the vendor process orders and claims; does it manage membership subscriptions; and does the vendor deal with consortial packages?

  - Renewal process—This is really a subsection of subscription management, but since renewals have their own workflows and timelines, it is useful to get a clear picture of how the vendor manages this key function.
  - Cancelations—This is also a subsection of subscription management but should be addressed separately. There are different kinds of cancelations—during the renewal process, after the renewal process, and format cancelations (e.g., canceling print but maintaining online). Be sure to ask how credits for cancelations are managed?

- Invoicing and reconciliation—This is another key aspect of the service provided by a serial vendor, and the library needs to know in great detail how the company manages invoices and how it handles account reconciliations. Important questions include:

  - when and how invoices are delivered to the library (print and/or online);
  - what information is included on invoices (will the library be able to track by fund codes, order numbers, subaccounts, reconciliation);
  - what is the turnaround time;
  - how does the vendor inform the library that the publisher has been paid for a library's subscription;
  - how long does the vendor retain invoice records; and
  - how easy is it to get historical subscription data.

- Electronic journals—If the vendor can activate online subscriptions on a library's behalf, the RFP response should include detailed information about the process and the services the vendor can provide in this area. How does the vendor manage communication between the library and the publisher, is it able to troubleshoot problems, and can the vendor deal with authentication and platform changes? The RFP should also address how the vendor deals with e-journal packages and e-journal database models—whether licensed directly by the library or through a consortium. Title reconciliation may or may not be part of this type of e-journal subscription, but the library will benefit greatly if the serial vendor keeps an audit of titles that move in and out of these journal packages and database models as publishers have a poor record of managing this accurately themselves.

- Transfers—If the library will be changing their serial vendor based on the RFP outcome, how does the company manage the process of transferring accounts between companies?

Vendor-Provided Online Resources (Database)

It is almost a given today that the majority of interactions between a serial vendor and a library will be electronic and that the vendor database will be key to managing all aspects of vendor–library communication. The database should track renewals, ordering, cancelations, invoicing, reconciliations, credits, access, claiming, as well as notifications and a host of other messages between the library and the vendor. The ease of use, accuracy, and consistency of data are all very important. How robust is the vendor's internal technical support to ensure that the database is maintained and regularly updated? How is the data protected and backed up? Is the training on the use of the database adequate or are there features of the database that present problems for libraries?

In the RFP instruction to vendors, the library should request guest access to the vendor-provided database—after all, how can the library evaluate this most important component of the vendor–library interaction if it cannot have access. PowerPoint presentations or screenshots are not a substitute for live testing.

Reports and Analytics

Libraries need many different types of reports related to their serial subscriptions. The RFP should ask for lists and examples of reports that can be generated at will by the library within the database environment, and to list and provide examples of the type of reports that require vendor intervention. Depending on local circumstances and serial history, the library may want to be very specific on the type of reports required or desired.

If the vendor can provide additional analytics that might be useful for the library, find out if these are part of the overall service fees or if there will be additional charges. For instance, if the vendor is able to provide usage statistics for electronic journals, will the vendor be able to provide these for all platforms or for just selected platforms?

Service Charges and Fees

Although it might be logical to make the service fee the main criterion for selecting a serial vendor, the library should think carefully about the whole package of services that a vendor can provide. The vendor should provide a very detailed list of all service charges and other fees for each of the years that the contract will be active, thus eliminating ambiguities and misunderstandings. The vendor should also indicate how they manage account prepays and credits as part of their service charge structure.

References

Preferably have vendors provide the library with a list of various references: recently added customers to evaluate how well the vendor handled transfers; long-term customers to evaluate how well the vendor deals with renewals and customer service in general; and customers with a similar account structure and size as your library to evaluate if the vendor is able to service the library's list of serials. If the RFP includes a special library (e.g., a law or medical library), one or more references should also be to a similar type of library.

Add additional main categories to the RFP or break out some of the categories suggested above into smaller sections. How you approach this depends on the experiences the library has had with current and past vendors. It is also possible that institutional procurement regulations require all companies wanting to do business with the university or the state to address additional questions unrelated to the specific RFP. For instance, at the University of New Mexico, in addition to providing proof of Small and Small Disadvantaged Business Certification, all companies that bid on contracts with the university must also answer questions on how they address environmental, equality, and human rights issues—for example, does the company provide health care or wellness programs for their employees?

VENDOR VISITS

Vendor visits are most likely to be a part of the RFP process, and, depending on what flexibility is allowed by procurement regulations and/or policies, these could be scheduled before the formal RFP starts, during the time the RFP is open for bid, or after the bid deadline has passed. Each has advantages and disadvantages.

If the vendor visits take place before the formal RFP process, it is up to the library to ensure that all likely vendors are informed that the library is planning to issue an RFP for a new serial contract. The advantage to visiting the library for the vendor is that it will give them a deeper understanding of the type of account involved, and if the vendor decides to respond to the RFP, they can address the issues that they identified as being the most important to the library in their responses. The advantage to the library is the opportunity to evaluate what each vendor is capable of doing. The preliminary vendor visit serves as a form of request for information (RFI), prior to the formal RFP.

If the vendor visit takes place during the time when the RFP is open for bid, there are undoubtedly rules that need to be followed—especially for public institutions. Most likely all vendors who are responding to the RFP will need to be invited (though not all may choose to accept the invitation). If procurement regulations stipulate the length of time that an RFP process is open, getting vendors to your library during this time frame can be a big challenge. The advantages for the vendor in visiting the library while the bid process is open are that they will have an opportunity to see what is important to the library and can address these issues directly in the presentation and also in their final bid. If the library is able to review bids as these are submitted to the procurement office—even as these are in draft form—the library could ask for clarification on vendor responses. The disadvantages to both the vendor and the library are that these visits will mostly likely be done on a very narrow timeline, not only creating scheduling difficulties for everybody but also increasing the cost to the vendor for visiting the library.

If the vendor visits take place after the bid process is closed, it is possible that the library may only invite the top contenders, based on preliminary evaluation and scoring. Most likely, regulations will dictate whether only some of the bidders or all of the bidders must be invited. The advantage to the library is that it has reviewed each vendor's responses and can ask for clarification where needed. The advantage to the vendor is that omissions or misunderstandings can be corrected.

EVALUATING AND SCORING RFP SUBMISSIONS

Once the response deadline has passed, it is time for the RFP committee to review all submissions. It is strongly recommended that the committee finalize a scoring matrix or rubric before the deadline—waiting until all the bids are in to create this matrix just further prolongs the RFP process and could give the appearance of being biased to favor one vendor over another. The committee will have to decide how much weight each of the main RFP categories (company background, customer service, vendor-provided database, reports and additional services, pricing, references, and any other required sections) will be assigned in the overall score, and they should also discuss how they want to evaluate and score all the detailed information provided within each of the broad categories. As the committee assigns weight to the various categories, bear in mind that it may not be in the institution's long-term interest to assign the highest weight to service fees. Considering the monetary size of the vendor account(s), it is probably more important that the library's subscription payments are transacted reliably and correctly. It is possible that the procurement office requires scoring of all submissions to be done in a certain manner. For public institutions it is especially important to follow a formal evaluation process as it is not uncommon for unsuccessful bidders to challenge the process.

Analyzing the different bids is a time-consuming process that should not be rushed. It takes time to review multiyear contracts (limits often set by regulations or policy) and to understand exactly what each of the bidding companies can and cannot do, what their strengths and weaknesses are, and what they charge for their different services. Whether each committee member scores each vendor individually, the committee scores each company as a group, or a combination of the two, it is very likely that the procurement office has additional policies and practices that regulate parts of this process.

Sometimes during this time the committee—and possibly everybody in the Acquisitions department—has had opportunities to work with the vendor-provided database to evaluate the strengths and weaknesses of these systems. The committee also needs to collect feedback from all who participated in vendor presentations for their evaluation of each of the companies.

Checking References

Each submitting bidder will have been asked to provide several references, and the committee should have developed a template of questions they want to ask each of the references. Using the outline of basic categories that the vendor had to address in the RFP, the reference calls may also want to address the following questions:

- How long has the library been with the vendor (new or well-established)?
- What is the size of the account (how does it compare to your account)?
- What do they like the best and what do they like the least about the company?
- How does the company address problems? Ask for examples and have the reference explain how the company addressed these.
- How do they like the vendor database—what works well and what not as much?
- Does the vendor provide additional value-added services? If so, explain/describe.
- Is there anything else the reference would like to add?

After the calls have been completed, these, too, need to be scored. If the committee splits up the work, it is a good idea to get the group back together to compare notes on the various calls.

Report and Decision

After the committee has evaluated each company's response to the RFP and assigned its scores, now comes the very important process of comparing scores and deciding which of the companies meet most of the library's expectations. If lucky, one company will outscore all the others but more likely—since there are now only a handful or so major serial vendors—expect the scores to be very close.

If only one library is participating in the RFP, the decision process might be fairly simple: Do we split the account and select two or more vendors to handle all serials, or do we select the highest scoring company to handle all serials? If multiple libraries are participating in the RFP, each library first needs to decide whether to split the account or to keep it with one company. Then each library has to decide which company/companies to select based on overall scoring. Expect to have several meetings to discuss the merit of each of the vendors and the different scenarios for the account structure.

If the library is the final decision maker, the work is basically done. One or more vendors are selected, and negotiations will start to finalize the service contract. A formal report should be prepared and kept on file. It will be useful to reacquaint library staff with the processes and decisions for when the library next has to renew or go out for a new RFP.

If, on the other hand, the library does not make the final decision, then a report needs to be prepared and sent to the procurement office to be forwarded to the person or body that makes the final determination—a sometimes lengthy process that hopefully was built into the timeline. The report should list the RFP committee members, provide information on why an RFP was needed for a serial vendor(s), a synopsis of the process and the evaluation criteria used, strengths and weaknesses of each of the bidding vendors, and each company's final score and the financial implications of the contract(s). The report also needs to reflect each participating library's preferences for the final award(s).

Using the RFP committee's report, the agency that makes contractual decisions will approve the recommendations in the report, reject the recommendations, or send the recommendations back to the committee for clarification. It is possible that a subcommittee (e.g., a finance committee) of the entity that makes the final decision will ask the RFP committee chair(s) to meet with the subcommittee to answer questions before the report is forwarded to the final decision-making body. Once the vendor(s) selection has been approved, the procurement office can contact the vendors letting them know the outcome.

THE NEW CONTRACT AND CONCLUSION

The RFP process is now complete. If a new vendor or vendors are selected, the library/libraries will start the often lengthy process of transferring titles from current to new vendor(s), as well as training, testing, and using the vendor database. If a current vendor is retained, the library may or may not have additional work before the new contract starts, but if the RFP process added additional services from the vendor, the library will want to get these started.

Selecting a serial vendor through an RFP process is often complex and lengthy, but with careful planning, it is possible to manage the complexity, and perhaps even reduce the time it takes from start to successful end.

Lessons Learned

- Timeline—timeline—timeline! The first step is to map out the RFP process. The more people and libraries that are involved, the more time it will take.
- Do your homework. Be familiar with the procurement rules and process at your institution.
- Consider inviting vendors to visit before the RFP starts. Solicit feedback on presentations from a variety of constituents.
- Do not hesitate to ask for sample RFP questions from colleagues at other libraries who have recently selected a serials vendor through the RFP process.
- Take the time to analyze the service charge proposals. The RFP response will become the terms of the contract with the serials vendor that is selected. Make sure you understand all the charges. You will likely have to do some work to translate them into a format that can be compared across vendors.
- Make time to call vendor references. Feedback received on the phone is often more candid and thoughtful than an e-mail response.
- Keep the scoring matrix as simple as possible. Scores given to a larger category of questions are more meaningful than scores produced by scoring lots of questions individually. Document why the RFP was scored as it was.
- Keep a file for the next time the serials vendor comes up for RFP. Assign someone to keep track of all products and services that are under RFP.

NOTES

1. Joseph A. Puccio, *Serials Reference Work* (Englewood, CO: Libraries Unlimited, Inc., 1989), 4.

2. "Vendor" and/or "vendors" will be used interchangeably throughout this chapter.

3. Association for Library Collections & Technical Services defines "serial vendors" as "a term used to refer to all types of suppliers of serial publications (i.e. both Continuation dealers and Subscription agents), and to distinguish them from suppliers of monographs. The term sometimes is used in a narrow sense to refer to vendors who supply serials other than periodicals (i.e., Continuation dealers) and to distinguish them from Subscription agents" (http://www.ala.org/alcts/sites/ala.org.alcts/files/content/resources/collect/serials/acqglossary/05seracq_glo.pdf p. 42). Accessed 4/9/18.

4. Albert Prior, "Acquiring and Accessing Serials Information—The Electronic Intermediary," *Interlending & Document Supply* 29, no. 2 (2001): 62–69.

5. One of the latest such bankruptcies in 2014 (Swets Information Services B.V.) cost libraries millions of dollars in lost subscriptions. See https://www.insidehighered.com/news/2015/01/02/swets-bankruptcy-will-cost-libraries-time-money (accessed May 24, 2017).

6. See Recent Updates at https://www.linkedin.com/company/association-of-subscription-agents (accessed May 24, 2017).

7. Ibid., 64.

8. Rachel Augello Erb and Nancy Hunter, "Prelude, Tumult, Aftermath: An Academic Library Perspective on the Swets B.V. Bankruptcy," *The Serials Librarian* 69, no. 3–4 (2015): 277–84.

9. NASPO, *Briefing Paper: Non-Competitive/Sole Source Procurement: Seven Questions* (Lexington, KY: National Association of State Procurement Officials, 2015), accessed May 24, 2017, http://www.naspo.org/SoleSourceProcurement/7-Question_Sole_Source_Procurement_briefing_paper-1-13-15.pdf.

10. Micheline Westfall, Justin Clarke, and Jeanne M. Langendorfer, "Selecting a Vendor: The Request for Proposal (RFP) from Library and Vendor perspectives," *The Serials Librarian* 68, no 1–4 (2013): 188–95.

11. Frances C. Wilkinson and Connie Capers Thorson, "Domestic and Foreign Serials," in *The RFP Process: Effective Management of the Acquisitions of Library Materials*, eds. Frances C. Wilkinson and Connie Capers Thorson (Santa Barbara, CA: Libraries Unlimited, 1998), 31–50.

12. Micheline Brown Westfall, "Using a Request for Proposal (RFP) to Select a Serials Vendor: The University of Tennessee Experience," *Serials Review* 37, no. 2 (2011): 87–92.

13 Debbie Schachter, "How to Manage the RFP Process," *Information Outlook* 8, no. 11 (2004): 10–12.

14. Helen Clegg and Susan Montgomery, "How to Write an RFP for Information Products," *Information Outlook* 10, no. 6 (2006): 23–33.

15. Matt Enis, "Swets Bankruptcy Recalls Fallout from RoweCom," *Library Journal* 139, no. 18 (November 1, 2014): 12.

16. *Lorraine Busby,* "Left Holding the Bag: A Tale of Two Companies," *The Serials Librarian* 67, no. 4 (2014): 355–62.

17. This is not a trivial question. When RoweCom/Faxon declared bankruptcy in 2002, it is estimated that libraries lost between $30 and $80 million in paid subscriptions that were not passed on to the publishers. See Sue Wiegand, "Financial Issues: Changes in Serials Acquisitions in the 21st Century," *The Serials Librarian* 49, no. 1/2 (2005): 244.

5

RFPS FOR PUBLIC LIBRARY COLLECTIONS

Dana D. Vinke

INTRODUCTION

The request for proposals (RFP) for public library collections is the formal process whereby an organization solicits vendor proposals for the procurement of library materials, such as books, journals, and media in various formats, based on stated standards and requirements. The process can be simple or complex depending on the needs and the requirements of the organization as well as governing body. Most institutions have well-established procurement procedures, contract service agreements, and detailed local guidelines for the RFP process. These should be consulted first before starting the RFP process.

The RFP process involves preparing and identifying the needs of the organization, writing the RFP, issuing the RFP, evaluating proposals, selecting a vendor, and awarding a contract. The RFP for library collections process, while challenging, can provide a unique opportunity for the library. A well-crafted and conducted RFP will select a vendor that is the most responsible and cost-effective, thus providing the organization more purchasing power and potentially enhancing the organizational workflow.

PREPARATION AND IDENTIFYING NEEDS

Timeline

The RFP process is usually initiated by the pending expiration of a current contract with a library materials vendor, an organization's dissatisfaction with a current vendor, or both. Establishing a timeline that ensures the continuation of services regardless of vendor selection is of the utmost importance. The project should begin at least one year in advance, and the timeline should encompass everything from the initial research phase to the anticipated contract start date, including allotted periods for surveying the needs of the organization, determining system requirements, and crafting and editing the RFP. The timeline should also incorporate milestones such as RFP release date, question period, proposal due dates, evaluation times, and award notification date while including buffer periods to account for delays in any step of the process.

RFP Committee

A team or committee should be established for the RFP design, evaluation, and selection portions of the process. Ideally, there should be a project manager for the team. This individual will coordinate meetings, facilitate discussions, and manage the overall project from initiation through to completion. The designated team should reflect the needs of various library departments and work units and be comprised of individuals who can best represent and elicit feedback from respective departments. Depending on the components of the RFP and staffing levels, representation may include individuals from the library's cataloging department, acquisitions department, and materials selectors (adult, youth, media, and print). Whether required by the organization or not, it is also a good idea to enlist one member outside of the library to provide objective input and evaluation, such as a departmental purchasing manager and finance analyst. Because the RFP process is labor-intensive, all team members should possess flexibility and time to commit to the process. In addition, there may be components such as vendor interviews or presentations that will require all team members be present.

Research

Librarians are familiar with performing research and usually have developed and honed these skills. The RFP provides an opportunity to utilize these skills for the benefit of the organization. Start by creating an online or network space to store research and collaborate with other members of the team. Create an e-mail distribution list among pertinent team members to share information. Begin researching by reviewing the organization's previous library collections bid. This is a good starting place because it will provide some historical perspective and bring to mind considerations that may not otherwise come to mind. If there are staff available who were involved directly in the earlier process, they may be able to give insights on topics or areas that were not addressed or possibly omitted previously. This will help avoid past errors or missteps.

Next, review and examine recent and relevant library materials RFPs from similarly sized organizations. This may be as simple as conducting an online search or contacting local systems of similar size and scope and requesting a copy of their RFP. The bid process is generally public information and retrievable from a library's administration or governing body. Consolidate documents for review by the team.

Another avenue of research is the library materials vendors themselves. Most vendors are willing to share copies of bids, proposals, or sample RFPs. Vendors may be consulted at conferences such as the American Library Association conference and Public Library Association conference or invited to the library to demo their services in advance of the RFP. Scheduling demos will provide insight and knowledge of new or current features and services. It is important to note that the vendors have an agenda and are likely to focus on the strengths of their ordering systems, fill rates, and depth of catalog rather than any shortcomings. Keeping a skeptical mind-set when reviewing vendor-sourced information will assist in evaluation. For example, if a vendor fails to provide any information on the provision of on-order records and the library utilizes them to notify patrons of forthcoming titles, then the team may inquire about or include in the RFP.

Surveys

Aside from the RFP team member's input and research, it will be useful to survey staff on the advantages and disadvantages of the current vendor and what features they would deem beneficial in the future. Doing so assists developing the technical requirements of the RFP as well as narrative questions. When surveying staff, be sure to use both ratings that are scalable and open-ended questions. Scalable ratings will help in weighing portions of the evaluation criteria. For example, staff may be asked, "Which is more important to a selector: depth of catalog or the discount price?" If staff continuously rank discount price as a higher priority (a 9 let's say, on a 1 to 10 scale with 10 being the highest) than depth of inventory (a 7), then the feedback can be incorporated in scoring and ranking the importance of price or inventory. Open-ended questions will help address issues that may not have been considered before and give staff the time to write in more detail their concerns or preferences.

WRITING THE RFP

When beginning to write the RFP, think of what the library would like to accomplish in terms of materials and services over the span of the pending contract period. Consider reviewing the library's mission statement or plan of service. If the RFP is crafted only in terms of the organization's present needs instead of future needs, the RFP may risk delaying plans, modifying the contract/agreement, or having to initiate a new RFP. A good example of this might be a library that seeks to open several branches in the next five years. A vendor is needed that can provide a quality, comprehensive, and cost-effective opening-day collection. In terms of the RFP, vendors would be requested to provide the extent of their ability to provide multiple opening-day collections over a five-year period.

Introduction and Statement of Purpose

The RFP should begin with an opening statement listing the intent and expectations, including the date the RFP is issued, the deadline for questions or clarifications, the date proposals are due, and the anticipated contract start date. The introduction should contain the library's mission statement or a brief summary of the plan of service highlighting major goals and objectives as they relate to the RFP.

Background

The background section provides an opportunity to introduce the organization to potential vendors. Typically, the section starts with a brief history of the library followed by the library's scope of services and library type (e.g., public, private, or some combination). The section would include the size of the library organization, number of staff, annual circulation, service points, and the role of the library in regard to the rest of the organization or community. For example, the RFP may state that the library is a medium-sized public library with 100 staff members and five branch locations and is part of the city's Parks and Recreation Department. The section should include other operational expenditures such as rental collections and approval plans and explain any cost that the library may expend on the outsourcing of cataloging and processing of materials. The section should also state whether the library practices centralized or decentralized collection development, maintain floating collections or utilize rental collections, and provide any significant plans for the near future such as radio-frequency identification (RFID) implementation or patron-driven acquisitions.

Additional operational data mentioned in the background section may be pertinent to potential vendors such as annual materials budget broken down by location, audiences, and physical material type. For example, see Table 5.1.

Table 5.1 Annual Materials Expenditure

Adult books	$300,000
Youth books	$150,000
Audiobooks (adult and youth)	$35,000
Music compact discs (adult and youth)	$25,000
DVDs (adult and youth)	$55,000

Definitions

Clearly define the technical terms or terminology presented in the RFP. Most fields of work have technical terms and acronyms, and libraries are no different. Library materials vendors and professional library staff are generally well versed in these terms; however, clearly defining terms will accomplish two things. First, it will eliminate confusion and ensure that both parties are on the same page. Second, it will help to explain the process and ultimate award of contract to those less familiar with the library's needs such as purchasing departments, finance managers, boards, and commissions. A contract award may need a board or council approval. Those organizations are typically made up of community members who are not as knowledgeable regarding a library's technical requirements. Presenting clearly defined terminology will help avoid long explanations later. Some terms to consider defining are ILS, RFID, MARC, EDI interface, and shelf-ready.

Evaluation Criteria

Evaluation criteria are the metrics used to assess, evaluate, and score each proposal individually, so they may be ultimately ranked objectively against one another. Each metric is directly related to the scope of service detailed in the RFP. Since an RFP is not a strict bid, the criteria for evaluation will include pricing and discounts, but the final decision will not be limited strictly to costs. Some key criteria for library material vendors may include inventory and catalog, fulfillment, ordering system, discounts off list price, cataloging and processing, vendor support and training, and relevant experience. The actual specifics of each criterion will be outlined in more detail in the technical requirements and narrative portions of the RFP.

For example:

DESCRIPTION OF EVALUATION CRITERIA
TOTAL POSSIBLE POINTS: 100

Selection of Materials (points possible 25)

The depth and breadth of available materials for purchase that meet the organization's requirements, as established by the proposal and as evaluated and examined by the RFP evaluation committee.

Cost (points possible 25)

Cost as determined by discount rates by material and format type, cost of processing and cataloging of materials, shipping and handling

---

costs, and other ancillary costs as offered in the proposal and as evaluated and examined by the RFP evaluation committee.

Online Ordering System (points possible 20)

Proposed ordering system must possess the software features and performance that align with the organization's requirements as demonstrated by the proposal and as evaluated and examined by the RFP evaluation committee.

Fulfillment (points possible 15)

Vendor's delivery methods, turnaround times, and fill rates offered in the proposal meet the organization's requirements, as demonstrated by the proposal and as evaluated and examined by the RFP evaluation committee.

Vendor Support and Services (points possible 10)

Vendor's documentation, training, and customer support meet the organization's requirements, as demonstrated by the proposal and as evaluated and examined by the RFP evaluation committee.

Recent, Relevant, and Prior Experience (points possible 5)

Vendor's experience in supplying materials of similar scale, scope, and complexity meets the organization's requirements, as offered in the proposal and as evaluated and examined by the RFP evaluation committee.

Scope of Services

In the scope of services section, vendors should be provided with an outline of materials and services being sought. The focus should be on the essentials of the RFP, and the technical aspects should be listed in the technical requirements section of the RFP. For example, a sample text could contain the following:

Anytown Public Library requires the services of a wholesale book distributor to provide the annual requirement of print books, audio, and video materials for a period of three (3) years with an option to renew annually for a total of five (5) years. Anytown Public Library is seeking a vendor(s) who will provide the following:

- Extremely competitive discount rates compared to retail and list prices
- Large and varied inventories with breadth and depth of collections
- Efficiencies in placing orders and processing payments to streamline workflow
- Integration with the library's ILS
- Material delivery options that include shelf-ready, fully processed, and cataloged materials
- Quick turnaround time from the ordering of materials to the receipt of materials
- Excellent fill rates
- Access to materials in a wide variety of popular languages
- Outstanding customer service and support

Partial Bids

It should be noted that RFPs for library materials may be inclusive or exclusive regarding format, age level, language, or subject specialty. In these cases, RFPs should specify whether partial bids will be accepted. Generally, partial bids are accepted when the library perceives an advantage in allocating the award to companies that may specialize in curating and providing materials in certain formats, age levels, language, or subject specialty. For example, certain distributors concentrate on a certain language specialty. This may be useful particularly since large distributors may not have the ability to cater to such specialization. In this instance, the decision may be to specify the languages that are in demand in the community and either generate a separate RFP or decide to accept partial bids for only these materials. The evaluation criteria for partial bid proposals should be developed in advance, so they can be evaluated equitably. While most vendors cannot provide all materials and formats, there are great benefits in having fewer materials vendors in terms of accounting, ordering, receiving, and workflow. The team should weigh all the pros and cons of a single materials RFP versus multiple RFPs.

Phraseology

Separate from terms and definitions, state requirements for prospective vendors as clearly and specifically as possible. Avoid terms like "should" and "support," and instead use terms like "must" and "necessary" when defining requirements. Terms like "should" and "support" can lead to ambiguity. For example, when telling a car salesperson that you need a car, would you say it *should* have brakes, or it *must* have brakes?

Attachments and Samples

For clarification purposes, it is often necessary that examples or samples be provided either by the library or by the vendor. For example, if the RFP requires full processing of materials, scanned examples of those specifications should be included in the RFP. Subsequently, the RFP may require that vendors provide examples of their ability to process materials according to the library's standards. The RFP should request that vendors supply any and all policies referenced in the bid document, including return and cancelation policies. These samples and attachments will be in addition to institutional requirements such as business licensing, insurance coverage, and liability.

Functional or Technical Requirements

The purpose of functional or technical requirements is to detail the exact needs of the organization or agency, which are nonnegotiable. Vendors must be able to provide the requirements, or their proposals are invalid. Numerate each requirement so that vendors can respond accordingly. Provide vendors the opportunity to respond with simple responses such as "complies," "does not comply," or "not applicable." The RFP may present vendors with the option to supply brief additional details regarding their response. The responses will help in reviewing and scoring RFPs.

In addition to functional and technical requirements checklist, the RFP should include narrative questions to offer an opportunity for more open-ended

Table 5.2 Examples of Technical Requirements and Narrative Questions

	Technical Requirement	Narrative Question
Interface	Vendor must provide an electronic, web-based ordering system with access to professional reviews.	List the professional review sources accessible through your interface.
Training	Vendor must provide ongoing training as needed for new employees and on new features, services, and upgrades.	Describe the process for requesting specific training for staff.
Cataloging	Vendor must provide on-order records in MARC and Resource Description and Access (RDA) formats.	Outline in detail how on-order records are accessed and loaded from your system to the integrated library system (ILS).
Processing	Vendor must be able to ship all hardcover books precovered with clear Mylar dust jackets.	Describe how the library would establish processing standards for shelf-ready materials.

questions and afford vendors the ability to provide more detailed and specialized answers. Most RFPs will have both, and each will cover the same major areas. For example, both the technical requirement section and narrative questions section will have topics that include acquisitions, cataloging, collection development tools, and processing. Table 5.2 contains examples of the same topics addressed differently by these sections. For the purposes of the chapter, we will address both technical requirements and narrative questions under each major component.

Defining Library Materials

Library materials, for the purposes of this section, refer to physical items a library purchases for the intent of internal and/or external circulation. These items include, but are not limited to, books, DVDs, CDs, readalongs, and audiobooks. Library materials, for the purposes of this section, do not refer to periodicals or electronic resources. In the technical requirement portion of the RFP, clearly define the materials being sought to purchase by criteria such as age group, reading level, format, and language. Specify the materials that are excluded from the RFP as well.

For example:

Vendor must provide materials suitable for adults and youth in all of the following formats:

Print Books:
- Hardcover books (adult and youth)
- Paperback books (trade and mass market)
- Graphic novels
- Books in library binding
- Large print books (hardcover and softcover)
- Board books
- Reference books

Audio Visual Materials:
- Audio CDs including current popular and classical music
- Book on CD (abridged and unabridged, standard and MP3)
- Prerecorded audio player
- Readalongs (hardback and paperback books with CD and page turn cues)
- Feature and educational DVDs (retail editions and rental editions)
- Feature and educational Blu-ray or Blu-ray Disc (BD) (retail editions and rental editions)
- Videogames

General Requirements

Shipping and Delivery

Shipping and delivery requirements are the specifications requested that determine when and how materials are sent to the library. Shipping requirements may include standards such as shipper, shipping rates, tracking, secure packaging to prevent damage, address labels, packing slips, and weight and size of containers. Designate physical location(s) and designate the days and times where materials will be received, including street address, floor, room number, and whether or not deliveries need to be inside or outside the facility. It is important to be as specific as possible and include any relevant details such as whether there is a security gate or door.

Delivery requirements also refer to the expected delivery time of stocked items within receipt of order. For example, the RFP may require that in-stock items be delivered within 48 hours of receiving an order. The RFP may also stipulate the receipt of items by publication/production date or street release date, whichever comes first.

Claims, Cancelations, and Back Orders

Material selectors may order items that are temporarily out of stock, permanently out of stock, or out of print. Items temporarily out of stock are referred to as back orders since the order cannot be filled by the supplier when placed but is instead awaiting availability. Publications may also be delayed or canceled for a variety of reasons. Detail how the vendors should handle all of these issues because order status is important for budgetary purposes and catalog maintenance. List the requirements in terms of handling claims, cancelations, and back orders in detail. Many libraries require vendors to automatically terminate orders that are on back order or delayed after an established time period (e.g., back-ordered items after 30 days will be canceled). Some libraries require periodical status reports of materials not received. The RFP should require that vendors provide their policy on cancelations when the library must cancel an order.

Substitutions

Substitutions occur when a vendor cannot fulfill a requested title. A vendor may substitute another item when a particular edition or binding is no longer available. Instruct vendors on when, if at all, the library is willing to accept substitutions.

Returns

Returns are materials the library has deemed unacceptable for reasons such as damaged or defective, not ordered, and not suitable for the collection.

Vendors should describe their return policy and describe the procedures for returning items, time limitations, nonreturnable items, and budget reconciliation in terms of credit, fund reimbursement, or replacement. Vendors should describe any restrictions on returns for shelf-ready items, including items that have been cataloged and processed. The vendor should also list any fees associated with returns such as shipping and restocking charges or fees.

Warranties and Replacements

Publishers may offer warranties or replacements depending on the material provided. Such knowledge is relevant mostly because sets or items with multiple parts may have components that if lost or damaged render the entire set or item unusable. Materials suppliers should provide information in their proposal on how third-party warranties or replacements are processed.

Invoicing

Accurate and timely invoicing is essential to a library's workflow. Include the library's requirements for receiving and processing invoices and receiving statements. Include the information necessary on each and how they should be itemized (title, ISBN, discount price, shipping). State whether the library requires print and/or electronic invoices and whether the library requires separate invoices for services such as processing and cataloging. Some requirements may include the provision of print and/or electronic (see ILS integration) invoices displaying the library's account number and itemization, including ISBN, binding, list and discount price, sales tax, and shipping costs. Vendors may be required to include a separate invoice detailing processing and cataloging charges. Depending on the organization, monthly statements may be required detailing all paid and outstanding invoices as well as all unfilled orders.

Size and Depth of Catalog

To ascertain the size and depth of the vendor's catalog, the RFP should solicit the names and numbers of publishers and imprints available in stock and available to order and the number of materials available in stock by age level, language, format, and binding. Request a list of any suppliers or types of suppliers the vendor is unable to offer. Be sure to request that items such as print-on-demand and self-published materials be listed separately.

Integrated Library System Integration

Integrated library system (ILS) integration refers to all aspects in which the vendor's online ordering system will interface with the library's ILS, including the public catalog, staff catalog, and acquisitions. This interface may be complex depending on the organization. For additional details on this topic, see the sections dedicated to cataloging and acquisitions.

Considerations include if, when, and how on-order records are loaded in the system to facilitate the placement of holds on forthcoming titles; if, when, and how full bibliographic records are loaded in the system; and if and how acquisitions transactions are processed through electronic data interchange (EDI).

EDI is a method of communicating orders, confirmation of orders, and invoices between the library's ILS and the library materials vendor. Systems utilizing an EDI interface can process purchase orders, claims, cancelations, invoices, and sometimes payment. Ideally, the library's ILS service representative will be consulted to provide clear and accurate data requirements for setting up an EDI interface with a prospective vendor. The RFP may require vendors provide a list of the ILS systems compliant with their product.

Interface

The vendor interface is the online system library staff use to browse, select, and order material. This is a critical element of the RFP as it can have direct impact on the library's workflow. Vendors have created quite robust systems and frequently add new features. When writing the interface portion of the RFP, consider which features are important to selectors. This assists in deciding whether these features are required or optional. Online ordering systems should be accessible and fully functional in the contemporary browser environments and on multiple device formats, including desktops and tablets. Vendors should also list any cost or limitations on the number of user accounts. The RFP may require that vendors provide unlimited simultaneous use of the interface at no cost. The RFP may also require that the vendor retain order histories for a defined amount of time.

To further solicit staff input, request guest access to the online ordering systems from vendors. Some key features to note include the search options, bibliographic data, cart/selection list management, and curated lists.

Search Options and Limits:
- Author/Title/Keyword
- Boolean search (use of operators such as AND, NOT, and OR)
- Format
- Publication date or date range
- Publisher
- Language
- BISAC browsing
- Demand
- Series information (links to other titles in a series)
- Reading level (e.g., Lexile® levels)

- Dewey or LC range
- Full-text reviews from professional journals (including starred reviews)
- Edition
- Price (list and discount)
- Stock status

Bibliographic Data:

- Title/Author
- Cover art
- ISBN/EAN
- Publisher
- Price
- Physical information (e.g., pagination, dimensions)
- Binding
- Publication date
- Annotation
- Stock availability, including on-hand, on-order, and warehouse
- Professional review sources (*Booklist, Kirkus, Publisher's Weekly, Library Journal,* and *School Library Journal,* etc.)
- Format options (links to all available formats)
- Ability to e-mail product information

Cart/Selection List Management:

- Ability to create and price lists in real time
- Ability to share and merge lists
- Ability to export selection lists to common electronic spreadsheet file formats
- Ability to add customized location and cataloging notes for individual items (e.g., this is a replacement copy)

Curated Selection Lists:

- Provide access to curated selection lists for books, audio, and audiovisual titles such as bestsellers, new titles, and award winners
- Ability for users to opt in and opt out of curated selections lists

Collection Development Services

Collection development services cover a range of services vendors provide that include notification of pending popular or subject-specific releases, curated selection lists, standing order plans, and book leasing programs. Curated selections are defined by the vendor with or without the input of the library and are designed to enhance selection and streamline workflow. For example, a curated selection list might be a monthly aggregated list of new science fiction titles or a list of new documentary films available in Blu-ray. A curated selection list may also include specific requisites provided by the library such as titles from specific publishers and unit price ranges.

Standing order plans consist of a selection of material that will automatically be provided by a vendor, either periodically or as published, on an ongoing basis. Most plans define the material type and conform to a predetermined set limit of materials, price, and delivery schedule. For example, a vendor may provide standing order plans for large print books. These plans have genre options (e.g., mystery, romance, inspirational), shipping, pricing, and title estimates (e.g., receive 36 hardcovers a year [monthly shipments] for approximately $1,173).

Book leasing programs offer popular titles such as bestsellers to meet patron demand on a rental basis. Once the demand is met, the books are returned to the vendor. Libraries typically have an option to retain these titles permanently if needed. A library agrees in advance to an annual plan based on the number of titles and quantity of books they wish to receive as well as the invoice method and interval (e.g., annual or quarterly). The discounts, selection, and quantity offered by these plans provide libraries with an economic way to meet patron demand.

Fill Rates

Fill rates refer to the ratio of orders to actual fulfillment. Depending on the vendor and the number of publishers contracted, fill rates will vary. Consider requesting fill rates based on material type, age level, and language. For example, the RFP may request fill rates for the following:

- General trade hardcover books (adult)
- General trade hardcover books (youth)
- Adult quality (trade) paperback books
- Adult mass market paperback books
- Youth mass market paperback books
- Large print books
- Publisher's library binding editions (youth)
- University press trade editions
- Audio CDs including current popular and classical music
- Books on CD (unabridged)
- Feature and educational Blu-ray/DVDs (retail and rental editions)
- Readalong books with CD
- Board books

Print on Demand

Print on demand (POD) refers to a process in which copies of books are not printed until the vendor obtains an order. This reduces publishing costs and allows for smaller or even singular print runs. Some major library materials vendors offer the service. While the service enjoys wide appeal, it is especially relevant to self-published authors or hard-to-find titles. If interested in this service, the RFP should request the POD standards from vendors, including paper quality, binding type, and processing costs.

Staff Accounts

Some vendors offer the provision of staff accounts, which means that staff can access many of the features the vendor offers the library in terms of selection, discounts, and shipping. The RFP needs to specify how these accounts are managed and kept separate from standard library accounts.

Customer Service and Support

Vendors should provide quality and timely customer service and support. Determine or clarify in the RFP the method and response time for resolving customer service issues. Consider requiring that vendors provide customer support via telephone, e-mail, and online chat as necessary and respond to all inquiries and questions within one business day. Take into consideration the library's hours of operation and various time zones. The RFP may also require the vendor to provide advanced notice of potential downtime for system updates, routine maintenance, and product enhancements.

Shelf-Ready Services

Shelf-ready services refer to the degree in which items arrive from the materials vendor processed, cataloged, and ready for circulation. Most vendors offer a variety of shelf-ready services, and these services generally fall into two categories: cataloging and physical processing. Cataloging ranges from providing access to brief on-order records to fully customized bibliographic records and call number assignment. Processing can include a variety of options including book covers, RFID tags, barcodes, antitheft security tags, spine labels, and property stamps. Services may be tailored to library needs and are usually established in advance with thorough testing. If the library requires shelf-ready services, define the terms in the RFP to ensure the library receives the level and quality desired. Include all shelf-ready required components in the price proposal and provide examples. The RFP may require or request vendors provide an average error rate in their cataloging and processing of materials. Even if the library does not currently use shelf-ready services, it may be prudent to request or require vendors provide such services to allow the library flexibility in the future.

Cataloging

Cataloging refers to the level, standards, and criteria to which the library expects the vendor to provide bibliographic records. For example, vendors may be required to provide MARC21 records that follow Anglo-American Cataloguing Rules, second edition (AACR2) and/or RDA standards. List additional requirements such as holdings statements, authority control, and any local practices such as call number and cutter specifications and local notes.

List requirements for the access and retrieval of bibliographic records from the vendor or other bibliographic databases. The vendor should detail their process for delivering these records and the origin of the records (e.g., OCLC, Library of Congress) in the proposal. The vendor should include detailed pricing in the cost proposal including appropriate costs for all types of formats for which cataloging services are provided.

Physical Processing

Libraries requiring vendors to partially or fully process materials will need to fully detail their exact specifications. Processing can include but is not limited to the application of property stamps and labels, call numbers, RFID tags, barcodes, and book covers. The specifics need to be represented in technical requirements as well as the cost proposal, including appropriate cost for all types of formats for which processing services are provided. Request that vendors provide samples of the processed materials, such as book covers and spine labels as well as the error rate in processing of materials.

Training and Documentation

Proper staff training and manuals or documentation are important both prior to implementation and ongoing especially when considering a change in a materials supplier. RFPs may specify the amount of time and type of training that is required each year. Taking into account the size of the library's staff, scheduling, and Internet infrastructure, the library or the RFP may require that instruction be on-site, online, or a combination of both. The subject of instruction should encompass all facets of operations including searching, selecting, and ordering materials; receiving and returning items; and invoicing. Vendors should stipulate any and all charges associated with training. The RFP may require that vendors assume the responsibility for all costs associated with training, including travel.

Most vendors offer some form of online support, and vendors may be required to demonstrate their offerings. The RFP should ask that vendors provide guest accounts, so staff can navigate the support site and review training modules and documentation for evaluation purposes. The RFP should require vendors send periodic notices in advance regarding new services, new features, and upgrades to their interface software. Vendors may be required to conduct ongoing training as needed for new employees.

Implementation Plan

The RFP should require vendors to submit an implementation plan to ensure a smooth transition in case of migration from one ordering system to another. The plan should incorporate an initial consultation with library staff to determine specific needs in terms of training, system configuration, and ILS integration. Vendors should provide an implementation schedule and a training schedule and include any cost in the cost proposal. The library should inquire as to whether order histories may be transferred to the new system.

References

RFPs generally require that vendors provide at least three customer references. The RFP may require references that are of similar size and scope to the institution and located in the same state or province.

Cost Proposals

The RFP process, separate from a simple bid process, allows for cost to be an important factor to the selection process but not necessarily the deciding factor. Vendors must submit a price or cost proposal, but the proposals will generally look different from standard bids in which there is simply an overall dollar amount. Instead, library material RFPs are primarily concerned with the discount rates from list prices offered by publishers, unit costs for cataloging and processing materials, additional cost such as shipping and delivery, access to the selection website, or access to full-text professional reviews. The RFP may request that vendors provide their average discount rates based on the material types and weigh discount rates on certain categories more heavily than others. For example, if the library materials budget is spent disproportionally higher on hardcover fiction, discount rates on hardcover fiction are more impactful than on academic titles.

To ensure accuracy and the ability to measure and compare vendor price proposals, the RFP should provide the material categories to vendors so that vendors provide their average discount.

For example:

- General trade hardcover books (adult)
- General trade hardcover books (juvenile)
- Adult quality (trade) paperback books (adult)
- Adult mass market paperback books (juvenile)

- Large print books
- University press trade editions
- Music CDs
- Books on CD (unabridged)
- Feature and educational DVDs (retail and rental editions)
- Feature and educational Blu-ray DVD (retail and rental editions)
- Board books

In terms of cataloging and processing, vendors should have to provide an itemized cost sheet based on the library's specific needs. For example:

Cataloging:

- Brief MARC records per item
- Original cataloging per item
- Copy cataloging per item
- Item records
- Add copy to existing record

Processing:

- Mylar cover and tape for hardcover books
- Laminate cover for paperback books
- Call number label on spine of books
- Property stamp on books
- RFID tags
- Barcode on books
- Spine labels
- 3M compatible tattle-tape
- 3M compatible security strips with overlay

ISSUING THE RFP

Issuing an RFP is its own process and typically includes the vendor list, date of release, question period, addendum, proposal due dates, and an estimated award notification date. It is important to note that municipalities may have overriding policy, procedures, or laws that dictate the terms of issuance of RFPs.

Vendor List

The team leader should establish a vendor list before the issuance of the RFP to ensure a robust, competitive, and varied response and to ensure transparency. A vendor list is comprised of library material suppliers with the appropriate identification and contact information for individuals responsible for responding to RFPs. Inclusivity is key in the process in terms of potential vendors, especially if accepting partial bids. As such, vendors may decline to offer a proposal or submit an insufficient or unsatisfactory proposal, but vendors cannot claim to have been excluded from the process.

Date of Release

The date of release refers to the date the RFP is made available to potential vendors as well as the general public. On this date, the RFP is physically posted, made available on the institution's web page for current bids and RFPs, and mailed or e-mailed to the vendor list. Institutions should request a confirmation of receipt from vendors.

Question Period

The question period refers to the period of time between the issuance of the RFP and an established deadline for submitting questions. During this period, vendors may submit inquiries, request clarification, and ask for additional information. Vendors receive formal responses after the question period is over. The formal response to vendor inquiries comes in terms of an addendum.

Addendum

Addendum refers to any modifications or clarifications made to the RFP during issuance. Addendums include the all vendor inquiries, all responses to vendor inquiries, additions or subtractions to the requirements, and any changes in terms or conditions. The addendum is sent as a formal response to all potential vendors and should require confirmation of receipt.

Proposal Due Date

The proposal due date refers to the deadline for vendors to submit a proposal. All proposals must conform to the terms of the RFP. As a rule, late or incomplete submissions are not accepted.

Award Notification Date

The award notification date refers to the date the organization plans to announce its intent or recommendation to award contract(s) for the RFP to a specific vendor or vendors. This announcement is made to all vendors who submitted a proposal as well as to the general public. Depending on the institution, there is a length of time and a process for vendors to protest or contest the award as well a formal process and governing board that subsequently approves or denies the recommendation.

EVALUATING THE PROPOSALS

Once proposals have been received, the team leader or project manager distributes copies to team members with detailed instructions and guidelines. Keep all original proposals stored safely for administrative purposes. Be sure to consult your organization's document retention policy since vendor proposals can be subject to document requests.

Each proposal should be read thoroughly and evaluated in accordance to the scope of service, technical requirements, narrative questions, and price proposals listed in the RFP. Proposals that do not meet the minimum necessary requirements should be documented and rejected.

Team members should score the elements of each proposal utilizing a standardized scoring scheme based on and weighted in accordance with the formal evaluation criteria presented in the RFP. Scoring the RFPs should be objective, and raters' scores should not differ significantly from each other. If scores differ greatly, the project manager should clarify instructions and attempt to resolve any discrepancies. To facilitate scoring, the project manager may create a grid comprised of vendor responses. For example, see Table 5.3.

Cost proposals should be scored using an equation or equations that can be applied equitably to all vendors and result in an individual score for each because cost is an objective measurement. A vendor should receive the same cost score regardless of reviewer.

Vendor references should be checked by a designated team member and reported back to the team. Ideally, all respondents should be asked the same questions. To facilitate scoring, use a Likert scale and ask responders to rate vendors on the evaluation criteria. A final follow-up question could include whether the reference would select the vendor again.

Table 5.3 Vendor Response Grid

	Vendor A	Vendor B	Vendor C
Allows returns to be claimed online	Yes	Yes	No
Provides chat support	Yes	No	Yes
Provides EDI	No	Yes	Yes
Will drop ship to each location	Yes	Yes	Yes

SELECTING A VENDOR AND AWARDING THE CONTRACT

Once team members have submitted their scores to the project manager, each vendor can be ranked. The vendor with the highest overall score is generally the intended awardee. All participating vendors must be notified of the results. The official award of contract process depends on the library's governing body and local city, county, or state law. For example, most municipalities have procedures for vendors to contest the results of the RFP before a contract can be awarded.

LESSONS LEARNED

- Start the process early. There is no way to anticipate all the delays that can and will present themselves; however, providing adequate time to respond and adjust accordingly will help mitigate the delays.
- Invite vendors to the process. Vendors are admittedly biased in favor of their own product, but they are also subject specialists and are uniquely aware of products, services, and issues that affect the supply, distribution, and selection of library materials.
- Do not focus on minutia, but rather focus on the library's goals and objectives when crafting the RFP. Details are important, but so are the library's plans for the future.
- Consider carefully the pros and cons of splitting the RFP. The cost savings in overhead (e.g., establishing and maintaining multiple purchase orders, navigating various vendor interfaces) may outweigh the savings on individual library materials.

BIBLIOGRAPHY

Bilal, Dania. 2014. *Library Automation: Core Concepts and Practical Systems Analysis.* Santa Barbara, CA: Libraries Unlimited.

Disher, Wayne. 2007. *Crash Course in Collection Development.* Westport, CT: Libraries Unlimited.

Disher, Wayne. 2010. *Crash Course in Public Administration.* Santa Barbara, CA: Libraries Unlimited.

Sandstrom, John. 2015. *Fundamentals of Technical Services.* Chicago: ALA Neal-Schuman.

Webber, Desiree. 2010. *Integrated Library Systems: Planning, Selecting, and Implementing.* Santa Barbara, CA: Libraries Unlimited.

6

RFPs for School Library Collections

Shannon D. Pearce

INTRODUCTION

It is a truth universally acknowledged that school libraries are not in possession of a good fortune and are always in want of books. The request for proposal (RFP) provides an avenue for school libraries to obtain materials for their library collections at a competitive price from qualified vendors that can meet the school or district's specifications and requirements while also satisfying federal, state, and local procurement requirements for competitive bidding. Soliciting proposals rather than simple bids allows the flexibility to evaluate vendors on multiple factors including price, rather than on price alone, and to select more than one vendor, if desired, in order to provide the greatest overall value to the libraries.

Strategic Partnerships

Every school, school district, or other educational institution, no matter the size, has its own particular maze of red tape when it comes to money. This encompasses local policies and procedures, as well as state and federal regulations. It is therefore important to involve the organization's procurement department in the RFP process, whether that department is a large office or a single business manager, to help navigate the maze and ensure that all regulations and procedures are respected.

The procurement department can also help with the nuts and bolts of the process. They can often provide a template for part or all of the RFP, including standardized "boilerplate" language for the regulatory sections. And in many cases, the procurement department will take the lead in some parts of the process such as issuing and advertising the RFP, notifying vendors, executing the contract, and other tasks.

It is also possible that, depending on the size and requirements of a school, district, or organization, and its estimated annual expenditure for library materials, it may be unnecessary or inefficient to issue an individual RFP. A small school or district could choose instead to join with others to form a library purchasing cooperative, in order to streamline administrative tasks and increase purchasing power. Another option is to purchase library materials through an existing contract or purchasing cooperative administered by a larger entity of which the school or district is a part, such as a regional education service center and or the state or federal government. Consultation with your organization's procurement department and with librarians in similar organizations can be useful in determining the best option for your particular situation.

Assembling the Team

At minimum, the team responsible for designing, issuing, and evaluating the RFP for library materials will include a librarian and a representative from the procurement or finance office. Depending on the size and structure of the organization, the library representative may be a library director or supervisor, a district or lead librarian, or a campus librarian. One person should be designated as the team lead, but it can be helpful to include several librarians on the team, particularly librarians who serve students at different levels (e.g., elementary, middle school, high school) since the collection needs of libraries at each level are different. If the scope of the RFP will include materials in Spanish and/or other languages, it is helpful to have at least one team member who is familiar with Spanish or another high-demand language.

Developing a Timeline

The answer to the question, "How long will it take?" is always "Longer than you think!" It is important to start planning for an RFP as early as possible, because some of the determining factors in the timeline do not offer much flexibility. First, decide when the contract resulting from the RFP should take effect. This is usually dictated by the expiration date of an existing contract, but it is also important to consider the timing for the transition to a new contract. For schools on a traditional calendar, it is best to schedule transitions to occur during the summer to avoid confusion caused by midyear changes in ordering procedures. However, some of the people involved may not work during the summer, in which case the RFP process would need to be completed before the end of one school year in order for the contract to be in effect for the following year.

Table 6.1 Timeline for the RFP Process

Date	Event	Person(s) Responsible
September 12	Initial team meeting	Lisa (lead librarian)
October–November	Gathering info and planning	Lisa, Chris, Deb, and Jill (librarians)
December–February	Writing the RFP	Lisa and Chris
February 20	RFP issued and advertised	Pat (procurement officer)
March 23	Official bid opening	Pat
March–April	Evaluating responses	Entire team
April 27	School board meeting	Lisa and Pat
May–June	Contract executed	Pat
July 1	New contract takes effect	–

Once the date for the contract to take effect has been established, the procurement department can provide information on other required benchmarks. For many school districts, the board of trustees or a similar entity must approve contracts over a certain dollar amount, which makes the next point to be set on the timeline dependent on that group's meeting schedule and how far in advance of each meeting the agenda items must be submitted. The date for the formal bid opening is then set far enough in advance of the board meeting to allow sufficient time for evaluating the proposals. Counting back from the date of the bid opening will determine when the RFP needs to be issued, based on established procedures and legal requirements, for example, the length of time a bid solicitation must be advertised.

The final step is to work backward from the projected issue date to determine a schedule for writing and editing the RFP, preceded by time for planning and gathering information. The more persons involved in this process, the longer it will take, so plan accordingly. As much as possible, build in extra time for contingencies such as meetings that must be rescheduled and other unexpected delays.

The timeline may also designate the person or persons responsible for each stage of the process. This will help each team member understand his or her role in the process and avoid confusion or delays, as in Table 6.1.

PLANNING AND DESIGN

It is tempting to jump right in and start writing the RFP, but while this may result in a well-written document, it is less likely to accomplish the true intent of the process. To get the results you truly want, the popular educational planning approach known as "Understanding by Design" recommends planning backward, starting with the results that you want and working back from there. For curriculum design, this means first deciding what you want students to know (desired results), then determining what products or activities will demonstrate that knowledge (evidence), and finally, crafting experiences and activities that will achieve the desired results (learning plan). (McTighe and Wiggins) For RFP design, this means first deciding what capabilities and characteristics you want the selected vendor to have (desired results), then determining what information from the vendor will demonstrate these qualities (evidence), and finally, crafting RFP questions to obtain that information effectively (learning plan). This approach ensures that the information provided in the RFP responses can be effectively and objectively evaluated to determine which vendor(s) will best meet the school or district's needs.

With an RFP, unlike a straightforward bid, the ultimate goal is not simply to obtain the best price (although this is an important factor) but to select the vendor that provides the best value overall for the organization. This requires taking the time to reflect on what is most valuable to the librarians and the students that they serve.

Gathering Data

The first step of the design process is to decide what you want the selected vendor to be able to provide and to do. One potential source of inspiration is RFPs previously issued by your own organization and by others, many of which can be found online or shared between colleagues. Examining and reflecting on these can provide examples of both what works well and what does not. It is helpful to read them with two perspectives in mind: that of a vendor tasked with responding to the questions and that of a team member tasked with evaluating the responses. Note the characteristics that are successful from both perspectives.

It is also useful to consider which vendor characteristics facilitate a successful ordering experience and which create barriers to the process. One way to do this is to survey the end users, in this case the librarians who will be ordering from the selected vendor, about their previous experiences. This can generate information about the levels of demand for various types of library materials, perspectives on customer service, feedback on the ordering system, and more. The survey may include questions such as:

- What types of library materials do you order most? What types of library materials do you order infrequently or not at all?
- What types of materials do you find difficult to obtain from the current vendor?
- How important is it to you that a vendor provides a local representative?

- How do you prefer to contact customer service—by phone, e-mail, or live chat?
- What is your favorite thing about the current vendor's ordering system?
- What do you wish the current vendor would change about their ordering system?

Setting the Parameters

Before proceeding with the planning process, it is important to determine what types and categories of library materials will and will not be included in this particular RFP, as this will affect all subsequent steps of the process. This decision is more complicated than it sounds on the surface; today, the definition of "library materials" for a school library goes far beyond a standard set of well-reviewed children's books. While still consisting largely of juvenile and young adult materials, school library collections now encompass a wide range of items, including print and audiovisual (AV) resources in not only physical formats but also an ever-increasing variety of digital formats. The content of the collection must support a comprehensive curriculum for students at multiple levels with multiple interests, cultures, and languages, as well as the specialized needs of schools with a particular focus, such as magnet programs, career-readiness tracks, dual-credit college courses, and more. Some school libraries also include curriculum kits, novel sets, makerspace tools and supplies, digital devices, and more in their collections.

It is tempting to make the parameters of the RFP very broad and include as many types of materials as possible. However, the larger the list of RFP requirements becomes, the smaller the pool of vendors who qualify to respond will be, and an effective RFP process requires a healthy number of responses. If only a couple of vendors are able to meet the requirements, competition is minimal at best. Conversely, if the parameters are set too narrow, the RFP will produce very little purchasing power for the hefty amount of administrative effort required. Finding the right balance in defining the scope of an RFP is key to the process.

Some types of materials may be used in the library but are not really library materials, such as AV equipment, digital devices, curriculum kits, leveled reading and reading intervention programs, test prep materials, and makerspace supplies. The specifications for these items and the criteria for evaluating them differ significantly from those used for books and AV materials, making it impractical to include them on the same RFP. eBooks likewise do not fit neatly into the evaluation framework for a standard library materials RFP; all digital resources have unique considerations and may be best considered separately.

Partial Bids

Some vendors do not offer a comprehensive array of bindings or formats and consequently do not meet all of the requirements of a general library materials RFP but may still offer materials that are of value to the library. These vendors that specialize in a particular type of resource can frequently offer a more robust selection in that specific area than the larger jobbers. In some cases, it is not necessary for these vendors to have a bid or contract agreement because orders to them are usually small. However, if aggregate purchases in the areas of specialty are anticipated to be significant, or if strict regulations restrict ordering from nonbid vendors, it can be useful to establish contracts with specialty vendors in addition to a jobber.

For example, a particular concern for many school libraries is the increasing need for materials in multiple languages. Most jobbers offer a selection of materials in Spanish and a varying number of other languages, but this is not sufficient for all schools or districts. Districts that offer dual-language programs or serve a significant population of immigrant students and English language learners may require a larger and more comprehensive selection of books in a particular language, or books in a wider variety of languages than the jobbers offer. Consequently, schools or districts that anticipate spending a significant amount of money on materials in languages other than English need access to vendors who specialize in these materials. These vendors typically do not offer a sufficient array of English materials (if any) to meet the specifications of the full RFP but can provide a deeper catalog of multilanguage materials.

Other types of vendors that may be of interest to school libraries include vendors that only offer books with one type of binding. Prebound book vendors remove the original publisher's cover (usually a paperback) from the book and apply a durable hardcover binding; school librarians appreciate the durability of these bindings, and the fact that the binding often comes with a replacement guarantee. Many vendors offer prebound books along with other bindings, but a few vendors offer mostly or only prebinds. Likewise, many educational publishers only offer books with reinforced library bindings. These vendors will likely not meet the minimum requirements for the full RFP but could submit partial bids.

When deciding whether to accept partial bids, carefully weigh the benefits of increased breadth and depth of available materials against the complications of awarding and ordering from multiple vendors. If the decision is to allow them, determine if all partial bids will be accepted, or only those from vendors in specific categories.

Looking Ahead

The contract resulting from an RFP can potentially be in effect for several years, so it is important to think ahead to significant events or changes projected to occur during that time period and how they might affect the requirements of the RFP. For example, if a district plans to open any new schools in the next several years and will be purchasing the opening-day collections

(ODCs) for the new libraries under this agreement instead of issuing a separate RFP, it may be helpful to include a question or two specifically about additional services and considerations provided for ODCs; these large orders would also affect the anticipated annual expenditures to the vendor. Or, if a district plans to significantly increase the number of schools offering dual-language Spanish programs, more partial bids from Spanish language vendors may be accepted, or a greater weight given to inventory of Spanish books in the evaluation.

Setting Priorities

At the end of the prewriting process, you should have in mind all of the qualities and capabilities that make up the perfect vendor. Since such a thing unfortunately does not exist, you can select the vendor(s) that will be the best fit for your school or district by prioritizing the desired qualities according to your organization's mission and goals, and survey data from the librarians. Keeping these priorities in mind will guide and inform the writing of the RFP.

WRITING THE RFP

The final step in the design process is to take all of the information you have gathered and translate it into an RFP document. The challenge in crafting the RFP is to ask for information in such a way that the responses can be evaluated and compared as objectively as possible; in other words, the responses should be apples and apples, not apples and oranges (or possibly kiwi). Educators know that the easiest types of assessments to grade are comprised of closed-ended questions where responses are limited to prescribed choices, such as true/false and multiple-multiple choice questions, which adapt readily for the RFP. Open-ended questions do not provide prescribed answers from which to choose; these can be informational or narrative.

True/False

On RFPs, the choices are usually yes/no rather than true/false, but the principle is the same. The RFP states a requirement, and the vendor states whether or not they can comply. A variation is to offer three choices—yes, yes with exceptions, and no—with space to state the exception.

Multiple-Multiple Choice

This format provides vendors with a list of choices, from which they select all that apply. For example, the RFP gives a list of types of materials (hardcover books, paperback books, prebound books, audiobook CDs, DVDs); the vendor selects all of the types they can supply.

Informational Open-Ended

This includes any question where the vendor must provide a specific piece of information, such as a discount percentage and number of titles in inventory. No prescribed answers are provided, so the question must be carefully worded to ensure consistency in responses. For example, instead of asking for a "discount percentage," ask for "average percent discount from list price."

Narrative Open-Ended

Narrative questions should focus on assessing the vendor's unique qualities and capabilities, not just restating an informational answer in complete sentences. For example, instead of asking "Describe your selection of materials in Spanish," consider, "An elementary school librarian contacts you for help with improving her Spanish collection; how would you respond?"

PUTTING IT TOGETHER

The various components that comprise an RFP document, what they are called, and how they are organized will differ for every situation, because each school or district operates under a unique combination of federal, state, and local policies. The following sections describe the typical building blocks of an RFP for school libraries, but the structure of each document will vary according to established procurement policies and the specific needs of the organization.

Introduction and Background

An introductory section provides a brief overview of the scope and purpose of the solicitation and the projected annual amount to be spent for library materials. There is usually a brief description of the requesting organization, including information such as the type of organization (e.g., public school district, private school, charter school system), number of students and grade levels served, number of campus libraries, and whether ordering will be centralized or decentralized.

Scope of Services

Clearly stating what is and what is not included in the parameters of the RFP will decrease the number of noncompliant responses received and make it straightforward to reject any that are submitted but clearly do not meet the requirements. If partial bids will be accepted, this should also be stated. For example, a sample text could read:

The Readerville Independent School District requires the services of a book wholesaler or jobber to provide juvenile and young adult print books suitable for use by K-12 students, professional books for educators, and non-digital AV materials (e.g., audiobooks on CD, DVDs) for a term of three (3) years with an option to renew annually for two (2) years. This solicitation does not include digital resources (e.g., eBooks, databases, etc.), curricular or test prep materials, leveled reading or reading intervention programs, computer software programs, periodical subscriptions (e.g., newspapers or magazines), or state adopted textbooks. The district is seeking a vendor(s) who can provide:

- A large and varied catalog of available titles in various bindings, including reinforced library, hardcover, paperback, and prebound
- Shelf-ready cataloging and processing services
- Highly competitive discount rates
- Excellent customer support

After reading the Background and Scope of Services sections, vendors should have a good sense of whether or not they meet the requirements of the RFP and will be able to submit a competitive proposal. In effect, these sections function as a "dating profile" for the RFP so that vendors can determine if they have the potential for a good match and wish to respond.

General Requirements

For each RFP, there are requirements that the vendor must meet and terms that the vendor must accept in order to be considered for award. Specific requirements related to the evaluation criteria (e.g., selection and fulfillment, cataloging, and processing) are discussed in those sections, but there are also general requirements with which the vendor is expected to comply. Often, the procurement department will have standard "boilerplate" language that can be used in this section to address requirements for shipping (make sure these requirements include inside delivery!), invoicing, returns, methods of payment, and similar items. It may be useful to add some items relating to library-specific situations, for example, to establish protocols for back-order shipments. Consult with the procurement department to coordinate this section of the RFP. Some examples of items in this section are as follow:

- Orders will be received from and shipped to multiple locations.
- Shipping shall be Free on Board Destination (FOB Destination) to include inside delivery, prepaid, and allowed.

- Unless otherwise noted, one initial shipment and one back order will be accepted.
- All items will be delivered by the "deliver by" date specified on the order, or, if no date is specified, within 60 days of the receipt of the order. At the time of the deadline or the end of the 60 days, the vendor will supply a list of unfilled titles and cancel the remaining order. The 60-day period may be extended by mutual agreement.

For this section, typically the requirements will be enumerated and vendors will be asked to state any exceptions, with a statement such as, "State any exceptions to the requirements as listed, referencing the number of the item. Stating exceptions will not disqualify a vendor from consideration; however, if no exceptions are stated, it is assumed that the vendor can and will comply with the requirements if selected." A point value may be assigned to this section, but more often it is not. However, if a vendor states exceptions, they should be reviewed by the procurement office to determine if any of the exceptions are extensive enough to disqualify the vendor. Vendors with less serious but still significant exceptions may not be disqualified but could be docked a point or two; if this is done, it must be consistent.

Evaluation Criteria

Unlike a simple bid, the RFP process evaluates vendors on multiple criteria, allowing the selection of vendor(s) that provide(s) the best overall value for the organization, not simply the best price. These criteria should reflect the goals and priorities established in the planning process. Establishing the evaluation criteria for the RFP fulfills the same function as creating a rubric or other assessment tool for a student project: it sets clear expectations of what will be assessed and by what standards, which is helpful for both the vendor (student) who is doing the work and the evaluator (teacher) who will assess the work.

Selection and Fulfillment

The most fundamental requirement of any RFP is that the vendor be able to provide the materials that are needed, so the desired result of this section is to identify vendors that can meet the requirements for library materials as defined in the Scope of Services. This can be demonstrated by the size of a vendor's catalog, the number of publishers represented, and the average number of items in stock in the warehouse from which the organization's orders will be filled. Another helpful number is the vendor's fulfillment or "fill" rate. Because the availability of print books can change rapidly, vendors are not always able to supply every title that is ordered; the fill rate is the average ratio

Table 6.2 Evaluation Criteria

Criteria	Standards	Points
Selection and Fulfillment	• Extensive catalog of juvenile and young adult materials in a variety of bindings/formats • Robust inventory • Significant catalog of materials in a variety of languages other than English • Excellent fill rate	35
Cataloging and Processing	• Shelf-ready cataloging/processing services • Compliance with district specifications	15
Ordering System	• User-friendly online ordering system • Variety of features for collection development • Smooth integration with existing systems • Efficient ordering processes	15
Cost Proposal	• Very competitive discounts from list price for purchase of materials • Attractive pricing for cataloging and processing, shipping, and other services	25
Vendor Capabilities	• Excellent customer service • Strong references from similar customers • Value-added services	10
	TOTAL POINTS POSSIBLE	100

of titles shipped to titles ordered, expressed as a percentage. You may wish to ask vendors for a list of publishers represented.

Because school libraries serve a specific population in terms of age, it can be helpful to request this information for each of several categories of materials typically found in K–12 school library collections, for example, juvenile and young adult materials. A general vendor that offers materials for all ages will come out ahead of a smaller vendor that focuses on K–12 libraries in overall number of titles, number of publishers, and inventory. But if specific categories of materials for children and teens are considered, the comparison between the two vendors is more equitable and better reflects their ability to supply the materials that school libraries need most.

The categories used should reflect the range of materials described in the Scope of Services. They may include, but are not limited to:

- Hardcover books—juvenile and young adult
- Prebound books—juvenile and young adult
- Paperback books—juvenile and young adult
- Books in languages other than English—juvenile and young adult, any binding

- Professional books—pedagogical, any binding
- Audiobooks on CD—juvenile and young adult
- DVDs

Cataloging and Processing

The staff for a typical school library is one librarian, who single-handedly fills the role of instruction librarian, reference librarian, clerk, page, and technical services department. Cataloging and processing services provided by vendors can lift part of that burden and provide significant value, as the charge for these services is minimal compared to the cost of the person-hours it would take for librarians to do it themselves. Available services include cataloging, which refers to the bibliographic record (i.e., MARC record) containing data about an item, and processing, which includes anything physically applied to the item such as spine labels, book covers, security strips, property stamps, genre labels, and book pockets. Shelf-ready processing means that the vendor applies all of the processing components before shipping so that the books arrive ready to come out of the box and go straight onto the shelf.

Libraries should have established cataloging and processing specifications; often, a school district will maintain standardized specifications that apply to all campus libraries. Cataloging specifications include requirements for the bibliographic record, including format, standards to be followed, subject heading preferences, call number specifications, and preferred method for records to be provided. Processing specifications provide detailed instructions on what components are required, and how and where to apply them, such as the location and orientation of the barcode label, if label protectors are required, and whether dust jackets that have been covered should be taped or glued. Attach a copy of the specifications to the RFP.

The RFP may include requirements for vendors to provide shelf-ready cataloging and processing according to the specifications provided, and to keep the specifications on file for each library, including barcode numbers used. It can be helpful to ask vendors to provide a sample catalog record and processed book in order to demonstrate that they can comply with the required specifications. If this is requested, provide detailed instructions about how these items should be submitted.

If partial bids for specialty categories such as foreign language materials will be accepted, there will likely be some smaller vendors that fit the category and can provide needed materials but do not offer cataloging and processing services. It may be necessary to make exceptions in order to access a sufficient vendor list for these specialty areas.

Ordering System

Another important consideration for school libraries is the functionality of a vendor's online ordering tools. Even large school districts rarely have a position specializing in library acquisitions; school librarians who do their own ordering must squeeze it in between teaching classes, collaborating with teachers, shelving, and a hundred other tasks, and even if ordering is done centrally, it is only one of many responsibilities being juggled by a library director or district librarian. So it is not surprising that school librarians place great value on an ordering system that is reliable and user-friendly, offers a big toolbox of features to assist with collection development, and does not require extensive training to use.

A requirement for this section could simply be to provide an online ordering system with access to the vendor's catalog. If the ordering system will need to interface with any of the organization's technical systems, the technical specifications required must be clearly stated.

Beyond basic requirements, vendors' ordering systems offer a wide array of features and functions. One way to assess the capabilities of each vendor's system is to provide a checklist of features that librarians have indicated are useful (e.g., on user surveys) and ask vendors to indicate which of these features are available in their systems. With this type of assessment, it is helpful to allow vendors to state exceptions; for example, if a vendor provides full-text reviews from three out of four journals required, the missing source can be listed as an exception and partial points awarded. For example, vendors could be asked if their ordering systems can:

- search for items by ISBN, title, author, publisher, and series;
- filter search results by reading level, interest level, language, and binding;
- provide access to full-text reviews from *School Library Journal* and *The Horn Book*;
- display real-time inventory;
- share carts between users;
- provide access to order status information and invoices;
- indicate if titles may already be in the collection (duplicate check);
- show accurate discounted pricing per the terms of the contract;
- automatically calculate cataloging/processing costs per specs on file; and
- submit orders online.

A narrative question for this section might ask vendors to describe how a librarian might use their system to find resources that support the curriculum for a particular subject and level. Vendors may also be asked to provide a guest or demo log-in for their ordering system to allow hands-on evaluation of its interface and functions. However, this type of evaluation can be very time-intensive, so it may not be feasible or needed in all situations.

Cost Proposal

Cost is not the only factor considered in the RFP process, but it is an important one, as school librarians continue to be asked to provide more resources for less money. The goal in this section is to determine which vendor can provide the materials needed at the lowest cost, which sounds straightforward enough, but the RFP must be carefully worded in order to elicit the required information in a way that allows effective comparison.

Discount Percentage

Rather than quoting a price for individual items, RFP responses typically propose a percentage of discount from the list price. But jobbers work with hundreds or even thousands of publishers and may have different agreements with each, so asking vendors to provide their best discount as an open-ended question will produce wildly varied results. Responses may include a discount range, such as "0–40 percent from list" or "5 percent from website prices which are already discounted 10–35 percent from list," both of which contain several numbers but no objective way to compare them. For a range of discounts, the median can be used to provide a single number for comparison, but this may give a skewed result, as a discount range of "0–40 percent " could mean that the average discount is 20 percent, or it could mean that one title is discounted 40 percent and the other 2 million titles in the catalog are discounted 0 percent. Requesting that the vendor provide an average discount is more helpful, but this too can be misleading as the overall average may be skewed by discounts offered on types of materials that would be minimally purchased by K–12 school libraries, such as music CDs or textbooks.

While no method is perfect, an acceptable approach is to request that vendors provide an average discount for various categories and types of materials likely to be most purchased. These categories will typically be similar if not identical to the categories described in the Selection and Fulfillment section described earlier in this chapter.

In addition to the stated discounts, it is important to ask if any other discounts are available under specific circumstances. Additional discounts are sometimes given for orders of multiple copies of the same title, or orders that exceed a specified minimum amount, or orders placed as part of an ODC.

Cataloging and Processing

The RFP should provide an itemized list of shelf-ready cataloging and processing elements to be priced by the vendor; list each item separately and be specific. If the organization's cataloging and processing specifications are included in the RFP document as an attachment (recommended), vendors can refer to them for additional details. Vendors may choose to attach a specification order form with prices; this can be helpful as supplemental information but should not take the place of the vendor's response to the RFP item.

Other Costs

Vendors should state the costs, if any, that will be charged for shipping orders in accordance with the specifications stated in the Requirements section of the RFP. They should also be asked to provide information on any other costs or fees associated with the ordering process, such as a subscription cost for the online ordering system, an upcharge for access to full-text reviews, or a data-disk fee for MARC records.

Vendor Capabilities

Most of an RFP's requirements focus on the product, which in this case is library materials—their availability, how they are ordered, how they are processed, how they are shipped, how much they cost, and so on. But it is also important to evaluate the vendors and the services they provide.

Customer Support

School librarians often feel isolated, being the only librarian on the campus and usually running the library single-handedly, so having access to responsive customer support for questions or issues with the ordering system is a high priority. It is difficult to quantify good customer service, but requirements in this section might include options for contacting customer service (e-mail, phone, chat) and average response time. If users were surveyed as part of the RFP planning process, the results can be used to focus questions on the services that users find most important. For example, if the survey indicates that most librarians place a high value on a relationship with a local sales representative, the RFP could ask vendors if there is a representative based within 150 miles of the organization's location, and if not, how the vendor provides personalized service from far away.

References

Vendors are typically asked to provide the name and contact information of three customers who can speak to the vendor's ability to provide the materials and services proposed. The RFP may indicate a preference or even requirement that the references be from school libraries or districts, and of a similar size and type (e.g., urban or rural) to the issuing entity.

Value Added

Vendors may offer considerations or services that are not part of the RFP requirements but that may be of value to the library, such as a sales representative who can bring sample books to the school for the librarian to review, a rewards program that lets customers receive free books, and personalized collection development services. Provide an opportunity for vendors to describe any of these services that they feel are relevant.

Required Forms

Provide any forms that the vendor may be asked to complete in order to comply with local policy or government requirements. These may include federal forms such as the W-9 and the Debarment, Suspension and Ineligibility Certification; state forms such as Texas's Notification of Criminal History of Contractor; or local forms such as conflict of interest statements.

Informational Attachments

Information to which the vendor must refer in order to respond to certain RFP items should be included as attachments. For example, if a requirement stated in the RFP is that the vendor provide cataloging and processing services according to established specifications, a copy of those specifications must be attached for reference. Another example would be to attach a copy of the district's standard service agreement.

ISSUING AND ADVERTISING THE RFP

The issuing of the RFP is part of the formal solicitation process, which must follow local, state, and federal requirements for procedures such as the minimum length of time between the issue date and the bid opening date and when public notices must be posted. Because this part of the process can be strictly regulated, whenever possible the procurement department should take the lead at this point.

The RFP is typically issued with a cover sheet with the name and number of the RFP along with the mandated information, such as the dates for the RFP issue, bid opening, and award; the procedure for questions and answers; instructions for submitting responses; and a contact person's name, e-mail, and phone number.

Questions

After the RFP has been issued, vendors will have a specified window of time in which they can submit questions or request clarification. These questions do not receive individual responses. Instead, they are collected and answered in writing; all of the questions and answers are published for all of the vendors to see so that all have exactly the same information and no vendor is advantaged over the others. The RFP document includes instructions for submitting questions, the deadline for doing so, and the date and method that the answers will be published.

Advertisement and Notification

Many vendors will see the RFP advertised in the newspaper and/or on the organization's website as required by policy, but notification of the opportunity can also be sent directly to vendors to encourage a variety of competitive responses. Notification may be sent to vendors with whom the organization has prior experience, vendors recommended by other schools or districts, vendors encountered at library conferences, and any others. This is particularly important if partial bids will be accepted from vendors in specialty categories, such as multilanguage materials. It is important to have adequate response in each category, and smaller vendors may not be actively searching for bid opportunities.

EVALUATING THE PROPOSALS

After the official bid opening when all of the proposals have been received, the responses must be evaluated and ranked. Depending on the situation, proposals may be evaluated by multiple team members (preferred) or by just one person. Either way, the method for awarding points in the evaluation should be laid out clearly and in detail so that the results are as objective and consistent as possible. This is particularly important if any of the evaluators are not librarians, as they will be unfamiliar with some of the unique requirements of purchasing library materials.

Keeping Score

Each member of the evaluation team is given a copy of each proposal along with detailed instructions and a summary sheet for each vendor. The evaluator will enter the points awarded for each item on the summary sheet; this form can also include a place for the evaluator's signature. The team leader will collect all completed summary sheets, tally and tabulate all of the scores, and rank the vendors accordingly. The score summaries and tabulation results must be documented and maintained on file as required by law.

The total number of points possible for each section of the RFP has already been established, as illustrated in Table 6.2; the scoring instructions will break down each section and assign a point value for individual items as shown in Table 6.3. Finally, the scoring method for each item is established and documented. Taking the time to carefully prepare the scoring instructions will lead to a smooth, consistent evaluation process.

Table 6.3 Point Values

Cost Proposal	Points
Discount from List Price	12
Cataloging/Processing Cost	8
Shipping Cost	4
Other	1
TOTAL	25

Scoring Instructions

The procedure for awarding points will vary with the type of questions. Yes or no questions are the simplest: the desirable answer (usually "yes") is awarded full points and the undesirable answer (usually "no") receives none. If there is an option to state exceptions, partial points could be awarded for a "yes" answer with exceptions. "Check all that apply" questions are just a long list of yes/no questions, so a similar principle applies. Divide the total point value of the question by the number of items in the list to calculate the "per item" point value, and then multiply it by the number of list items that the vendor has checked to calculate the number of points awarded.

When vendors supply their own answers rather than selecting from a prescribed list, it is just a bit more complicated. Informational items such as "State the percentage of discount from list price offered for this type of item" can be evaluated using a "scorecard," which assigns points based on the range of responses. For example, if a question is worth 12 points and the vendor responses range from 0 to 35 percent, the scorecard might look like Table 6.4.

Table 6.4 Points by Discount Range

Discount from List Price (%)	Points
0	0
1–10	2
11–15	4
16–20	6
21–25	8
26–30	10
31 and up	12

Most school librarians were once classroom teachers, and most classroom teachers have at some point in their careers had to grade short-answer essay questions. Open-ended narrative questions in the RFP are very similar to these and can best be evaluated in the same way: with a rubric that defines the level of performance for each point value.

Evaluating Samples

Vendors may be asked to submit materials to provide evidence of their qualifications, such as a sample MARC record and processed library book to demonstrate that the vendor can meet the required cataloging and processing specifications. These items may require specialized expertise to evaluate; for example, procurement office personnel cannot be expected to be familiar with MARC records, and even librarians who do not do their own cataloging may have difficulty. A cataloging librarian or library technology specialist, if the district has these, or a district librarian, or a campus librarian with cataloging experience may be tasked with completing this part of the evaluation and sharing the results with the team.

Vendors might also be asked to provide a guest log-in for their online ordering system to demonstrate its features and usability. This can be an effective method when the evaluation is done by the librarians who will be using the system; however, testing a complex ordering system is a time-consuming process, especially if a large number of vendors submit responses. To keep this task from becoming overwhelming, create a specific list of tasks to be performed to test each system. Alternately, the vendors can be divided up between the team members to reduce the number that each must evaluate, or additional librarians can be recruited to help with this part of the process. Or, vendors could be scored according to all other criteria first, and this in-depth evaluation is done only for the highest scoring vendors.

Checking References

One person may be designated to check the vendor-provided references. This should be done as early as possible in the evaluation process to allow time for responses to be received and tabulated. For consistency, contact all references the same way, for example, e-mail or phone, and ask the same questions to each. References may be asked to rate a vendor's performance on a four- or five-point scale on various criteria such as available selection of materials, order fulfillment, and customer service. References may also be asked to name one or two of the vendor's strengths or suggest something that could be improved. The final question is usually a yes/no question that is some variation of "Would you use this vendor again?" or "Would you recommend this vendor?"

SELECTING AND NOTIFYING THE VENDOR(S)

The team lead will collect the evaluation sheets from the committee (if there is one) and tally the results. If any responses have been identified that do not comply with the scope and requirements of the RFP, the insufficiency should be documented before the response is removed from consideration. All remaining vendors can be ranked according to the number of points awarded and the vendor(s) with the highest score awarded.

If multiple vendors will be awarded, the criteria for doing this must be established. The top two or three or more vendors can be awarded, or a threshold can be set and all vendors who score above that level are awarded. If partial bids for specific categories of materials have been accepted, the same methods can be applied to the vendors in each category to select one or more of them to award. Document the scores received by each vendor and the criteria for award.

The team lead will usually submit the recommendation for award and documentation to the procurement department, who will notify all vendors of the results.

PRESENTING THE RECOMMENDATION

Typically, before a contract can be signed, a formal recommendation from the RFP team must be presented to the board of trustees or similar governing body for approval. This recommendation is prepared in accordance with established policies and procedures and an agenda item for the meeting submitted by the appropriate deadline. The recommendation may include a brief statement of the purpose of the RFP, the vendor(s) recommended for award, the term of the contract, and the estimated dollar amount that will be spent. A representative of the team may want to attend the meeting where the vote will take place in case there are questions.

ESTABLISHING THE CONTRACT

Once the required approvals and ratifications have been obtained, the procurement office will execute a contract with the selected vendor(s) according to the terms of the RFP response. If the term of the contract includes optional renewal periods, check with the procurement department in advance of the renewal date. If the vendor's performance has been satisfactory, it can be renewed; the procurement department usually takes care of the paperwork for this.

LESSONS LEARNED

- Collaborating with the procurement department saves time and energy. Before you spend time working on something, check with them—they may have boilerplate all ready to go!

- Do not try to do too much with one RFP. It can be tempting to include as much as possible in one RFP so that you do not have to do as many. But it can actually be more efficient to do two moderately sized RFPs with a clear focus (e.g., print library materials and eBooks) rather than one big, complicated one that tries to compare apples to oranges to penguins.
- Document, document, document! Vendors who do not get the award can ask to see the evaluation results, and sometimes they do.
- Always bring snacks to the RFP team meetings.

BIBLIOGRAPHY

McTighe, Jay, and Grant Wiggins. *Understanding by Design Framework.* Alexandria, VA: 2012. ASCD.

Morris, Betty J. 2010. *Administering the School Library.* Santa Barbara, CA: Libraries Unlimited.

Smith, Andrew J. M., and Nancy J. Brown. 2013. "Crossing the Language Barrier." In *School Libraries Matter*, edited by Mirah J. Dow, 137–49. Santa Barbara, CA: Libraries Unlimited.

Wools, Blanche, Ann C. Weeks, and Sharon Coatney. 2014. *The School Library Manager.* Santa Barbara, CA: Libraries Unlimited.

7

NEGOTIATING COLLECTIONS FOR CONSORTIA: RFIS/RFQS

Anne E. McKee

In Part II of this book, Chapters 3 through 6 dealt with issuing request for proposals (RFPs) to purchase collections for academic, public, and school libraries. Chapters 8 and 9 addressed RFPs for selecting integrated library systems (ILSs) for academic and public libraries and consortia. Negotiating for collections on behalf of a consortium is different because it generally requires negotiating directly with a publisher rather than with a vendor. For this reason, when negotiating for consortial collections, a request for information (RFI) or request for quotation (RFQ) is more appropriate than an RFP. This does not preclude issuing an RFP if multiple sources can provide the product, but typically these kinds of negotiations occur with a single publisher. Therefore, this chapter discusses the use of RFIs or RFQs for purchasing collections for consortia.

INTRODUCTION

Consortium staff who negotiate on behalf of its members are a hardy breed; they can handle anything, at anytime, anywhere. They will tell a vendor, publisher, or content provider, "No, the members of our consortium will not agree to that." When the providers push back and try to claim that "other consortia" may have agreed to a clause or term, the consortium negotiator will say, "Well, we are not like other consortia—please remove the offending clause now." They cannot be fazed. This chapter will discuss alternative solutions to an RFP, but to understand the reasoning, we must appreciate consortia, what they offer, how they operate, how they differ from individual libraries, and what they can accomplish for their members.

WHAT ARE CONSORTIA?

Consortia comprise many different types and models. There are statewide consortia, higher education consortia, public library consortia, and multi-type library consortia (public, private, K–12, and higher education). There are geographical consortia, medical and hospital consortia, and outside of the United States, even countrywide consortia. Consortia are formed when there is a perceived need or acceptance of commonly held goals. Consortia bring libraries together to address specific needs. For example, there are consortia dedicated to shared collection development and interlibrary loan (ILL). In these cases typically libraries within a region either in a state or among neighboring states can develop robust and efficient ILL services. Other consortia focus on digitization. Often libraries in a region contain materials of interest to the region that they need to digitize, preserve, and share with each other and the larger research community. There are also instances when libraries from different countries have formed consortia to address specific needs such as digital preservation and electronic resource sharing. Another common type of consortium is when libraries share an ILS. Still other consortia specialize in the acquisition of materials, which is the focus of this chapter. Buying as a group often enables consortia to obtain discounts that are not available if libraries do it alone.

The founding of a consortium usually starts informally and grows organically. A few librarians might begin a discussion about a particularly thorny issue that one of them is facing and much to their satisfaction—and typically outright relief—they discover that other librarians have that same interest or problem. Librarians are deft at networking, and soon more librarians want to be included in the discussion. For example, one consortium the author is familiar with evolved from a group of library directors meeting in the evening at a library conference and discussing their problems over drinks and dinner.

Consortia Staffing

Usually when a consortium is formed, an institution or two will step up and volunteer librarian staff time to help run the consortium's needs. This is often looked at as a payment in kind, in which case the existing library staff add another job duty. These types of consortia can find that it is challenging to make progress on shared objectives since there is no staff dedicated 100 percent to the needs of the consortium. At some point, as consortia grow and mature, a consortium will need to decide if it should continue to run as a volunteer organization or if it should implement a dues structure to either assign some consortium duties to internal staff or hire paid consortium staff. Although each choice has its own challenges, eventually consortia will typically hire staff to conduct their business, including negotiating with publishers.

NEGOTIATING ON BEHALF OF A CONSORTIUM

Consortia with paid staff have robust negotiations and licensing programs. There is usually one staff member whose position focuses almost exclusively on liaising among content providers, publishers, vendors, and the member libraries. It takes expertise, good communication skills, and even humor to address these needs. It is imperative for all members to understand and accept that this negotiator liaison does have the authority to make decisions. Nothing can kill negotiating power faster than having the consortium's members second guess the liaison's ability to make good decisions. It is only at this juncture that the consortium should decide how to proceed when acquiring collections for member libraries.

More Than One Type of Request

There are definitely times when sending out one type of request is preferred over another. Each type of request is distinctly different, and consortium staff and members need to understand these differences. Knowing when to select one type of request over another is usually learned through experience and over many years of trial and error. By understanding when and how to use each type of request, the consortium can succeed in acquiring the needed content for the best possible price.

RFIs and RFQs Are Different

In consortia, when there is a need for a service or product, a fairly formalized process begins. The least formal is the RFI. RFIs are issued to find out if the desired product is available and get a description of what the product can do, what is included, and so forth. It is important to note that when an RFI is issued, it does not constitute a commitment to purchase a product. It is merely a way for the library to "float" the idea or discover if the needed product is available in the marketplace. RFI responses do not need to be in the rigid, prescribed format that is usually required for other types of proposals such as RFQs to determine pricing.

The RFQ asks for a quotation for a product or service, in the case of consortia, generally from the publisher. Typically, it seeks a list of prices for a product that is well defined, in this case for a package of titles. It may include built-in annual inflation for multiyear contracts as well as other terms and conditions. Unless the quotation is "best and final," the consortium staff negotiate terms and conditions of the contract on behalf of member libraries.

The Selection Committee

For a consortium, it is important to confer with all the members in the initial stages of the RFI or RFQ process. Consortium members typically comprise libraries of varying sizes, some with large staffs and budgets and some with much more limited resources. Naturally, everyone's interests in a service or product will not be identical. When buying content such as databases and journal packages, a large academic library's interests will be much wider than those of a small community college library. Some libraries in the consortium may not be interested in a particular product at all. For this reason, negotiating on behalf of a consortium adds the complexity of identifying each member library's needs by ensuring that each member library has representation and a voice in the process.

Involving an Institution's Purchasing Office

In a statewide consortium, it may be possible to turn to the purchasing office of one of the libraries for assistance. It may even prove wise to discuss having the purchasing agent write, distribute, and receive the information or quotes/bids.

Although a purchasing office can be helpful to the libraries in a consortium, be aware that allowing the purchasing office into the process may prove to be a detriment in the long run. Sometimes, once the purchasing office handles an RFI or RFQ, it is reluctant to turn back "control" of the process to the consortia. The purchasing agent may attempt to place him or herself in the current process as well as any other request processes in the future.

Communicating with Vendors

Unlike negotiations directly with the publisher of a title or package, it is usually the norm that once the RFI or RFQ has been released to multiple vendors, no one may discuss the whys and wherefores of it outside of the designated channels. Know the appropriate laws because for a state-supported institution, it may actually be illegal to respond to questions when multiple vendors are involved once the request has been released. It is customary to appoint one person to respond to vendor questions about the RFI or RFQ, usually the consortium staff negotiator. However, these questions should really only center on clarifications or problems within the document or concerning the process. Consortium staff should never respond to questions such as the following: How many other vendors/publishers received the RFI or RFQ? Would you be willing to put in a "good word" for us? Can you promise to give us the business? These types of requests are unethical at best and downright dishonest at worst. Further, no communication should occur between the individual libraries and vendors responding to the RFI or RFQ during the process. Generally, the consortium staff member collects the RFI or RFQ responses as they arrive, coordinates any product demonstrations, and finally is the point person for officially awarding of the contract on behalf of the consortium.

If a Vendor Questions or Contests the Award

Do not be surprised if other vendors who submitted proposals but were not awarded the contract ask to see all the competing bids. There are many reasons why this is done: sometimes to see what products their competitors are offering or to learn ways they could improve their own proposals with other customers in the future. Sometimes, it is a check to see if there were any irregularities in the process, such as a competitor having inside information to craft their proposal to better meet the needs of the RFI requirements.

NITTY-GRITTY NEGOTIATION POINTS TO CONSIDER AND EMPLOY

- Always, view the publisher/content provider/vendor as a partner. Express your desire for shared synergies; banish the "us-versus them" mentality as this can cause instant animosity. Instead, use language that helps to create a win-win situation for both sides.
- Respect the other side: this does not mean to lie down and let the publisher or vendor stomp on you with cleats. Rather, make sure the other side understands that both of you are equals. You respect their expertise. Quietly, but confidently, expect them to respect yours!
- Be frank, bold, honest, and open about your requirements without projecting an aggressive manner in your requests. You can be frank without being obnoxious. You can project a business-like demeanor without being unpleasant. You must understand that you are their equal.
- Never assume the answer is "no." Even if you believe your request is a shot in the dark, you will never know for sure until it is verbalized.
- A "no" is just a "no." Do not take it personally. It does NOT demean you, it does NOT mean that all negotiations must cease, and it does not even mean that the "no" cannot be turned to a "yes" later on. Just take the "no," and rephrase, reconstruct, and resubmit the request in another way. This is where viewing the publisher or vendor as a partner could aid you in obtaining the needed "yes."
- Know who the real decision maker is on the side of the publisher or vendor. Do not begin negotiations with your local sales representative if the person who makes the decision is the vice president of the company. Be up-front; ask who the decision maker is on behalf of the publisher or vendor. Then firmly request that you must negotiate with the decision maker. If he or she is unwilling to work with you, then it is probably not a company you should select to work with you.
- Inquire as to when the publisher or vendor's fiscal year ends. These content providers are all usually more willing to "cut a deal" (better discount, sweeten the compensations offer, etc.) in the last quarter of their fiscal year. Ask if there is an early adopter's discount that can be extended, for

example, over the next three years. The more you know about the vendor, the more tools you have in your arsenal to work with.

- It is imperative to know the financial strengths or weaknesses of the provider. Do your research: read the business articles, perform an environmental scan, check their references, and read their annual report. If the financials sound somewhat shaky, but they are the only company that can provide what you want, state the parameters necessary to get your business. For instance, the provider must be willing to accept the payment in chunks in a mutually agreed upon schedule. Inquire about utilizing a lockbox at the vendor's financial institution of choice. Request due diligence on their financial records. Ensure in writing, that any agreement includes various ways you can terminate the contract without prejudice or legal ramifications.

CONCLUSION

Be informed, be succinct, be bold, and be professional regarding your needs in all negotiations. Regardless of the type of request format the consortium chooses to utilize, the most crucial point to acknowledge is that the consortium is in the driver's seat. It may be a marathon rather than a quick dash, but do not panic or give up. The consortium leadership now has the tools to decide which kind of "request for" document is best to issue. If a quick, informal product survey is desired; the RFI is appropriate, if just a price quote is necessary, an RFQ can be used. Typically, consortia shopping for collections do not issue RFPs, but they may pursue this option if a very formal proposal from multiple vendors is deemed necessary. The RFI, RFQ, or RFP process is designed to create predictable situations, an even playing field, and an open and transparent process in which both the consortium and the publisher or vendor benefit. It is a win-win situation for both sides.

WRITING AND EVALUATING SPECIFIC TYPES OF RFPS: INTEGRATED LIBRARY SYSTEMS

8

ACADEMIC LIBRARIES AND ACADEMIC LIBRARY CONSORTIA PROPOSAL PROCESS FOR INTEGRATED LIBRARY SYSTEMS

Lea J. Briggs

INTRODUCTION

Purchasing and migrating to a new integrated library system (ILS) requires a significant investment of an institution's funds and staff time, so libraries typically keep the same system for many years. In many public institutions, major purchases are managed using a request for proposal (RFP) process. An RFP is a formal process used in many industries to solicit bids from vendors. In this case, it details specifications for the ILS and provides a framework for evaluating competing proposals. The RFP is an announcement to vendors asking them to submit responses to a library's stated system needs. Although time-consuming to write, the final document is one that clearly states your library's needs and expectations. The RFP will help determine system suitability and can be an important tool for gaining team consensus when choosing a future library system.

No matter the library type (academic, public, or school library), steps of the RFP process remain generally the same for public institutions. A selection team is created and drafts the RFP, which is posted for a set period of time under the guidance of the institution's procurement department. The team develops questions and evaluation criteria, arranges product demonstrations, contacts references, evaluates complete proposal packages, reviews and rates vendor responses, and identifies a preferred vendor and product. The contract is then negotiated and awarded.

The process does not end after a contract has been signed but shifts to implementation. Implementation involves the actual migration of data and workflows from the old system to the new one, and beginning to operate in the new environment. This is where you put to the test the work done in previous RFP steps. A postmortem at the end of the implementation will provide an assessment of strengths and weaknesses of the new system in meeting your needs as well as of the RFP process, which will help guide future ILS selections.

Purchasing regulations vary, and some institutions choose to engage in a system selection process that does not utilize an RFP. One such alternative approach is considered goal- or vision-oriented and can allow for an open-ended review and evaluation process. Included in an appendix to this chapter is a case study using an alternative approach to ILS selection from the Private Academic Library Network of Indiana (PALNI).

DETERMINING A NEED FOR A NEW ILS

Maybe staff members are at your door daily to complain about the current ILS. Maybe you have heard of wonderful functionality from peers at institutions using different systems or have seen interesting demonstrations at a professional conference. Or maybe your current ILS contract term is nearing expiration or the vendor is ceasing its support. Whatever the case, one day you will begin to think about what a new management system might bring to your organization. Looking around, even if you do not buy, is a good chance to see what is available in the current market and will help a library gauge the right time to take advantage of newer technology or negotiate enhancements with the existing vendor.

Assessing Strengths and Weaknesses of the Current System

Purchasing and migrating to a new library system is a significant expenditure of funds, staff time, and institutional energy. Due to these costs, most libraries stay with a system for several years, so the purchase decision should not be taken lightly. Understanding the library, as well as what works well and what needs improvement in the current system, can provide a useful grounding in the search for a new system. Not every library problem can be solved by technology. It is important to understand your current system's functionality and local library work processes to determine if a new system will actually remedy the shortcomings of the current environment or if they could be resolved another way. A needs assessment or evaluation of the library provides enlightening information on the current facility, staff, and collection in order to better focus questions and envision an ideal solution.

Begin with an evaluation of the library itself, noting things like types and sizes of collection materials held, types of patrons served and their needs, functionality needed, availability and technical skills of staff, reliability of high-speed Internet access, and future plans for new services, library growth, or collaboration. Couple the library evaluation with an assessment that looks at strengths and weaknesses of the current ILS in meeting library needs, as well as note current trends in the industry and future desires of the library. Consider how well the current system helps the library align with its strategic plan or direction. Feedback from users can be vital to better meeting their needs from a system perspective. Staff surveys or interviews are options for gathering additional input. The system librarian or the local support ticketing system can also be a good source of information about common complaints from staff using the current ILS. This review and evaluation helps give some objective data to what can be a rather subjective topic. Information from this data-gathering process will help form the list of critical features for the new system.

Reviewing Industry Trends

Become aware of opportunities the new systems on the market may offer. Read reviews and articles in the literature, attend demonstrations at professional conferences, and consult with peers using other systems to learn about existing functionality and what is new and soon to come to the market. Well-known library consultant Marshall Breeding's annual report of library systems in *American Libraries* is an excellent source for learning about industry offerings and trends. Cloud computing is causing shifts in the market, and the drive for interoperability with campus enterprise systems is also gaining traction in the academic world (Richardson and Hopkins 2004).

The shift to web-based and cloud-based library management systems is changing the ILS game by allowing for more collaboration and sharing while sometimes reducing the need for local technology skills. Some libraries issue a request for information (RFI) to vendors to learn about current market offerings and use that information in crafting the RFP.

Keeping an eye on nascent technology can help determine when to move or what types of enhancements to request of your current vendor. Useful questions to ask yourself during this phase include the following: Do you anticipate joining or creating a consortium? Are you hoping to further integrate the ILS with other campus systems, such as Bursar or Assessment?

Standards—How Does the Current System Rate?

Three significant areas to review in the current system are cataloging, data, and accessibility. What are absolute needs for cataloging functionality, authority control, and metadata? Does the system support MARC, Dublin Core, RDA, or other XML standards? Is it ready for BIBFRAME and beyond? Also review data security and interoperability with other systems. How secure are data in your current system, and what data standards do connected systems meet? What are campus requirements related to third parties handling student or financial data? Richardson and Hopkins (2004, 5) emphasize:

> Because the ILMS [Integrated Library Management System] will be a major component of a much larger network of library-related systems and services, it is imperative that the system has adopted key standards for library data and interoperability with other systems. The continued growth of networked-based services and initiatives emphasizes the importance of compliance with established standards, incorporation of new standards, and support for emerging ones.

Accessibility is mainly a concern in the public access catalog but also considers staff-side implications. Related to accessibility is the issue of responsive design to accommodate access with a variety of electronic devices. Evaluate how your current system measures up, and determine where you would like it to be in the future.

Lessons Learned

Not performing a needs assessment leaves a hole in the objective knowledge about the current system. It also makes comparison and decision making more difficult in later stages of the RFP process.

RFP PROCESS FOR AN ILS

An RFP for an ILS is a formal expression of design specifications in the form of a call to vendors in the marketplace for a proposal demonstrating how their products and services meet your stated needs. This process is opened to potential vendors for a set period of time and follows a scripted process, generally under the watchful eye of the institution's purchasing or procurement department.

Create a selection committee to lead this project, understanding that its composition is vital to the success of the process. This team will identify the selection criteria, evaluate the proposals and demonstrations, and make a recommendation for purchase. The contract is then negotiated and awarded. Once a contract is signed, planning for migration and implementation of the new system begins. Work will be negotiated, milestones set, and the migration process begun in earnest. After implementation, evaluations of the new system and of the RFP process should be conducted to help inform the next system change effort.

Getting Ready

Three keys to a successful RFP process found by Calvert and Read (2006) were communication, preparation, and documentation. Communication is essential at all levels of the organization and with all stakeholders. Transparency and openness of documentation goes a long way toward alleviating misunderstandings. Published timelines keep processes on schedule. Preparation covers everything from the initial discussions of library goals to reviewing the existing system and library workflows to reviewing industry trends and knowing the market to involving stakeholders throughout the process. Documentation has three main rules: be clear, be concise, and be accurate. State your goals clearly, do not repeat questions, and review documents for errors. Aim to ensure these three areas are addressed as you work your way through the process.

Using a consultant to help draft the RFP may bring a needed outside perspective. However, they often use generic templates and do not know useful details about the local institution. Carefully weigh the benefits and shortcomings of contracting with a consultant.

Another issue to consider as you prepare is that a change in systems will affect nearly every staff member. Therefore, it is never too early to begin change management conversations. Helping everyone begin the adjustment process as early as possible will ultimately help ease the transition when it happens.

Appointing the Selection/Project Team

Establishing a selection team is an early critical stage of the RFP process. Work the selection committee will complete includes determining the goal (aligning with strategic goals of the library) or desired outcomes, writing the questions to vendors, scoring the RFP responses, and evaluating the vendor demonstrations. The committee also contacts references, evaluates complete proposal packages, and identifies a preferred vendor and product. The systems librarian is often charged with leading the team. Team membership should include staff from technical services, information technologies, public services, and all the functional areas of the library, along with administration/finance. Determine if specific roles are needed or if there is a useful way to share the work the committee will do. For example, perhaps one person could manage the arrangements for the on-site demonstrations, whereas another could coordinate the reference contacts. The team should not be too large, but it does need to be comprehensive in representation. Participation in the process will enhance buy-in when the choice is made and change is imminent.

It may be useful to have the committee break into subgroups to solicit suggested questions and scenarios from employees not on the committee. This will broaden participation in the process and enhance the quality of the final product. As Manifold (2000, 122) notes, "The system selection and migration processes are much stronger with the involvement of all staff." The system ultimately affects nearly everyone in the library, so find ways to be inclusive.

What Is Your Goal?

To paraphrase from *Alice in Wonderland* by Lewis Carroll (1865): If you don't know where you are going, any road will get you there. So defining your goals prevents this confusion. What are you expecting a new system to accomplish for the library? Being able to articulate the goals for the system helps vendors organize their proposals around your specific needs and also helps provide clarity during the evaluation stage.

Depending on the expectations of the institution and requirements of its procurement office, some libraries may opt for a more vision-oriented approach to the RFP process where the library describes high-level expectations and general characteristics and asks vendors to describe options for meeting those expectations. Other institutions might develop a more detailed document outlining general goals while also delineating specific requirements and functionality (Breeding 2015b). The approach taken will inform the evaluation process used.

Special considerations for academic libraries include heavy use of electronic resources of various types; heavy interlibrary loan (ILL) needs; interoperability with other campus systems such as student registration, bursar, and accounts payable; and user need for the ability to generate or capture citations and seamlessly search across many resources. Consortium needs might include the ability for shared functionality such as circulation, collection development, and electronic resources management, along with robust individual and consortium-level analytics and reporting of statistics and usage. Consider the specific needs of your institution as you set your goals.

Open-source systems are usually considered during high-level strategy discussions. Currently, the only real open-source library management system option on the market is Kuali OLE (Breeding 2015b). Open-source systems are unique enough that they may qualify as sole-source purchases and not need to go through a traditional RFP process.

Working with Local Purchasing and Procurement Rules

Every institution will have procurement procedures and regulations to follow. Contact the appropriate representative early on, and have that person meet with the selection team so that everyone has the same understanding and expectations of the rules and required processes. Discuss where there is flexibility. It is now common for entities to have online systems for posting and responding to RFPs. Public institutions usually have rigid guidelines and timetables that must be followed for large purchases in the interest of transparency and accountability. Be sure to follow the rules completely. Your procurement officer is experienced in this area and may have good advice to benefit the team related to phrasing of questions or the flow of the process.

Planning Evaluation and Scoring Proposals

Determining parameters ahead of time makes for easier work later in the review process by enabling the selection committee to identify the most critical elements on which to base the evaluation. Setting the selection criteria before receiving responses also makes it a fairer process. Note the broad areas of performance and functionality that are critical to your institution. Some common sections may include system functionality, training and support, on-site demonstrations, financial stability of the vendor, cost, and references.

Not all areas of the ILS count equally in the overall scoring. For example, an institution with significant digital holdings may value highly robust electronic resources management functionality and score that functionality with extra weight, whereas an institution without those types of holdings may find it of little importance and not choose to include it in the scoring at all. Official references may carry less weight relative to system functionality for any library. Cost should not be the most important factor for any institution. The scoring should be weighted to emphasize the areas most critical to your local situation and needs.

Create a scoring tool based on RFP categories to allow for comparison of responses. A grid with categories and vendors each taking an axis works well and allows for direct scoring comparisons. Choose either points or percentages as the base for calculating the final score. Assign a maximum value to each category. Include a section for notes to help clarify scoring decisions.

Sample Evaluation Criteria and Scoring Grid		
Evaluation Criteria		
	Initial Scoring	**Possible Points**
A.	Functionality: Products, Services, Performance, and Security. (Scope of Work Section A, and Scope of Work Overview-Preferred Functionality)	40 points
B.	Total Cost: Start-up, Recurring, Licensing Models (Scope of Work Section B)	30 points
C.	Experience/Qualifications (Scope of Work Section C)	10 points
D.	Implementation, Training (Scope of Work Section D)	20 points
	Subtotals	**100 points max**
	FINAL SCORING—IF INTERVIEWS REQUIRED	
E.	Vendor Interviews/Demo	30 points
	Total	**130 points max**

Figure 8.1 Evaluation Criteria and Scoring Grid from the University of New Mexico's RFP for an ILS, 2013

Determine which committee members will participate in the scoring and voting processes. Discuss with the group how consensus will be reached, how ties will be broken, and how disagreements among members will be handled. It is possible there will not be unanimous support of a single product in the end. Discussion should happen ahead of time about how such a situation will be managed.

Writing the RFP

This section discusses the mechanisms of actually crafting the RFP document. Many example RFPs are found from a simple web search. Organizations often use a template for RFPs, particularly if the submission system is online, so check to see if one is available or even required by your institution. Consult with your procurement agent or purchasing officer to understand what flexibility you have crafting the RFP. You want to be able to customize it enough to reflect your individual situation and to solicit information from vendors that is useful to your decision-making process.

When developing the RFP document, ensure it is measurable and informative. Focus on the final evaluation and on solutions. All vendors provide basic functionality; how will unique solutions be discovered? Will the selection committee be able to compare responses and make a choice? Refrain from the temptation to ask all yes/no questions or to try to detail every possible functional aspect of a system. This approach tends to limit options based on existing system knowledge and may not expose exciting new developments or potential solutions. "Checklists of functionality can be misleading relative to the actual performance of any given system in its daily operation in a library" (Breeding 2015a, 5). The industry trend is to be more general and to look for flexibility and opportunities for growth, as noted by Calvert and Read (2006, 657), who investigated best practices for writing and using RFPs. They asked librarians and vendors the same set of questions around what they found most useful about the RFP, what they believed worked well in practice and what did not, and for suggestions to improve the process. Among the most common responses given were the following:

- Do not limit the RFP to yes/no answers. Allow vendors the opportunity to detail how their system performs various functions.
- Note fixed technical requirements (e.g., the need to run on Linux) early on.
- Be sure to tailor the RFP to the needs of the specific library. Do not use a sample document without customizing it to reflect your situation.
- Have vendors elaborate on their development plans for the next two to three years. Look for clearly detailed paths.
- Create questions that elicit responses noting unique and value-added features of each system.

Writing good questions is vital to getting good responses and the best outcome. Properly worded questions help make scoring more objective and clearcut. Something that will impact the daily lives of staff members can be an emotional topic, so it helps to be as objective as possible.

Distinguish between businesses processes (staff-side) and user needs and experiences (public-side) (Bahr 2007). Create questions that address each. Academic libraries should include detailed questions that address the unique needs of their users, such as management of electronic resources, ILL functionality, and interoperability with other campus systems. Consortia will want to focus on items centric to their needs, such as options for shared functionality in circulation, resource sharing, collection development or electronic resources management, and robust reporting capabilities.

Take the time now to develop scenarios of processes you would have vendors walk through during on-site demonstrations (e.g., running a complex statistical report). The demonstrations should also be scored and considered in the final evaluation. You may find the need to make script adjustments once you have the RFP responses in hand, but it is good to have an outline of scenarios to address at the ready.

Descriptions of common sections of ILS RFPs follow. Not every section will be included in the scoring matrix.

Background and Description of the Library/Consortium

Provide vendors a description of your library, its type, whether you have branches, size and types of holdings, and size and types of the user population served. Get fairly detailed about types of electronic packages and items held (i.e., downloadable, streaming, video, audio, and music collections). Note your current system and how long you have used it. Also describe any strategic plans for predicted growth, expansion or change in service levels, or potential consolidation or collaboration with other institutions. Some sources also encourage an institution to include an available budget for the system. They advocate that knowing your existing system, budget, and plans for the future will help a vendor provide more detailed information about meeting the library's needs and what the migration process will look like. Other sources believe that the budget should not be shared with the vendors so as to allow for greater flexibility in the final price negotiations.

Company Data

In an era of market consolidation and buyouts, ask questions to elicit details about the vendor's primary market, ownership, financial health, vision, operating practices, and long-term interest in the market. Learn about the quality of their products and the size of their market share. Do they have a proven record of working with libraries of your type and size?

References

Ask vendors to provide contact information for references of current customers similar to your library's size and audience, but recognize those contacts will be carefully selected. Ask for three to five references to get a variety of perspectives on each company and its product.

System Specifications

Involve technology experts and note minimum specifications so that you do not end up with outdated systems quickly. Industry trends now have software moving to the cloud or to contracting for Software as a Service (SaaS), in which there is no local hosting or ownership of the software. Questions to ask yourself are the following: Do you have the trained staff to host a system locally or to make customizations if the software allows? Does your institution have any restrictions on third-party systems holding patron data? Consider the following:

- Hardware requirements—Vendors must articulate any hardware requirements for their products, from staff computers to barcode readers and label printers.
- System upgrades—Require information to be given on frequency and method of system upgrades, including anticipated downtimes.
- System performance requirements and remedies—Lay out your system performance requirements, and have the vendor list remedies for when there are problems.
- Source code—Who owns the source code? How can you get your records out of the system in the future? Are there associated costs?
- Data security—Note any institutional requirements related to security of data. Have the vendor describe how they meet security standards.

Functionality

While most systems cover the basics, Breeding (2016) advises that the library must specify the modules and functionality desired. Do not assume something will exist in the system. Minimum critical system functionality includes the ability to get material records into the database, for users to be able to search that database easily and find holdings, for access to materials to be seamless, and to be able to track items that are checked out.

How questions are written determines the answers given. What makes a good question? Open-ended questions are usually better than those that will yield a simple yes or no answer though some questions of that type can be useful. Try not to close off opportunity or impose limits with the phrasing of questions. For example, asking "Does the system do X (Yes/No)?" is less informative than asking "How does the system do X (describe)?" Allow for some flexibility for the vendor to recommend alternative solutions that may be more efficient and economical. As Calvert and Read (2006) note, question writing can be difficult. If members of the evaluation committee have limited experience with other systems or in other libraries, it may be challenging for them to consider other ways to do certain work beyond how it is handled in the current system, which may influence how questions are worded. It can be useful to solicit questions from staff members who have experience using other vendor systems or to review other recently issued RFPs for wording ideas.

If you choose to go the route of an RFP that asks more detailed questions, rather than a high-level vision piece, consider questions in some or all of the areas as discussed next. The list is not exhaustive, and you may have additional critical questions.

- Cataloging—An accurate database of holdings is vital for an institution, both to account for assets and for successful searching of held items. Ask questions about how data are composed in the new system and what happens to data during its migration from the old system to the new one. What standards does the new system support? Have vendors describe the structures of various record types. If a library has older formatted data, how will it migrate? What do holdings statements look like? How are bibliographic data imported and exported? How are single-part, multi-part, and serial items managed? Do records have needed fields for ILL? How are notes fields created, managed, and migrated? Is electronic data interchange (EDI) present for bindery systems, acquisitions, and claiming? Which barcode schemes are supported?
- Public access catalog/discovery—Being able to easily search for and find materials is critically important. Intuitive interface design is a help to patrons. Planners should be aware of their users' needs related to searching. Consider the existing levels of search, display, linking, and ILL or hold buttons, as well as what ability is made available for local customization. Note functionality from the patron side, such as ability to see current account information, checkouts, bills, and saving and sharing lists. Some systems are built with the expectation that another discovery layer will be added to provide an enhanced search experience. Consider your goals in this area, articulate expectations, and ask questions accordingly.
- Circulation—Circulating materials comprises a significant amount of a library's activities. The circulation module needs to be simple and easy to use to prevent errors. Have vendors describe how their product handles patron record creation or batch loading, fining, billing, notices, as well as holds and recalls.
- Acquisitions—Describe how purchases and renewals of electronic packages (monograph and serials) as well as print materials are handled. Ask

about online ordering partners and options for EDI with vendors and campus financial systems. Have the vendor provide samples of reports and screenshots of interfaces.

- Electronic resources management—Have the vendor describe how electronic resources are managed, including linking, license tracking, electronic rights management (ERM), renewals, and purchasing/cost information. Which components are included in the system, and which are available at an added cost?
- Reports and statistics—Being able to account for items and quantify activity are critical abilities. Ask the vendor to describe standard, or canned, reports and ad hoc reporting capabilities. Ask for samples, including reports of traditional things like circulation by patron type, date, and more. Also ask about analytics options, including collection overlap (comparing content of electronic package to electronic package and/or print to electronic package), collection age, cost per use, and more. How is inventorying of the collection managed?
- Multiple branches or locations—If appropriate, describe desired functionality useful to libraries with multiple branches, whether on the same campus or satellites in other cities. This may include the ability to easily identify and move groups of materials in the database from one location to another, to run statistical reports at a granular location level, or to have branches operate with different hours or circulation policies.
- Enhancements—A system should undergo regular enhancements to adjust to changing demands in the field. A library is not well served by a product that remains static, so enquire about development plans and timelines. Learning about past performance meeting enhancement schedules can be useful. Ask about any costs related to enhancements.
- Add-ons—Resource sharing and ILL management (define formats and protocols for exchanging electronic documents), serials module, inventory module, online acquisitions, radio-frequency identification, self-checkout options, federated searching tools, room or computer reservations, and interoperability with the local patron registration system or bursar's office are all areas of possible interest. Ask about robust, full-featured application program interfaces (APIs) to allow communication with the ILS and provide for true interoperability with external enterprise systems. Request a list of released and planned-for release APIs. Who is responsible for developing or maintaining existing APIs? Be sure to indicate expectations of your library for functionality beyond the absolute system basics.

Training and Support/Customer Service

Staff change over time. Problems arise. Ask vendors to describe how training and support are provided, noting method, timing, and cost. Many vendors provide online materials and webinars to educate staff members about using their product. Will trainers come on-site, or will all training be done remotely? Are trainings customizable to your institution? Is there a cost?

Project Deliverables and Requirements

Clearly articulate expectations about deliverables, requirements, anticipated timelines, and deadlines. Ask for clarification about which party is responsible for each step of the process.

Cost proposal

Ask for a detailed cost proposal. Be sure the costs of system add-ons are clearly indicated. As Karetzky notes, "A low bid that appears to be a money saver may in fact result in higher costs" (1998, 44). Maintenance and support should include system patches and upgrades. Ask for details on terms for renewal or contract extension.

Boilerplate from Purchasing

The institution's procurement office normally requires the inclusion of standard text related to legal obligations. Common items include submission method, deadlines, procedures for submitting questions, duration of contract, renewal and exit options, data ownership (bibliographic and patron), applicable law/public records requirements, and assignment of rights.

Evaluation Process

Evaluate the vendor submissions by comparing the systems across the various predetermined dimensions. Allow ample time for a thorough review of each proposal during this critical evaluation process. Keep in mind that items such as overall system performance, customer service, available features, adaptability, and flexibility may be as important as price in the long run. Include feedback from other library staff and users whenever possible.

Scoring Responses

Each committee member with a vote needs to review every proposal and score all categories using the previously created grid. Keep notes. After all scoring is completed, meet as a group to talk about the scores so that any differences in understanding or experience can be discussed. If the group has questions about a proposal, ask for clarification from the vendor. Do not make assumptions. Scores should be compiled and top ranking vendors identified.

On-Site Demonstrations

The top-ranking vendors should be brought on-site for product demonstrations. This allows for a bit of a look under the hood of the product and gives opportunities for further questioning about details of the product's functionality.

Plan the agenda well. Give vendors breaks; they are human, too. Invite as many library staff as possible to the demonstrations. Administrators will have questions as well. Provide attendees evaluation sheets. Make sure staff are engaged and prepared to watch, listen, and ask questions during the presentations. It is best if there is a core group of appropriate staff able to attend all presentations to help ensure a fair comparison. Include their feedback in the overall scoring.

It can be one thing to read a list of steps to complete a process and quite another to watch the steps demonstrated live. Watch for logical flow of operations. How many clicks or screen changes does it take to do the work in high-volume functions? How is the system response time? Ask to be shown how to customize areas or set defaults. Be skeptical. The vendor should not bring only sales staff to demonstrations. Someone should be available to explain why a system works the way it does.

Evaluate each demonstration as soon as possible after completion while it is fresh in people's memories. If questions arise, follow the established process to get clarification or more information from the vendor.

Testing

It is a benefit if a test area or sandbox space is available to experiment in an environment that more closely replicates the live software. Ask about limited-time access for staff to kick the tires and take the product for a spin.

References

The vendor should supply contact information for current customers similar to your institution. Remember, these references are usually carefully chosen by the vendor. Phone calls may elicit more candid responses than written responses; however, both are useful. Be considerate when contacting references. It may be tempting to ask a long list of detailed questions. However, a handful of general questions may give you the information you need. Possible questions include:

- What were your priorities or one or two main goals you hoped to achieve when moving to the product? How well do you feel they were achieved?
- If you had to do it all over again, would you still select the same system?
- How satisfied is your library with the product? Please explain.

- How did the implementation and migration process go? What should we look out for? Please explain what went well and what did not go as planned, including any hidden costs, vendor involvement and reliability, and realistic timelines. What might you do differently if you were to migrate and implement now?
- How well does the system interoperate with other systems and does it make best use of standards?
- Can you get the reports and statistics you need from the system? Please explain.
- If hosted, how satisfied is your library with this service, including system availability and response time? Please explain.
- How satisfied is your library with the responsiveness of the vendor and the customer service and support provided? Do you have any concerns with the vendor? Please explain.
- How satisfied is your library with the level of local customization available in the product, both in the staff and public interfaces? Please explain, including what was not possible.
- Have costs been predictable and as expected?
- What overall advice would you have for us if we migrated to the product?

Members of consortia may also want to ask questions such as the following:

- Describe your experience managing bibliographic, authority, and electronic records of the product as a consortium.
- Are you able to get reports and statistics at the institutional level that each member needs? Please explain.

Be sure to also do some of your own investigations and talk to your own library contacts as well as those provided by the vendor.

Site Visits

Consider making site visits to institutions using the products of the vendors on your short list. Talk to staff there to see firsthand how it works in real-life situations. Understand that local libraries operate and make choices differently than yours might. Wrap this information into the overall evaluation.

Contract

Contract negotiations are beyond the scope of the RFP and will likely be handled mainly by the institution's purchasing department. However, there are some important items to ensure are included in the contract.

Components

Clearly state which components are included in the package, including add-ons such as training and optional modules.

Data Ownership and Exit Options

Discussing exit strategies and costs is often overlooked when negotiating a new system contract. This is likely not the library's final ILS vendor relationship, so detail how data can be extracted for migration to a future ILS. Indicate clearly who owns what data, including bibliographic and patron data. Also note what can be done with the data and any restrictions on use (you may wish to retain the rights to use it in other campus systems, for example).

Timeline

Discuss implementation timelines, as well as penalties or bonuses related to completion time for the project.

Data Migration and Implementation

Detail the work done by each party related to the migration of existing system data and implementation of the new system.

Lessons Learned

Writing and evaluating the RFP are critical to the success of the project. Take the time to do it well. Cover details, but don't get too far into the weeds. Avoid checklists! Don't box yourself in by using limiting questions. Leave vendors an opportunity to talk about functionality you didn't specifically ask for, but that may provide a solution to your stated problems. Do not be tempted to purchase a product based on price or functionality alone but on the basis of the entire package of what it offers and how well it meets your goals.

IMPLEMENTATION AND EVALUATION OF A NEW ILS

After the contract has been signed, the implementation phase begins. Implementation includes mapping and migrating existing data from the old to the new system, training staff on the new system, adjusting workflows, and shifting to live work in the new environment. Wrapping up the whole process is the evaluation of the product and the selection process to inform your next purchase.

Implementation

Discussions with the vendor will begin in earnest about an array of work to be completed in order to get your institution operational on the new system. A point of contact, usually an implementation manager, will be assigned by the vendor, and one should be selected from the library, often the systems librarian or director of technical services. It can be useful to employ a migration project manager to facilitate the process from the library's side. This person is the primary contact with the vendor and will coordinate all details of the process, including scheduling meetings, facilitating decision making, completing documentation, and ensuring work is completed in a timely manner by both sides. Existing staff already have a heavy workload ahead of them, setting up and learning a new system while keeping up with the existing work in the old system, and a project manager could lighten that load. With or without a project manager, a library implementation team should be created to lead the various functional areas through the transition, make decisions, and create new workflows. This team's membership is probably different than the RFP team but may have some crossover. Items to work out with the vendor include, but are not limited to:

- Scope of work, project plan and milestones, responsibilities of each party, and timeline
- Training (vendor-supplied or in-house)
- Premigration data cleanup and/or retrospective conversion
- Data discovery, conversion, review, and testing
- Change management
- Communication

Implementation involves decisions about what existing data to migrate and, nearly as importantly, what data not to migrate (Jost 2016). Some data may not map into the new system, and some may be too incomplete to migrate. Review workflows and refer back to the needs assessment to see if some processes are now past their time. Do the data collected still serve a practical purpose? Of the data items you will keep, map the migration and project timeline. Prioritize what goes first. Common data types to migrate, as possible, include bibliographic, patron, outstanding orders, serials check-in, accounting transactions, bindery, and patron circulation/billing history. Once the data have migrated, it will need to be reviewed for accuracy.

As you train staff and discuss new workflows, there will be a temptation to do things just like you have always done. It does a disservice to try to fit the old processes into the new system. Embrace the new system to take advantage of its fullest offerings. This change will require a period of adjustment. Change is hard, even for those who desire it. It can be particularly challenging for staff who are resistant. Have mechanisms in place to support everyone to ensure the best outcome.

Discuss whether to run both systems live for a period of time. There is often a period of time where library work continues to happen while data are being processed off-site, resulting in a gap in current information. Dual systems might be the easiest way to manage this. Consider arranging access to old data files in the native system for a period of time or creating an archive in case data need to be reloaded. Once the new system is stable, sign off on the project and consider the implementation complete.

Evaluation

According to Jost (2016, 37), at project closeout, "what the library should be trying to accomplish is a 360 degree view of the project, encompassing the aspects of what went well and those areas that could have been improved." At the beginning of the RFP process, you articulated what you wanted the system to be. Now you need to determine how closely it matches that set of desires.

After the system has been live for a few months and the initial learning curve has been managed, ask library staff and patrons how well the new system is performing. Does it meet the original goals set when writing the RFP? What went well during migration and implementation and what could have been improved?

Likewise, get input on the effectiveness of the selection process. Were the right people on the selection team? Were the right kinds of questions asked on the RFP? Were any key questions omitted? What went well and what would make that part of the process better?

Lessons Learned

Fully embrace the new system in order to take advantage of all it offers. Do not try to distort the new system to match old workflows. Review processes used to improve them for the next purchase.

SUMMARY

The ILS is the backbone of library work and a critical component to the success of a library. The RFP process is a tremendous undertaking, requiring resources from funding to staff energy. "One of the benefits of an RFP is that you will have in writing from the vendor what the integrated library system will and will not do" (Webber and Peters 2010, 87). The system needs to be able to grow with your library and change with the times. The system is critical to the daily functioning of the library, so choose the product that best meets the needs of the library, today and into the foreseeable future, not simply the least expensive one available. Saving a dollar today may cost tenfold in work-around costs or lost opportunities over the lifetime of the contract.

REFERENCES

Bahr, Ellen. 2007. "Dreaming of a Better ILS." *Computers in Libraries* 27 (9): 10–14.

Breeding, Marshall. 2015a. "Introduction and Concepts." *Library Technology Reports* 51 (4): 5–19.

Breeding, Marshall. 2015b. "Selection and Procurement Strategies." *Library Technology Reports* 51 (4): 20–21.

Breeding, Marshall. 2016. *Library Technology Buying Strategies*. Chicago: ALA Editions.

Calvert, Philip, and Marion Read. 2006. "RFPs: A Necessary Evil or Indispensable Tool?" *The Electronic Library* 24 (5): 649–61. doi:10.1108/02640470610707259.

Carroll, Lewis. 1865. *Alice in Wonderland*. Auckland: Floating Press.

Jost, Richard. 2016. *Selecting and Implementing an Integrated Library System: The Most Important Decision You Will Ever Make*. Chandos Information Professional Series. Amsterdam: Elsevier.

Karetzky, Stephen. 1998. "Choosing an Automated System." *Library Journal* 123 (11): 42.

Manifold, Alan. 2000. "A Principled Approach to Selecting an Automated Library System." *Library Hi Tech* 18 (2): 119–29.

Richardson, Joanna P., and Peta J. Hopkins. 2004. "Selecting an ILMS for a Future You Can't Imagine." http://epublications.bond.edu.au/cgi/viewcontent.cgi?article=1000&context=library_pubs.

Webber, Desiree, and Andrew Peters. 2010. *Integrated Library Systems: Planning, Selecting, and Implementing*. Santa Barbara, CA: Libraries Unlimited.

CASE STUDY

Not all institutions desire, or are required, to utilize an RFP selection process on major purchases. Private institutions, in particular, have more flexibility in this arena. The following case study of the Private Academic Library Network of Indiana details an alternative approach to ILS selection, which is goal- or vision-oriented, allowing for a more flexible review and evaluation process.

PALNI WEB-SCALE REVIEW: A "NON-RFP" PROCESS

Kirsten Leonard

In September 2012, the Private Academic Library Network of Indiana (PALNI) began exploring next generation ILSs that are designed to operate on the web. Developers of these solutions tout system design that allows for speedier and less problematic software upgrades, more efficient and less complex workflows, integration with external data and analytics sources, and increased ability to remain relevant in the information field through scaled operations. PALNI institutions struggled to manage updates and utilize software capabilities of our centrally hosted Aleph system. PALNI also had a key goal to recover resources dedicated to ILS activities and redeploy those resources to develop additional services and gain substantive business analytics/intelligence to provide service development direction. Web-scale systems also increase the opportunity for collaborative and aggregated technical services, sharing of other human resources/expertise, collaborative collection development, shared storage, and increased resource sharing. None of these collaborative goals was served by our current system. Because of our desire to move in completely new directions, the PALNI executive director, PALNI board, and PALNI team leaders felt that a traditional RFP would put the organization in danger of replicating our current system rather than taking advantage of the new opportunities presented by web scale and the opportunity to advance deep collaboration among the PALNI libraries. While PALNI did form committees, develop high-level goals and questions, ask for bids, and have criteria for a decision, the fact that the consortium is comprised of private colleges with no formal process requirements allowed PALNI to use a more iterative and evolving informal process to envision the future.

PALNI is a 501(c)(3) owned by the twenty-two supported private academic institutions. The founding concept of PALNI is to collaborate to enhance teaching and learning through optimizing library resources and services. The PALNI solution to escalating financial pressures is to collaborate not only with other private academic institutions in Indiana, but also to partner with other groups and consortia to reduce costs and compete academically through innovative services. As the internet and information services landscape has changed, so have PALNI systems and services at the strategic direction of all twenty-two library deans and directors who sit on the PALNI Board. Through our move to a web-scale system that freed up resources, staff time, and staff expertise, PALNI has expanded beyond providing primarily a resource management system to sharing expertise, staff, and resources in many areas including strategic planning, marketing, application and programming development, usability and user needs analysis, reference, information fluency, outreach, data management and configuration, and collection management. (PALNI, About Us n.d.)

In 2014, immediately after the launch of our new system, the PALNI board voted in the PALNI-wide Commitment to Deep Collaboration to become more deliberate and expand the ways in which the PALNI libraries worked together.

In the fall of 2012, several people came together to develop the plan for review of web-scale systems to ensure that overall goals were met. The PALNI board developed a survey to clarify areas of agreement and convergence of board members/library directors. The overall board goals for the system selection were the following:

- Prefer simplicity when there are trade-offs.
- Be sure PALNI is not reacting to our current frustrations and issues, and be sure of what we would be getting/giving up.
- Configurability is not as important as reliability and data management.
- Reducing time and the learning curve to perform workflows is important because shrinking employee full-time equivalent (FTE) makes workflow more difficult, especially for smaller libraries (Leonard 2014).

Given our goal to increase the ability to collaborate with the system, the board also asked that reports from the functional areas should include the extent that the prospective system facilitates:

- shared collection management (retrospective and new acquisitions),
- shared processing,
- consortium eBook purchases/licensing, and
- the ability to default a shared discovery solution to PALNI-wide while allowing individual libraries to boost local holdings.

Other desirable characteristics were "integrated and logical workflows, robust statistical information on holdings, circulation etc., and a unified resource management system that includes a robust Electronic Resource Management component" (Leonard 2014). Characteristics that had more mixed responses across the libraries included a preference for back-end simplicity over extensive customizability, but some libraries would not give up more robust functionality for back-end simplicity. Therefore, the board requested that task forces indicate what functions are included and their impact on back-end complexity. The board could also not provide clear direction on whether lower cost was preferable to more robust functionality and whether all product modules must come from a single vendor. They preferred to see the details in the report and weigh all aspects together.

The review process included the following modules: ILS, Discovery Layer, KB/OpenURL Linker, Federated Search, ERMS, and Digital Asset Management (if provided). The level of interoperability and standards-based development between these modules within a single vendor and across vendors was evaluated. Products were required to be web-based and multitenant and included ExLibris; OCLC, including EBSCO EDS working with OCLC WMS; and Intota with Serials Solutions and EBSCO EDS as discovery layers.

The project timeline was accelerated with the time from planning for evaluation through implementation being less than 21 months. The project steps are noted in Figure 8.2.

The work of the evaluation was divided into the following functional groups: Systems, Discovery, Acquisitions & Cataloging, Circulation/Patron, Electronic Resource Management, and Digital Projects. Each functional area developed a list of goals to determine how well each system can accomplish the board-defined goals. This was explicitly not an exhaustive list of specifications or specific steps to allow for the possibility of increased efficiency or benefit in the new designs. The groups also reviewed the Orbis Cascade Alliance specifications and adapted areas applicable to PALNI goals to build on evaluation processes developed by a similar consortium. Each group developed a list of overall strengths and drawbacks of each vendor option. They researched the vendor's future planning, quality control, ease of use, and overall efficiency for each of their functional areas. Each group had a chair and report committee. The groups solicited input PALNI-wide from those working in the functional area, including an official vote from those working in the functional area on the scenarios of product options.

Figure 8.2 Web-Scale Timeline Plan

Each committee report included the level that each product met the PALNI-wide goals and any limitations that would prevent PALNI from selecting a particular product. The groups provided a current status overview of functionality (in terms of broad goals) and the pros and cons of the products reviewed.

The combined reports from each of the functional groups were extensive (358 pages) and time-consuming to write, and, given the fast-paced development process of web scale, they were immediately out of date. However, the process was essential not only for making the final selection but also for all staff to begin to understand the profound differences between the web-scale systems and our current system. The time and depth of their review assisted in the process of stepping back and being open to new ways of providing current services and new services. The broad areas of inquiry for each group are noted in the Appendix. Each group scheduled webinars with the vendors and requested that they demonstrate how to do sample tasks or processes so that we could gauge the level of functionality, complexity, and efficiency. Groups followed up with written questions that vendors responded to in writing.

The initial plan included the development of a rubric to weigh the varying reports from the functional areas and costs from the PALNI board, executive committee, and executive director. However, as we began to understand the opportunity and complexity of the products, it was felt that any weighting we could develop at that time would be arbitrary and unnecessarily constrictive. The board requested that the executive director develop a marketplace and proposal analysis. The analysis included reports on vendor development plans, governance and business structures, agreements with content providers and linked data, resources allocated to the project, and resource scaling plans as more institutions adopt the product, as well as opportunities for development partnerships. In 2012, most of the systems were new and rapidly evolving. The products were not mature, and in the case of Intota, not even released, adding to the complexity of making a decision. The analysis also included PALNI direct costs to maintain the current system as estimates on staff time to use and run the system—that is, the cost of staying put, and the impact on the budget for each of the received proposals.

To make the final decision, the board reviewed the combined reports and recommendations from the functional groups, the analysis of the marketplace from the executive director, and the written proposals from the vendors in a two-day retreat facilitated by former Earlham College board member, Tom Kirk. The review of the executive director report set the stage to look at the wider marketplace and service impact. Small groups then evaluated the functional reports, noting the level of readiness and the impact of the most recent release on key service needs. Several of the functional reports had noted key services that were not yet available. Thus, the executive director and many board members expected that a decision would be delayed. However, a recent release of WorldShare Management Services (WMS) met a majority of those needs. In addition, the PALNI treasurer prepared a financial analysis on individual institution fees showing the financial benefit of making a decision immediately. And finally, the use of clickers and skillful facilitation allowed for fast input and articulation of concerns from the entire 22-member board. Surprisingly, we quickly developed a high level of agreement to move forward with contract negotiations once a final round of functional "Day 1 must-haves" was gathered from the functional groups.

Given that our goals for the new system were radically different and focused on collaboration, the process used to select a system differed from the typical RFI/RFP process. Our process was more goal-driven rather than detailed workflow specifications. As we learned more about the systems, we adjusted our expectations and investigated the new opportunities presented. Rather than linear, this was a highly iterative process. There were some areas of disagreement and some needs were unmet, but all PALNI libraries have stayed together and continue to deepen our collaboration and look for ways to provide services together. The systems continue to mature and develop, and we look forward to more collaborative opportunities.

REFERENCES

Leonard, Kirsten. "The PALNI Experience OCLC WMS (PowerPoint)." November 18, 2014. http://www.slideshare.net/KirstenLeonard/palni-experience.
PALNI. n.d. "About Us." http://www.palni.org/about-palni.

Appendix

RESEARCH AREAS

Cost

- Cost for implementation and ongoing cost—Amount and pricing model. Is there an additional cost for new modules?
- Cost for staff time for implementation, ongoing training, and ongoing maintenance
- Workflow savings (if any)—Speed and task success rates, number of steps in processes, screen space utilization, functional usable design

Quality Control/Reliability

- Quality control for software development and knowledgebase data—Stability, speed, success rates, error rates, quality of experience
- Quality control of platform—Downtimes, upgrade impact, reliability, security
- Community/PALNI development quality control

New Library Services Value

- Services provided that are new to PALNI, that is, business intelligence modules, Electronic Resource Management System (ERMS), support for sharing human resources/expertise, collaborative collection development and shared storage, and increased resource sharing. New services that PALNI may provide to its users.

Resources

- Business model, for example, open source, member driven, for profit
- Functional robustness/Configurability (determined by Group Deep Dives)
- PALNI-initiated configurability—Amount of DIY capabilities (determined by Group Deep Dives)

- Research and development resources—Development map, number of research personnel, partnerships for development
- Support structure—Location, number of support staff, knowledge of support staff, helpfulness, communication skills, scaling capabilities, communication method, training support
- Cloud infrastructure/Platform robustness—Scalability, cost, robustness, interoperability, standardization
- Community bibliographic data quality control, size
- Partnerships/Agreements with publishers/content providers
- Partnerships for linked data
- Community of users—How many, how active, how much like us, what resources do they bring
- Community development—App factory, knowledge threshold to develop

Interoperability

- Interoperability and ease/cost of integration with campus systems
- Support for interoperability with other systems
- API support—Documentation, communication on development changes that impact APIs
- Data use functionality—Ability to get our data out easily, cheaply, and in a usable format, both during contract and at contract cease

Legal

- Contract data use/Ownership restrictions
- Liability issues
- Governance structure for development on the systems

9

PUBLIC LIBRARIES AND PUBLIC LIBRARY CONSORTIA PROPOSAL PROCESS FOR INTEGRATED LIBRARY SYSTEMS

Christopher Holly

INTRODUCTION

This chapter is designed to be a supplement to the previous chapter, "Academic Libraries and Academic Library Consortia Proposal Process for Integrated Library Systems." Much of the integrated library system (ILS) request for proposal (RFP) process transcends library type, and the prior chapter outlines a solid structure for any ILS RFP. While there are nuances to consider with the ILS RFP for any library, this chapter focuses on some of the distinctions with ILS RFPs in public libraries and public library consortia. Depending on the services offered and nature of the organization, an academic library may also find utility in the topics discussed in this section.

The examples and lessons described in this chapter are sourced from the experiences of Cooperative Computer Services (CCS). It ends with a case study of a single public library's experience with an RFP.

Headquartered in Arlington Heights, Illinois, CCS is a group of 24 public libraries in the north and northwest suburbs of Chicago that share an ILS. From 2016 to 2017, CCS created a new strategic plan followed by a comprehensive needs analysis as part of its ILS RFP process.

The author would like to thank his successor as executive director of CCS, Rebecca Malinowski. While in the thick of a busy implementation, Rebecca provided input and a careful review of this chapter.

DETERMINING A NEED FOR A NEW SYSTEM

The renewal of ILS maintenance contracts is an obvious practicality that often dictates the next RFP cycle based upon local procurement rules. Whether it is a three-, five, or even seven-plus-year renewal cycle, appropriate planning and institutional reflection are integral to determining a need for a new system. Rather than being forced by a procurement cycle, proactive planning will help instill confidence in the decision of whether to go to RFP.

Isn't This Just Trading One Set of Problems for Another?

At the time of writing this chapter, the state of the ILS industry is one of consolidation. As a result of consolidation, there are fewer choices in the marketplace, and this lack of competition is slowing the wheels of innovation. Some progress is underway, such as the shift of ILSs to more open library services platforms, but many of the same decades-old processes are still a fundamental part of the current systems. Marshall Breeding echoes these sentiments in the *Library Systems Report 2017*:

> Not only have technology-focused companies consolidated themselves, they have become subsumed within higher-level organizations with broad portfolios of diverse business activities. The survivors of this transformed industry now bear responsibility to deliver innovation from their amassed capacity. Modern web-based systems delivering traditional library automation and discovery capabilities are now merely table stakes.
>
> Real progress depends on building out these platforms to support the new areas of service emerging within each type of library. (Breeding 2017)

The need for support in emerging areas of service is especially the case for public libraries, which do not typically focus on the same kinds of electronic resource management needs as academic libraries and still encounter high transaction volume for traditional circulation functions. This is also the case for consortia, which often require more complex system options in order to accommodate the varied needs of their members.

The state of relative status quo in the ILS marketplace often leads to the common feeling, "Aren't we just trading one set of problems for another?" While this turn of phrase is an easy way to deflect a potentially overwhelming RFP process, it also shields an organization from necessary reflection. Instead of deflecting, organizations should ask questions such as the following: How does the current ILS allow the library to uphold the focus and direction of its strategic plan or mission? What are the current problems? Has the library or library consortium regularly reviewed options and workflows? With the feature-rich ILSs that exist, would revisiting system configurations solve some problems? If you were going to ask for new features and functions, what would those be? These questions and more are crucial for organizations to consider to determine the need for an ILS RFP.

A variety of tools exist to help organizations analyze their operations and needs. At the comprehensive level, libraries could apply continual improvement strategies like Six Sigma or Kaizen in order to regularly work on process improvement. However, a needs analysis could be as simple as a set of questions in a staff survey or an e-mail alias to which library staff can send suggestions. The nature of your analysis depends on where you are as an organization. *The Memory Jogger 2: Tools for Continuous Improvement and Effective Planning* provides a set of diagnostic tools divided into typical improvement situations: working with ideas, working with numbers, and working in teams. Some tools that are typically helpful in a needs analysis are Flowcharts, Force Field Analyses, Cause and Effect/Fishbone diagrams, and Pareto Charts.

Defining the nature of need is key. For example, does it primarily lie with people, process, or technology? While it is easy to blame the aging ILS as the culprit, there may also be other factors at play that take precedence. Jeffrey Berk in *Champions of Change: The Manager's Guide to Creating Sustainable Business Process Improvements* outlines five categories of change that can affect an organization: Strategic Change, Process Change, Personnel Change, Technology Change, and External Shifts (Berk 2004). By thinking through the influence of these areas on an organization, it can become evident whether there is a need for a new ILS.

Strategic Planning—A CCS Example

A strategic planning process preceded the ILS RFP at CCS, and the new strategic plan provided a clear focus for the high priorities in the ILS RFP. CCS had traditionally created a long-range plan that was more tactical in nature. After a recent change in its executive director's position, the CCS leadership felt that it was important to conduct a more expansive, visionary plan. CCS hired an analytical consulting company focused on nonprofits to facilitate the process, analyze the situation, and identify the influential factors. The CCS Governing Board welcomed a complementary point of view by selecting a company that specializes in fostering best practices within the nonprofit world but does not focus solely on libraries.

The consulting company conducted interviews with the CCS Long Range Planning Committee, CCS library directors, CCS staff, and related organizations like Reaching across Illinois Library System (RAILS). The main purpose of these interviews was to gather information on the current state of affairs, pain points, needs, and trends. The consultants consolidated and analyzed the information gathered through the interviews, and they used the data to suggest broad strategic initiatives for CCS. After receiving the final analysis, the Long Range Planning Committee, CCS executive director, and CCS staff created the full strategic plan.

The consultants identified eight major areas of importance to the consortium in their assessment. These areas apply both to public library and consortial trends: (1) "relevance" issue, (2) funding constraints, (3) need for training, (4) "what's out there?" uncertainty, (5) new building and renovation trend, (6) patron-centric versus staff-centric focus, (7) eBooks and media, and (8) existing strengths. From these areas of assessment, CCS developed organizational goals, potential activities, and targets based on seven strategic initiatives: (1) Shore Up Current Value, (2) Formalize CCS Posture, (3) Increase Shared Learning, (4) Make the Data Useful, (5) Answer the "What's Out There?" Question, (6) Consider Structural Reorganization, and (7) Develop a Clear Digital Content Strategy.

With or without a consultant, a library or consortium can follow a similar process. The benefit of using a consulting company for the process at CCS was that the consulting company provided a neutral point of view and pointed out related areas that insiders may have overlooked. One example of an overlooked area was the importance of library renovation projects. While everyone was aware of these projects, not as much consideration had gone into the implications for building planning and the ILS.

Strategic Planning—Lessons Learned

- Identify your stakeholders and find out what they want. For public libraries, stakeholders would usually be the community. With a consortium, there may be additional levels of stakeholders; for example, primary stakeholders are typically related to the governance and who chooses to join or leave a consortium, whereas secondary stakeholders may be those who directly deal with some of the services of the consortium like the library staff and/or patrons. CCS defined its primary stakeholders as the member library directors, since the director has a significant influence on whether the library would remain a member of the consortium and determines what services the library would seek from the consortium. Naturally a focus on the library user is important for the consortial office; however, the focus on how to serve a library user is typically defined by the individual library missions and strategic plans.

- Identify the users of your services. Even though CCS's primary stakeholders are the library directors, the work is being done by the library staff for the users of the library. As a result, CCS formalized an education initiative for library staff and developed a key tenet of the public library patron as the North Star. When ranking the importance of ILS functionality, these separate orientations provided a clear guide.

- Take the time to analyze and reflect. CCS spent six months on its strategic planning process, which took place two and half years before the ILS maintenance contract was up for renewal. By planning ahead, CCS had the time to analyze and reflect on their needs and where they wanted to go.
- Involve as many people as possible. It is important for people to feel that their voices are heard, especially as members of a consortium. While the library directors were formally interviewed, their staff participated through internal library discussions and technical group meetings. In order to help the library directors facilitate internal library discussions, the consultants and executive director prepared a list of suggested questions to consider in those meetings.

---

1. What are some of the biggest challenges you face in fulfilling your library mission?
2. What do you expect CCS to accomplish for you currently?
3. How well is CCS fulfilling those accomplishments (in question 2)?
4. What library functions does CCS perform well for your patrons?
5. What library functions does CCS need to improve for your patrons?
6.
   a. In the future, what sorts of capabilities should CCS be adding to create a better library experience for you as staff?
   b. In the future, what sorts of capabilities should CCS be adding to create a better library experience for your patrons?
7.
   a. How would you like to collaborate with other libraries?
   b. How could greater collaboration help overcome some of those challenges in question 1?
8. What is your desire for greater collaboration with other libraries around shared technology?
9. What other things could CCS conceivably do—which it currently is not doing—to support you?

- Understand the ramifications of the status quo. What is at risk if there is no change? In the case of public libraries, it could mean local relevance and funding. In the case of consortia, it could mean losing member libraries.

RFP PROCESS

Communication, preparation, and documentation are three overarching themes mentioned in the prior chapter that are key for any RFP process. The prior chapter also referred to the significant time and resource commitment of a library or consortium in this process. Given its comprehensive nature of looking at the overall business practices of a library, the ILS RFP process can be an opportunity to work on other organizational development needs. For example, CCS had undergone internal staffing changes as well as changes in the member library directors themselves with almost half of the libraries having hired a new director within the past five years. The ILS RFP process became an opportune time in which to reestablish communication and collaboration within the consortium. This section outlines the first phase of this process focused on education and needs analysis.

Getting Ready—A Rising Tide Lifts All Boats

As with all software applications, the ILS has its proponents and critics. Because the ILS incorporates a broad range of library functions, library staff will make compromises in some areas to accommodate other areas of higher importance. Over time, frustrations tend to develop, priorities change, and people lose sight of the original priorities. Focusing on education prior to writing an RFP helps to address these issues as well as make the RFP writing process much easier. As mentioned in the previous chapter, a request for information (RFI) can also be part of an education phase. While the RFI can offer a structured way to obtain information, be careful that it is not too rigid and allows room for new ideas.

Before jumping too deeply into an RFP process, it is more important to initially foster an environment of education for staff members or member libraries, in the case of consortia. Like brainstorming a research paper before writing it, this education phase will serve as a creative testing ground for ideas, needs, and priorities. This education phase can also be used as a tool to help address other needs of the organization, for example, developing better cross-departmental communication. All in all, the rising tide of organization-wide education will help raise everyone to a common understanding and approach for writing the RFP.

In structuring this period of education, finding ample time may be an issue. It is important to at least devote a month, though preferably several months, to learning about what is available from larger vendors to smaller vendors. In fact, you may learn about components from some vendors that will require interoperability with others. Sometimes more creative and innovative ideas come from vendors that are smaller newcomers, who can often develop more nimbly. During this time, set up high-level demonstrations from vendors, refer to RFPs from other institutions, and do not take anything for granted. Let staff or member libraries communicate with vendors directly in order to freely explore topics and gather ideas. Just make sure that they know how to frame where the organization is in its investigation process so as to properly represent the library or consortium.

As people gather information and answer questions, an integral piece of the structure is classifying the findings. No matter how you gather this information, time should be spent organizing those details into at least three categories: existing functionality turned on, existing functionality turned off, and functionality not available in current system. This activity is crucial to properly define the "as is" versus the "should be" state of the system.

An education phase may feel extraneous or unnecessary, but it is an important step to precede a successful needs analysis. The ILS is so closely tied to all elements of the business of running a library that it can be difficult to uncouple true needs from system design. This education process can help people think outside of their current workflows, especially if most of the staff people only know the system that is currently in use. If an organization conducts a proper education phase and subsequent needs analysis, the RFP should write itself, so this time spent up front will pay off down the road.

A Collaborative RFP Process—A CCS Example

After approximately 15 years of using the same ILS, concerns and frustrations were increasing among CCS library staff. The concerns and frustrations ranged from feelings of dirty data, messy policies, and overcustomization that might be causing other problems, not to mention long-term supportability to general feelings of wanting more autonomy. The complexities of the system made it difficult to pinpoint whether specific concerns were system based, policy based, consortia related, library related, or were even valid. Therefore, it was important to develop a process that allowed library directors and staff to better understand the underlying causes to their frustrations.

The executive director proposed a multiphase, yearlong process to explore these issues called Project Laulima. "Laulima" is a core principle of cooperation in Hawaiian culture that literally means "many hands working together." While as a cooperative, CCS members are always working together, the process of deciding what the primary cooperative tool (ILS) should be is the epitome of how the cooperative works together; hence Laulima. The goals of Project Laulima included creating needs assessment of CCS Libraries, communicating these needs among member library leadership and staff, engaging directors in the process to help foster the collective vision, informing the RFP, and evaluating the RFP. CCS started Project Laulima in March 2016 and concluded approximately one year later.

Phase one of Project Laulima preceded the RFP writing phase. The purpose of Phase one was to provide consortium members with a set of topics on which to explore and gather information. Essentially this was a more extensive RFI process with open vendor dialogue. This methodical approach brought all of the library representatives up to the same level of understanding on system issues. The information that the teams gathered would then be used to create a more focused RFP based on agreed-upon consortial needs.

Phase one involved seven project teams comprised of 48 people in total. Each team was led by a member library director and contained subject matter experts from different member libraries and a variety of functional areas (public services, tech services, IT, etc.). These Project Laulima teams looked at different ILS architectural models as well as how the data were used in the current system for reports and other outputs. The key question that they needed to answer was "What ILS consortial architecture best matches the needs of the consortium?" These teams looked at both single-instance ILS setups and separate/multiple instances of ILS. With each of these options, the teams weighted the pros and cons based on levels of library autonomy and levels of patron efficiency.

The Project Laulima teams convened over a three-month period, during which they answered RFI-like questions and directly interacted with the vendors to learn more about their systems. This process created a fluid dialog between the teams and the vendors in a way that formal RFIs often do not. While every library had at least one representative on the Laulima project teams, the consortium also arranged vendor presentations so that everyone in the consortium had a chance to learn about and explore the different systems.

In addition to the formal work that the project teams were doing, the consortial office created an e-mail alias so that anyone within the consortium could provide feedback, thoughts, suggestions, and ideas related to system needs. Member library staff submitted everything from features that the current system did well to wish list items. Because all of the staff had access to e-mail, the e-mail alias made it quick to send off an idea as someone had it. A central office staff person then compiled the suggestions sent to the list.

After the three-month period, the project team directors met to recommend an ILS architecture for the RFP. This decision process reaffirmed for the directors and the full Governing Board what model would best support the consortium into the future. In addition to learning more about the systems, the consortium benefited from new interpersonal relationships between directors and a variety of staff from the member libraries. This result ties into the concept of creating a common heartbeat that Sutton and Rao discuss in *Scaling Up Excellence*:

> When people share the same daily, weekly, monthly, and seasonal rhythms, connections among them form faster and stay stronger. The people trust each other more deeply, and coordination becomes easier because they see and experience the world in the same way. (Sutton and Rao 2014)

A Collaborative RFP Process—Lessons Learned

- Determine the "should be/as is gap" at both a strategic and technical level. The strategic plan established the organizational priorities to more clearly articulate where the organization could go and what was missing to get them there. The needs analysis provided more specific technical points to support what was missing to get to the achieved state.
- Develop a unique name for the project that does not have connotations to anything else. Not only does it help make the project unique, but it also makes for an easy-to-search filter.
- The schedule of topics to research started with a series of questions sent out on a weekly basis with one week to answer them. This ended up being too short of a turnaround time. The teams needed more time to gather answers and analyze responses. As a result, the original phase one timeline was pushed back from two months to three months. In hindsight, two to three weeks per question area would have been more reasonable.
- As the teams gather information, adapt as necessary. Some of the teams came to conclusions early in their investigations about what architectures would not work for CCS. As a result, it was difficult for them to continue to explore for the sake of learning when it started to seem obvious that those architectural options did not suit CCS.
- The CCS office staff separately considered issues from the member library teams so that the needs exploration came from the libraries themselves. This created a stronger sense of buy-in as decisions were made. In some cases, it was tough for some members to draw their own conclusions when they usually relied on the consortial office for guidance, so it became an empowering situation.
- Develop a glossary of terms to help keep everyone at the same level of discourse. Remind participants to ask questions when they do not know what something means and create an environment that encourages open dialogue. ABC-CLIO offers a good start with their *Dictionary of Library and Information Science*: http://www.abc-clio.com/ODLIS/odlis_A.aspx.

WRITING AND EVALUATING THE RFP

Vendors and librarians alike are tired of the endless functional checklists in RFPs. It is common to hear, "Every system checks out books. We want to focus on what is important to our library." There are also plenty of public record RFP responses available to easily gather stock responses from vendors. In order to avoid getting buried in endless checklists, distill questions down to those which will have the most influence on your decision. For example, system interoperability is an important factor for many institutions. In that case, ask about how specific interoperability is achieved along with plans for future integrations, for example, the version and detail behind an implementation of Standard Interchange Protocol (SIP2), Security Assertion Markup Language (SAML), or NISO Circulation Interchange Protocol (NCIP).

Beyond Checking Out Books—Topics for Consideration

As public libraries continue to expand their services to include a range of things from passport processing to makerspaces, the need for interoperability grows. While not meant to be comprehensive, here are lists of considerations for both public libraries and public library consortia.

Considerations for public libraries could include events calendar, summer reading, makerspace, room reservations, visibility of electronic resources, volume of checkouts and hold requests, user engagement, website management, mobile apps, content management, digitization, and ease of authentication.

Considerations for public library consortia could include ease of system upgrades, transaction volume, temporary versus permanent staffing to handle this project, system architecture options, resource sharing functionality, levels of autonomy at the library level, superuser management capability, granular permissions, what settings must be shared, what settings must be separate, what services must be handled centrally, can discovery be a per-library decision, how do different e-holdings packages get managed per library, and how are patron authorizations handled differently per library.

Writing the RFP—A CCS Example

Phase two of Project Laulima encompassed both the writing and evaluation portions of the RFP process. With this second phase, the teams reconfigured by area of expertise so that they could work together as functional units. Each participating director now led a team focused on a specific area of the library, for example, Circulation and Cataloging. The teams generated a lot of useful data and feedback from their phase one work, and this information provided the backbone for the RFP. To help put this information in perspective, the output from phase one was also categorized into four categories: what the current system already does, what the current system could do if configured differently, what is on the development plan for the current system, and what the current system cannot do. While it took a lot of time to collate and consolidate that information into the RFP, the RFP essentially wrote itself because the teams had already done extensive information gathering and analysis.

Parallel to this point in the process, the current executive director announced his departure from CCS. There was discussion about whether to put the process on hold or to continue as planned. The general philosophy was that this was to be a membership-driven decision and the executive director would be the steward of that decision. Timeliness of the gathered data was also important. Therefore, the process continued along as planned. In order to provide consistency and continuity in the process during this transition, CCS hired a consultant to assist with the final stages: writing the RFP, evaluating the RFP, and contract negotiation.

The CCS Governing Board tasked the consultant and executive director with providing the written RFP prior to the executive director's departure. Originally the format was envisioned to be no more than 10 key questions of most importance to CCS. The logic being that any system could circulate a book and compromises would need to be made on some aspects of functionality. However, as the consultant and executive director combed through the phase one analysis, it became clear that it was important to include questions on specific functional areas. The additional questions confirmed functional depth to ensure that certain levels of consortial sophistication were available.

In the end, CCS developed a comprehensive RFP covering 10 key questions and no more than 20 top questions per major functional area. These functional areas included General ILS Functionality, Acquisitions and Serials, Cataloging, Authorities and Record Processing, Circulation, Public Interface/ Discovery, Reporting, Systems/IT, Third-Party Integration, Implementation Migration and Support, and Vendor Stability and Experience. While the key questions were weighted most heavily, the functional questions were given Low, Medium, and High designations for levels of importance in order to keep them in perspective. These designations were visible to the vendors so that they could understand the consortial priorities.

The 10 key questions encompassed 1 question for the cover letter and 9 questions in the "Key Functionality" section. These questions represented the primary needs of the cooperative based upon the feedback and discussions from phase one. When writing these questions, it was also important to create questions that were nuanced enough to invoke thoughtful responses from the vendors and not simply invite boilerplate, stock responses. The overarching themes of the key questions focused on vendor partnership and future plans specific to certain areas like staff interface development, third-party integration, application programming interfaces (APIs), reporting, and workflow consultation services.

Writing the RFP—Lessons Learned

- With a large organization, such as a consortium, a crowd-sourced RFP can be a great way to gather information and see trends. It is still important for those more familiar with ILS operations and industry trends to provide questions that might be missing from the crowdsourcing.
- Take the time to clarify what may be possible with the current system now. There might be quick wins with patrons and library staff by adjusting settings or setting up functionality in the short term.

- A consultant can provide fresh eyes to all of the input and help tease out any sacred cows.
- The original plan was for the executive director to manage the entire process without a consultant. In retrospect, a consultant would have been useful to have regardless of whether there was a transition in leadership or not.
- Depending on organizational bandwidth, it may be helpful to hire temporary assistance during this phase to collate team output and organize that information into the RFP.
- It is rewarding for the team members to see their work reflected in the RFP.
- This process emphasized the importance of creating the RFP from scratch and not just selecting questions on a stock RFP. CCS was able to develop questions that truly resonated with the consortium. Because these questions were uniquely created, there was not as much of a tendency toward copy-and-pasted responses from the vendors that would be typical of an out-of-the-box RFP.

Evaluating Responses—A CCS Example

After receiving the vendor responses, the functional teams established in phase two of Project Laulima continued their work with scoring. The member library directors were also invited to score the "Key Functionality" questions. The consultant collated the individual scores to develop aggregate total scores per vendor response. In order to help communicate the scoring process across the system and facilitate consistency in scoring, the consultant provided web-based meetings with the CCS membership.

After the RFP scoring, the leadership team opened up feedback from everyone. This helped establish questions for the evaluation of the finalists. In order to make sure that everyone had a chance to interact with the finalists, a series of web presentations were set up with each finalist. The final evaluation focused primarily on unanswered questions, the vendor relationship, the vendor's plan for the future, and how those might play out into the implementation and beyond. In the end, by getting a full range of library input throughout the process, the final ILS choice was truly a member-driven decision.

Evaluating Responses—Lessons Learned

- Solicit primary stakeholder feedback as part of your scoring to ensure buy-in.
- Carefully consider how much time will be needed both to set up vendor meetings and to set up follow-up internal meetings. This can be particularly challenging during holiday periods.

- CCS considered whether a traditional points-based scoring system per question was useful or if scorers should just rank each response as a whole, relative to one another. While the impartiality of any scoring system can be debated, scoring provides a formula from which to more consistently compare results.
- Consider breaking out the cost proposal from the rest of the RFP so that scorers can evaluate functionality without the influence of cost. High cost does not always imply high functionality.

CONCLUSION

As of this writing, CCS is one-third of the way through its implementation process. Overall, the general theme is clear communication with the membership. The CCS ILS project team set the expectation with membership for where to get information and when, and they communicate with the member libraries on a regular schedule. CCS developed a migration portal and provides weekly migration updates, including library task lists. Each member library has a designated point person for the implementation who ensures that specific library tasks are completed. To help understand and ensure involvement, the CCS office tracks interest and engagement via online tools. Overall, this process achieved much more than just issuing a successful RFP. By using the RFP as a focal point to bring the 24 libraries to the table to discuss issues of common concern, it enables CCS to reinvent itself as a vibrant and well-functioning consortium.

REFERENCES

Berk, Jeffrey. 2004. *Champions of Change: The Manager's Guide to Creating Sustainable Business Process Improvements.* Tarentum, PA: Word Association Publishers.

Breeding, Marshall. 2017, May. "Library Systems Report 2017: Competing Vision for Technology, Openness, and Workflow." *American Libraries* 48 (5): 22–35.

Sutton, Robert I., and Hayagreeva Rao. 2014. *Scaling Up Excellence: Getting to More without Settling for Less.* New York: Crown Business.

CASE STUDY

Analyzing and articulating the needs of the organization are integral to a successful and satisfying RFP process. The following case study illustrates the importance of developing meaningful questions that resonate with the focus of an organization. Kitchener Public Library shows how interoperability with complementary technology and services can be just as important in the evaluation as the ILS functionality itself.

KITCHENER PUBLIC LIBRARY ILS RFP (LCCMS)

Mary Chevreau

Background

Kitchener Public Library (KPL) is a medium-sized public library in Kitchener, Ontario, Canada. The system consists of a central library and four additional community libraries, serving a population of 250,000. A fifth library is currently slated for construction in 2019.

KPL has been an Innovative Interfaces, Inc. (III) customer since 1992. It was the first Canadian library to select III and one of the first public libraries to implement III. Over the years, the library upgraded, enhanced, and expanded the III system. We are currently using Millennium with Encore as the discovery layer. The KPL has hosted and supported Waterloo Public Library (population 105,000) on a shared Millennium system since 2000.

Decision to Look at the Market

Public libraries, including KPL, are challenged with changing the perception of who we are and what we do. We know we are not simply a repository of books and databases, with a transactional relationship with our customers. Yet, in spite of our surveys, focus groups, marketing, and outreach, we continue to hear the same things from our community, such as "Wow, I didn't know you did that," or "Wow, I didn't know you had that," or "I had no idea you have such a great space—I should come here more often." In other words, we are struggling to reach our customers in ways that resonate with them and compel them to use the library. Our usage statistics are average or above average for a system of our size, but we know they can be much better.

In order to help us change this perception, we implemented a number of initiatives, including realigning our marketing department to support additional messaging through social media; developing a new customer channel focusing specifically on our millennial customers; moving our more traditional, core programs from print to online; and creating a glossy, magazine-style calendar for our special events and 85 Queen cultural series. However, we still believe that we are not reaching our customers in meaningful and specific ways and have identified challenges in having effective metrics to measure customer engagement. Staff identified the need for a new tool or module to track and manage customer engagement, including direct marketing based on customer profiles, targeted e-mails and communication based on specific customer activities and interests, and outcome-based assessment through direct customer feedback on programming and events. Ideally, the product would integrate with the ILS patron/customer database so that staff can move seamlessly between the transactional relationship and the promotional engagement side.

So what, one might ask, does this have to do with an ILS RFP? The answer is everything. It became clear that this library is not looking for an ILS, or even a library management system (LMS), but rather, an integrated library customer and content management system (LCCMS).

System Review and RFP Development

Staff performed a review of the ILS marketplace as well as recent RFP formats. As neither the marketplace nor standard RFP templates addressed our needs, staff developed a custom template. The KPL template is based on the assumption that all vendors invited to respond to the RFP have proven "core" library management modules, with hundreds of implementations throughout North America. "Core" modules are defined as Cataloging, Circulation, Acquisitions, Serials, and an OPAC or Discovery layer. Vendor references were given high points, as the selection committee believed strongly that the testimonials and conversations with libraries provided a significant bellwether for our overall success. ILS functional questions focused on pain points, critical functionality missing in the current system, or desired functionality expected in a next-generation LCCMS.

The RFP was issued on May 26, 2017, to specific ILS vendors, as well as posted online. Letters of Intent to bid were due June 5, 2017, with final submissions due June 29, 2017. The RFP contained sections on the core modules, plus a significant section on customer relationship management (CRM). The RFP requirements further listed the CRM portion of the solution as a mandatory requirement and that if a vendor's current product "does not" support this functionality, to collaborate with a company who can.

The library received valid submissions from four ILS vendors and two CRM companies. All four ILS vendors partnered with at least one of the CRM companies, although each CRM company also submitted a stand-alone bid.

KPL system review team consists of representatives from technical services, IT, web and content services, and public services.

The responses were assessed using the following points system:

Corporate Background and Vision	10 points
References	30 points
Cost	20 points
CRM	15 points
User Experience	15 points
Implementation and Training	10 points
Staff and Technical Functionality	15 points
Compatibility with Third-Party Services	10 points

Short-List and Demonstrations

The ILS review team members independently reviewed and scored each response over a period of five weeks and met once as a group for the final short-list discussion and selection. The team selected a short list of two ILS vendors and two CRM vendors based on responses, references, and overall scores. The team was disappointed with the lack of integration between the ILS and the CRM vendor responses. While each ILS vendor did follow the mandatory requirement of partnering with a CRM vendor, the CRM responses were simply inserted as a section, with no visible evidence of actual collaboration or integration. In fact, the two CRM stand-alone responses were *identical* to the responses provided within the ILS RFPs, which also suggested that there was little collaboration between vendors. However, the selection team decided that they could still work with the responses and would be able to explore the ILS–CRM collaboration in more detail during the on-site presentations.

The team decided to invite the CRM vendors in *before* the ILS vendors so that they could develop informed questions for the ILS vendors. Each CRM vendor will be given a half day to present their vision and solution.

Each short-listed ILS vendor has been asked to prepare for a two-day on-site meeting/demonstration. The focus of the meetings will be for staff and the library executive team to understand the product road map and vision of the company, and through live demonstrations, understand the functionality defined in the RFP. Each ILS vendor will be given a half day to present a corporate overview, as well as to demonstrate their solutions in whichever way they like. The rest of the time will be dedicated to answering specific questions from the RFP.

Key outcomes for the review include:

- better understanding of how each vendor will address the pain points, future functional needs for the libraries;
- confidence that the vendors understand the CRM integration and needs of the library;
- vendor's commitment and preparedness for the demo, including staff and executives who attend;
- clear sense of the road map and direction of the company;
- confidence that the ILS company has a named implementation and support team with evidence of competency and knowledge;
- evidence of financial stability through financial statements; and
- proof of stability and commitment at the ownership and executive level.

Summary

Staff believe the decision to focus on pain points and new emerging workflows and technology allowed them to write a succinct RFP. They were able to quickly list the pros and cons of each solution and develop a short list for vendor demonstrations. Staff were disappointed in the lack of collaboration between the ILS and CRM vendors, but we are charting new territory, and it will be up to the library to build this partnership. Regardless, staff believe that the LCCMS is integral to our success and the way of the future for libraries and well worth pursuing.

Final Selection and Outcome

After careful consideration, the review team decided that none of the short-listed ILS vendors were able to provide a compelling reason to migrate to a new ILS. Therefore, a decision was made to delay the ILS for 6–8 months, with a timeline to review and select pushed to 2019.

The KPL team was able to move forward with a CRM solution, and unanimously selected Third Chapter Partners to deliver their Patron Point solution http://www.patronpoint.com, which is currently in implementation.

Writing and Evaluating Specific Types of RFPs: Other RFPs for Libraries

10

RADIO-FREQUENCY IDENTIFICATION SECURITY AND INVENTORY SYSTEMS: THE REQUEST FOR QUOTATION

Catherine Jannik Downey

INTRODUCTION

Georgia Gwinnett College (GGC) opened its doors for the fall semester 2006. The college did not spring up in the woods near Lawrenceville, Georgia, for that opening group of 118 students; the Gwinnett University Center preceded GGC at the same location, serving as a satellite campus for area colleges and universities. The GGC Library and Learning Center remained in a small portion of the campus's signature building along with classrooms, offices, the college administration, and a coffee shop. The majority of the books were acquired by the main campuses, which had hosted classes in Lawrenceville. In 2008 the process of building a stand-alone library, slated to open in 2010, began. The new college opened with the inherited collection of approximately 40,000 volumes and added an opening-day collection of an additional 30,000 in the move from the signature building into the new building, which in 2016 was named the Daniel J. Kaufman Library and Learning Center in honor of the school's first president. Staff were asked to envision a library to serve the "Campus of Tomorrow" as GGC was branded. One of the innovative technologies was radio-frequency identification (RFID), a security and inventory solution. Some of the librarians had worked with the county system that employed the technology, and it was a good fit for GGC's new library building.

The GGC Library was in a unique position to deploy a new security system. Staff were lean and were expected to remain so as the college grew, so inventory, shelf reading, and lost and missing searches needed to be handled more easily with the robust RFID systems than with previous, more manual methods. Funding for the conversion to RFID could be incorporated into the cost of the new building and would likely not be otherwise available at any time in the future.

At GGC, the request for quotation (RFQ) process was chosen for procurement of the RFID system for a number of reasons. As a college opened in 2006, staff had a vested interest in using relevant, advanced technologies in building the new library but were not particularly interested in putting an RFP together for any security and inventory system that would include responses using something other than RFID. The systems librarian spoke to an existing vendor who could provide RFID to get an idea of what costs might be for installation, training, and maintenance. Those cost estimates fit within the budget for the new construction. With this preliminary information, four vendors were invited to campus in early 2009. Each of the vendors gave their sales pitch and supplied valuable information regarding RFID and their particular products. None of the staff had been through the request for proposal (RFP)/RFQ/request for information (RFI) process before and were unclear of the process. Were we required to go through the RFP process for a security solution, RFID, or otherwise? Could proposals be limited to RFID vendors? Staff knowledge of RFID systems meant no need for a formal information-gathering step provided by an RFP or RFI. The library then met with GGC's Logistical Services department for guidance. At their suggestion, by only soliciting quotes from the vendors that could provide RFID saved a great deal of work. The RFQ can be a part of or follow an RFP, but the RFP is not a necessary precursor. From there, an RFQ was crafted.

WHAT TO INCLUDE IN THE RFQ

The Logistical Services department provided guidance regarding the format of the document. The "Specifications for the Georgia Gwinnett College Library Radio Frequency Identification (RFID) Security Detection and Inventory System" is a simple document consisting of a brief description of the required system:

> The Georgia Gwinnett College Library requires a system for the inventory and security of its collections. Radio Frequency Identification or RFID is the system proposed to allow both inventory control and security of the Library's holdings. Each item in the collection will have affixed a tag that when activated by a reader/antenna emits a radio signal used to retrieve inventory information from the Library's integrated library system. These tags also have a security bit which is detected by gates at the doors of the

library if the material has not been properly checked out and the bit disabled thus alerting staff to an item being removed in an irregular manner. Specifications within this document are minimum requirements for the RFID system.

Thirteen sections outlining particular requirements followed the introduction. Each section, contained in the appendix, addressed components of the system to install in the new library. Following are the sections used with descriptions and some suggestions for how they might be applied to other libraries.

Gates

An adjustable, audible, and visible alarm and an ability to count patrons are standard features for library security gates and no different for those used with RFID. An RFID system allows greater functionality such as an interface with the integrated library system (ILS) and the ability to alert and report to staff workstations information such as items stolen. Additionally, gates can be customizable to coordinate with the interior design of the library, should be American Disabilities Act compliant and mounted with buried cables, and have network-down functionality. Specifications should include information regarding the local ILS and address current International Organization for Standardization (ISO) or other applicable standards and be data-model independent should the RFID tag or system supplier change at some later date.

Book Returns

Determine the number of book returns needed and whether each will be RFID enabled. If the return is RFID enabled, determine if it will also be attached to a materials handling system. Returns mounted on exterior walls must be secure and weatherproof, and returns should be customizable in keeping with the design of the building. Determine if items returned must be updated in the ILS in real time through Standard Interchange Protocol (SIP), Standard Interchange Protocol 2 (SIP2), and NISO Circulation Interchange Protocol (NCIP), and if the return must reactivate security tags or print hold notices. Indicate if the return system must include an appropriate workstation and whether and what type of book carts are required.

Self-Check-Out

A number of GGC employees had worked with self-check-out stations in the past and wanted them to be part of the circulation desk. With only one public entrance, it did not require an unmonitored, stand-alone kiosk. Previous experience made staff wary of installing a self-check-out solution that could only be seen from the patron's side of the desk. A desktop solution that could be monitored from both sides—patrons on one side, staff on the other—was requested in order to minimize the number of trips around the desk staff would make to troubleshoot issues. This required 19-inch touch screens for patrons and a keyboard and mouse for staff. If these stations would be part of the millwork of a desk, would the RFID antennae be incorporated into the desk or would it sit atop? With an eye to the future, the antennae needed to sit on the surface of the desk so that as technology changed, present furnishings would not become obsolete. It seems that currently most libraries prefer a stand-alone kiosk station in which case dimensions and accessibility specifications may be included in the RFQ. For either solution in your library, you will need to include how the station accepts patron information: by some manner of card reader or optical input or keying in identification information. If you do not want the kiosk solution, you will need to request that a receipt printer be part of the quote as well.

Software

As discussed in the section about Gates, the software provided by the RFID vendor should be SIP, SIP2, and NCIP compliant for communication with the current ILS. The system should be able to read and adapt to multiple data models in the event your library changes RFID vendors in the future.

RFID Tags

RFID tags should be included in your RFQ since if you are doing a retrospective conversion of your collection, tags should also be sent to your book jobber for the opening-day collection. At GGC, unprinted, low acid adhesive, ISO compliant, 13.5 MHz tags were requested, and they had to be printable, reprogrammable/rewriteable, and data-model independent. Ensure that defective tags will be replaced and compatible with an expected standard (ISO 28560–2:2014).

RFID Inventory Wand

The inventory wand should also be ISO standard compliant, data-model independent, and provide security bit scans and shelf checking. It should interact with, search, and display titles from the ILS, be portable and lightweight, and have storage capacity, acoustic and visual indicators, and a read range of approximately four to five inches. Portable may mean something different to each vendor, and the mechanism by which a display is delivered could also vary. Wands change a great deal over time and may vary widely. They come in different sizes, able to be completely handheld or require an attached laptop on a cart, and may have different read-range capabilities.

Conversion Station

Doing the retrospective tagging of the 40,000 volumes, a portable station, leased for a month to do the bulk of the tagging, was available. Had a leasing option not been available, the tagging station needs to be one of the workstations being purchased. The conversion station and one of the workstations described next were on hand to do the retrospective tagging.

Workstations

In this section, request all the antennae needed for the number of stations needed. The GGC Library needed five staff workstations: two at the circulation desk; one station for the technical services department; one for quick tagging, retagging, and ingestion of new books; and one for processing of resource-sharing materials. Compatibility was requested with the particular versions of software installed on the library's new computers as well as two receipt printers and two swipe card readers for the circulation desk stations.

Installation

In this section, spell out exactly who should perform the installation of each component of the solution and if there was some other entity with which coordination was necessary. The conversion station should be handled by the vendor. The security gates, book drops, and self-check stations should be handled by the vendor and, in the case of GGC, the building contractors. The workstations require the vendor to work in conjunction with the college and library technology departments. Some companies do not handle the installation of specific portions such as book drops. Schematics may be supplied in the response to the RFQ, and installation may be coordinated with local facilities managers for old construction.

Training

In this section of the proposal, the training for staff is requested. GCC requested two days of training based on our single branch, small staff, and knowledge gained in our information-gathering visits with vendors. Because RFID is a relatively low-threshold technology to adopt, the support following installation could be provided by phone consultation and does not require an extended training period. Make sure to request manuals and training materials for all software, workstations, self-check machines, and gates.

Support

GGC required a minimum one-year, renewable support contract with service expectations for a four-hour or shorter response time by toll-free number and twenty-four-hour or shorter response time for any routine parts or service. Your vendor should also provide a listing of any applicable warranties and a timeline and explanation of any planned upgrades.

Contractor Experience

Other authors in this book have mentioned checking the contractors' experiences. GGC required that the contractor must have been in the business of supplying RFID systems to libraries for a minimum of five years and list their five most recent system installations. Based on this experience, you should ask each vendor to list their five most recent installations and list all installations working with the ILS your library uses.

Time Frame

This section will depend on whether you are remodeling, just installing a book drop or check-out kiosk and some workstations, or building a new library. If you are building, the installation must be coordinated with the construction and conclude by the completion of the new library building. A large portion of your time frame will be determined by working with the building contractors and being scheduled into the Gantt chart of the construction project. This determines the date for the delivery and installation of the conversion station in the existing library. A two-week estimated window for gate installation and the same for the self-check components to be installed meant installation at the time the desk millwork was completed.

If you are in an existing building, your time schedule will be much different and the component parts will come at your convenience. The deliveries will be between you and the vendor.

The Logistical Services department entered the RFQ into their system that allows electronic quotations, and notice was sent to a list of vendors. This list of over 50 companies was created by the Logistical Services department at GGC from a search of possible library vendors. In truth, only a small number of these vendors could supply the full RFID system as specified in our RFQ. The closing date for submission of quotes was four weeks from issue of the RFQ. During this time, prospective vendors could submit questions to get clarification on what we wanted. Some of the questions were about what was meant by "double corridor" gates. These gates were three pedestals allowing two streams of patrons side by side through the gates, an in and out lane though either could be ingress or egress. Of the four companies invited to present a proposal at the beginning of this process, only two responded.

In examining the two responses, two problems surfaced. These are discussed during the evaluation phase.

EVALUATION PHASE

In order to evaluate the 30- to 70-page responses effectively, a specifications chart was created for comparison. Each of the 13 sections listed previously was broken down into individual specifications, the quote total, and second-year costs. This seemed like a relatively straightforward step; however, it was more complicated and time-consuming than anticipated. The first two responses received seemed comparable though one was quite a bit more expensive than the other. Logistical Services advised to remember that if both vendors met the requirement, the one providing the lowest bid would be awarded the contract. Upon further, detailed inspection, each of the vendors had not met at least one of the specifications making both vendors "nonresponsive." One vendor did not provide pricing for a depressible, soft-drop, lined book cart for the book drop, receipt printers, and swipe card readers for the staff stations or a two-sided self-check-out option, indicating that they did not see any reason for the dual-sided setup as specified. Additionally, their response was vague in regard to or did not specifically mention some of the specifications from the RFQ. The other vendor indicated that their inventory wand did not have a touch screen and there was no ability for the self-check to alert staff to patron problems as specified in the RFQ. After discussions with the Logistical Services department, neither response was technically complete, so neither company could be awarded. Upon reflection and further research, both the touch screen inventory wand and staff notification feature of the self-check stations were options that were not universally available and neither was necessary to have a successful RFID solution, so they were removed from our specifications. However, the dual-sided self-check station was not negotiable. In order to meet legal and ethical standards for this process, it was important for the RFQ to conform to what was technically possible from our anticipated vendors and reissue.

The reissued RFQ elicited responses from the same two companies as the first as well as one from a third vendor. Hopefully the original two vendors had fully responded to the rewritten request. The updated specifications chart was used to determine whether the responses were full and compliant. The vendor that had not supplied a quote for the dual-sided self-check-out machine in the first round had failed to do so in the second response as well. They submitted a response that was deficient in the same areas and vague on the same topics; they had submitted the exact response as in the first round changing only the bid number and due date on the cover sheet. They were deemed nonresponsive. The new vendor made substitutions for requested screen sizes and duration of training and did not provide for the dual-sided self-check stations. They were also determined to be nonresponsive. The second of our original vendors was now able to comply fully with the inventory wand specifications since we had removed the touch screen requirement. Taking out the staff notification requirement of the self-check machines, they were able to meet that specification as well.

After working through the evaluation process and the specifications chart, only one vendor met all the criteria in the RFQ. Erring on the side of caution, the Logistical Services department asked that we explain in detail how the two nonresponsive vendors failed to meet our specifications. We used the same specifications chart, but instead of indicating only compliance or noncompliance and a page number of the bid, there was a prose explanation, and each vendor's response was handled in a separate document later shared with the nonresponsive companies. An example of one such explanation was in relation to the requested dual-sided self-check-out stations. Our third vendor's response did not include this option, and noted that the computer mouse and keyboard requirement for each was part of the dual-sided check-out set-up that was something the vendor would not provide. The vendor responses are reproduced in Table 10.1 below.

Specifications	Vendor A	Vendor B	Vendor C
1. Gates			
Buried cable mounting	X	X	X
Double corridor, ADA compliant	X	X	X
Customizable look in keeping with the design of the library	X	X	X
RFID	X	X	X
Patron counter	X	X	X
Adjustable audio and visual stolen item alert	X	X	X
ILS system stolen items reporting	X	X	X
Compatible with ISO 15693 and ISO 18000-3 RFID chips	X	X	X
CAT5e or CAT6 Ethernet communication interface	X	X	X
"Network-down" functionality	X	X	X
Data-model independent	X	X	X
2. Book Vendor e Returns			
a. Return 1—RFID Return			
Exterior in-wall, weatherproof and secure	X	X	X

Figure 10.1 Downey, Catherine Jannik, "Comparison of Responses 06102009," June 10, 2009.

Lockable	X	X	X
Real-time check in/database updates	X	X	X
Reactivates security tag	X	X (p. 34)	X
Prints hold notices	X	X	X
Appropriate workstation (or connection to a workstation) as necessary	X	X	X
Sorting not necessary	X	X	X
"Network-down" functionality	X	X	X
Faceplate should be in keeping with the design of the library and say "Book Return"	X	X	X
SIP2, SIP, NCIP compliant	X	X (p. 35)	X
Data-model independent	X	X	X
b. Return 2—Traditional Return			
Secure	X	X	X
Lockable	X	X	X
Able to be upgraded to RFID in the future	X	X	X
Faceplate should be in keeping with the design of the library and say "Book Return"	X	X	X
c. Book carts for the returns (2)			
150–180 books, depressible/cushioned/soft-drop/padded/lined book cart	**NO p. 7**	X	X
3. Self-Check-Out (2)			
Swipe-type card readers (2)	Not mentioned	X	X
Antennae (2) data-model independent, 8–12" read range (single or dual)	X	X	X
Receipt printers (2) with formatable printing (does this belong with software?)	X	X	X
Flat touch screens at least 19" diagonal with integrated speakers (2)	NO	NO p. 36	X
Flat screens at least 17" diagonal (2)	NO	X	X
Keyboards (2)	NO	NO	X
Mouse (2)	NO	NO	X
"Network-down" functionality	X	X	X

Figure 10.1 (Continued)

4. Software			
SIP2, SIP, NCIP compliant	X	X (p. 38)	X
Data model adaptable	X	X	X
Can read multiple data models	X	X	X
Must interface with current ILS (Voyager)	X	X	X
5. RFID Tags			
100,000 standard, unprinted tags	X	X	X
ISO 15693/18000-3 compliant	X	X	X
13.56 MHz	X	X	X
Reprogrammable/rewriteable	X	X	X
Data-model independent	X	X	X
Low acid adhesive	X	X	X
Printable	X	X	X
Guaranteed/replaceable if defective	X	X	X
Able to move to ISO Tag Data Standard (when approved)	X	X	X
6. RFID Inventory Wand			
ISO 15693/18000-3 compliant	X	X	X
Portable	X	X	X
Lightweight—(Weight approximately 1–2 lbs.?)	X	X	X
Handheld	X	X	X
Displays titles	X	X	X
ILS interactive	X	X	X
ILS-based search capability	X	X	X
Capable of shelf order checking	X	X	X
Can provide security bit scans	X	X	X
Read range of approximately 4–5"	X	X	X
Adjustable acoustic and visual indicators	X	X	X
Data-model independent	X	X	X
Storage capacity	X	X	X
7. Conversion Station			
Leasable (approx. one month) or convertible to a workstation	X	X	X
Reader/Antenna (single or dual) or equivalent technology	X	X	X

Figure 10.1 (Continued)

Barcode scanner	X	X	X
Mobile cart	X	X	X
Able to interact with the ILS but stand-alone when needed	X	X	X
Able to print tags as they are programmed	X	NO	X
8. Workstations			
XP/Vista compatible	Not mentioned	X	X
Six antennae	X	X	X
Two receipt printers	NO	X	X
Two swipe-type card readers	NO p. 12	X	X
9. Installation			
Gates done by vendor in coordination with building contractors	X	X	X
Book drops done by vendor in coordination with building contractors	X	X	X
Self-check done by vendor in coordination with building contractors	X	X	X
Workstations done by vendor in coordination with GGC Educational Technology and Library Systems departments	X	X	X
Conversion station done by vendor	X	X	X
10. Training			
Two days	Unclear	NO pp. 26–27	X
Manuals and training materials for all software, workstations, self-check machines, and gates	X	X	X
11. Support			
Support contract for a minimum of one-year, renewable annually	X	X	X
Less than four-hour response time by phone (toll-free number?)	Not stated	X	X
Less than 24-hour response time with routine parts and service	Not stated	X	X
Please list any applicable warranties	p. 19	p. 44	p. 66
Please address any planned upgrades	None stated	pp. 44–45	p. 41

Figure 10.1 (Continued)

12. Contractor Experience			
Contractor must have been in the business of supplying RFID systems to libraries for a minimum of five (5) years and list their five (5) most recent system installations	X	X	X
13. Timeframe (all dates are subject to change)			
Installation complete by Library completion	X	X	X
Conversion station installed in the existing GGC Library—August 2009	X	X	X
Gates installed at resilient flooring and base—estimated 3/09/2010–3/22/2010	X	X	X
Self-check components installed at millwork installation—estimated 2/25/2010–3/08/2010	X	X	X
Workstations installed at library move in—July 19, 2010	X	X	X
Quote			
Total	$mid	$low	$high
Second year	unknown	$mid	$low

Note: Page numbers refer to the page numbers of the vendor's responses to the RFQ.

Figure 10.1 (Continued)

Once the compliant vendor was determined, a notice of intent to award the contract was issued by the Logistical Services department. This notice was followed by a 10-day protest period in which a vendor not selected in the process could protest the decision. One vendor representative indicated that a company response would be provided because they were certain they met all the requirements of the RFQ. This representative erroneously explained that not replying to a criterion because they did not recommend that solution did not constitute noncompliance. We never received their promised response.

CONCLUSION

The RFQ process is different than the RFP process, but each has its place. In the case of GGC Library's need for a new security and inventory system to be implemented in a new building, an RFQ was the right decision. The type of system was identified, and there was no need to solicit proposals for non-RFID-based solutions. Experience with RFID gave the ability to describe what was wanted and how it should work. Two things would have made the experience with RFID better: a wand with more up-to-date technology would improve the shelf reading experience and less obvious RFID tags might make it more difficult for thieves to identify and remove the security measures. In the end, the GGC system performs as expected and has made staff-assisted and self-check-outs and some aspects of shelf management more efficient as well as making lost items' searches easier.

APPENDIX

SPECIFICATIONS FOR THE GEORGIA GWINNETT COLLEGE LIBRARY RADIO FREQUENCY IDENTIFICATION (RFID) SECURITY DETECTION AND INVENTORY SYSTEM

1. Gates

   Security gates for detecting improperly checked-out material. They provide an audible and visible alarm, interface with the ILS system, alert and report to workstations, and count patrons.

   Buried cable mounting

   Double corridor, ADA compliant

   Customizable look in keeping with the design of the library

   RFID

   Patron Counter

   Adjustable audio and visual stolen item alert

   ILS system stolen items reporting

   Compatible with ISO 15693 and ISO 18000-3 RFID chips

   CAT5e or CAT6 Ethernet communication interface

   "Network down" functionality

   Data model independent

2. Book Returns

   One RFID enabled (exterior) and one traditional book return (interior) able to be upgraded to RFID in the future, both with appropriate carts for collecting the books.

   a. Return 1—RFID Return

      Exterior in-wall, weather proof and secure

      Lockable

      Real time check in/database updates

      Reactivates security tag

      Prints hold notices

      Appropriate work station (or connection to a workstation) as necessary

      Sorting not necessary

      "Network down" functionality

Faceplate should be in keeping with the design of the library and say "Book Return"

SIP2, SIP, NCIP compliant

Data model independent

b.   Return 2—Traditional Return

Secure

Lockable

Able to be upgraded to RFID in the future

Faceplate should be in keeping with the design of the library and say "Book Return"

c.   Book carts for the returns (2)

150–180 book, depressible/cushioned/soft-drop/padded/lined book cart

3.   Self Check-Out (2)

Two self check-out stations which will sit at the circulation desk and be approachable from both sides; patrons on one side, staff on the other. Each station should have a touch screen for patrons and a keyboard and a mouse for staff. No kiosk necessary, components will be installed on contractor built millwork with double swing arm monitor mounts provided by architects.

Swipe-type card readers (2)

Antennae (2) Data model independent, 8–12" read range (single or dual)

Receipt printers (2) with formatable printing (does this belong with software?)

Flat touch screens at least 19" diagonal with integrated speakers (2)

Flat screens at least 17" diagonal (2)

Keyboards (2)

Mouse (2)

"Network down" functionality

4.   Software

SIP2, SIP, NCIP compliant

Data model adaptable

Can read multiple data models

Must interface with current ILS (Voyager)

5.   RFID Tags

100,000 Standard, unprinted tags

ISO 15693/18000-3 Compliant

13.56 MHz

Re-programmable/re-writeable

Data model independent

Low acid adhesive

Printable

Guaranteed/replaceable if defective
Able to move to ISO Tag Data Standard (when approved)

6. RFID Inventory Wand
   ISO 15693/18000-3 Compliant
   Portable
   Lightweight—(Weight approximately 1–2 lbs.?)
   Handheld
   Displays titles
   ILS interactive
   ILS based search capability
   Capable of shelf order checking
   Can provide security bit scans
   Read range of approximately 4–5"
   Adjustable acoustic and visual indicators
   Data model independent
   Storage capacity

7. Conversion Station
   Leasable (approx. 1 month) or convertible to a workstation
   Reader/Antenna (single or dual) or equivalent technology
   Barcode scanner
   Mobile cart
   Able to interact with the ILS but stand-alone when needed
   Able to print tags as they are programmed

8. Workstations
   XP/Vista compatible
   6 antennae
   2 receipt printers
   2 Swipe type card readers

9. Installation
   Gates done by vendor in coordination with building contractors
   Book drops done by vendor in coordination with building contractors
   Self-check done by vendor in coordination with building contractors
   Workstations done by vendor in coordination with GGC Educational
      Technology and Library Systems departments
   Conversion station done by vendor

10. Training
    2 days
    Manuals and training materials for all software, workstations, self-check
       machines, and gates

11. Support
     Support contract for a minimum of one year, renewable annually
     < 4-hour response time by phone (toll free number?)
     < 24-hour response time with routine parts and service
     Please list any applicable warranties
     Please address any planned upgrades

12. Contractor Experience
     Contractor must have been in the business of supplying RFID systems
       to libraries for a minimum of five (5) years and list their five (5) most
       recent system installations

13. Timeframe (all dates are subject to change)
     Installation complete by library completion
     Conversion station installed in the existing GGC Library—August 2009
     Gates installed at resilient flooring and base—estimated 3/09/2010–
       3/22/2010
     Self-check components installed at millwork installation—estimated
       2/25/2010–3/08/2010
     Workstations installed at Library move in—July 19, 2010

11

PROCURING DIGITIZATION SERVICES FOR LIBRARY COLLECTIONS: A PRACTICAL OVERVIEW

Kyle R. Rimkus

INTRODUCTION

Seeking formal procurement for the digitization of library collections is challenging and fraught with pitfalls. It takes months of effort to plan and execute a successful request for proposal (RFP), and librarians who are not careful at each step of the process risk signing contracts with vendors whose services will fall short of expectations. A well-crafted RFP, however, distinguished by a cogent statement of need and clear technical and business requirements, often leads to a mutually satisfactory relationship between library and vendor. This chapter provides an overview of essential elements to such a call for proposals, supplemented by concrete examples drawn from solicitation documents recently issued by the author's home institution, the University of Illinois at Urbana-Champaign Library.

LIBRARY DIGITIZATION

The term "library digitization" comprises the creation of digital surrogates for any items a library may hold in its circulating or noncirculating collections. Most often, these are bound materials such as books and periodicals from general collections, bound and unbound books and manuscripts from special collections, newspapers in print or microfilm format, maps, photographs, photographic negatives, slides, other visual materials, audio materials, and moving image materials. Libraries have many reasons for wishing to digitize materials, but they tend to fall under the categories of access and preservation (Lopatin 2006). Libraries may want to make print collections in the public domain freely available in digital format on the web or simply to create digital surrogates for reasons of preservation, exercising their legal prerogative under section 108 of the U.S. copyright code or similar provisions in other countries, to reformat items in the process of physical degradation that are no longer available for purchase. In either case, files created from digitization efforts usually end up in some sort of digital library system where they are publicly available to patrons, a digital preservation repository where they are accessible to select library staff, or both. While many libraries choose to build staff and technical capacity in-house by establishing their own digitization labs, this is a costly investment, and many prefer to utilize vended services for the reformatting of their materials. In fact, even libraries that manage their own labs sometimes have recourse to vended services in order to provide higher production capacity or to deal with difficult material types.

WHY AN RFP?

Before issuing a call for proposals, the librarian ought to determine whether the formal procurement process is necessary at all. Many libraries are subject to regulations stating how much money they can spend with a single vendor per year before running afoul of their institutional procurement guidelines. Such regulations differ from one institution to another, but for the sake of example, if a state-funded library in Illinois intends to spend more than $80,000 on a given service in the course of a year, it has an obligation to initiate a call for competitive pricing among external vendors for that service (University of Illinois Office of Business and Financial Services 2016). But if said library does not intend to spend over the regulated threshold, its staff may pick and choose vended services in an informal, unregulated manner. When given the option, many librarians prefer to canvas trusted colleagues for references to competent, reasonably priced vendors, rather than to run the gauntlet of a formal procurement process, daunting as this usually is.

The advantage of formal procurement is that, if done right, the library is able to ensure all qualified vendors a fair and equitable shot at a remunerative contract while looking out for its own financial and staff interests. Much of this hinges on the quality of the call for proposals itself. If the call document accurately represents the work to be done, clearly states the library's quality standards, and includes sufficient protections for the library in case the vendor submits subpar work, the proposal has an excellent chance of working out well for the library.

Before crafting said procurement document, however, the library must decide what type of call is best. Many institutions distinguish between an RFP and a call for competitive bids. The precise distinction between an RFP and a bid, as well as the terms used to identify them, may vary from one institution to another, but broadly speaking, an RFP is issued for specialized work in which price is not the overwhelming deciding factor, whereas a bid is issued for clearly definable work that a broad spectrum of vendors is assumed capable of fulfilling and is thus awarded to the lowest bidder. In an RFP, one might include language similar to the following on the evaluation of proposals (this and other subsequent sample texts are adapted for brevity and clarity from two digitization solicitation documents from the author's home institution [University of Illinois at Urbana Champaign 2011, 2015]): "The following evaluation factors, grouped by relative order of importance, will be used in determining the best-qualified offers: response to technical specifications, price, experience, proposed delivery schedule, customer support, viability of proposer(s), overall quality and completeness of response." By contrast, an invitation to bid will have price as its bottom line, paired of course with meeting the essential requirements of the proposal: "The library will rank responses in order of price to determine the lowest priced response that meets requirements of responsiveness and responsibility."

At the author's home institution, digitization falls into a gray area between the bid and RFP categories. Procurement staff at the university and its oversight officers have at times allowed library digitization services to be solicited as RFP while insisting more recently that digitization procurement—due to their view of digitization as a clearly definable process with specific technical specifications that a broad spectrum of vendors should be able to meet—should go out as a bid.

In the author's experience, library staff have been more satisfied with contracts garnered from RFP than from competitive bidding. An RFP allows the library to place significant weight on such intangible qualities as experience, customer support, and the perceived viability of the proposer. These qualities, which essentially translate to reliability and professionalism, are of great importance. Indeed, vendors who charge above the lowest going rate but do excellent work and understand how to communicate with librarians as valued clients often end up saving libraries money in the long run, compared to the high personnel costs incurred by having to tidy the messes caused by less competent competitors with lower prices.

Cut-rate operators in the digitization business sometimes rise to the top of the vendor pool in a poorly structured bid. Many of these companies provide digitization services to companies in the corporate sphere who wish to do away with filing cabinets and maintain legacy paper records in digital format. While these digitization companies have a niche to fill, the priorities of their clients differ from those of libraries. Subsequently, the staff of these digitization vendors often lack training in the careful handling of cultural heritage materials, not to mention knowledge of file format standards in libraries. Digitization vendors that service libraries, by contrast, train their staff in the care and proper handling of books and manuscripts, understand something of library file formats and metadata, stay abreast of changing technical and metadata standards, and maintain professional contact with librarians and archivists through regular attendance at national conferences.

Keeping these factors in mind, it is advised, if given the choice, to issue an RFP with weight given to professionalism and reliability rather than a call for the lowest bidder for library digitization. Should circumstances require the librarian to issue a bid rather than an RFP, great care must be taken to state all work and business requirements in detail so that the call is stringent enough to attract only the most qualified vendors. In both the case of an RFP or call for lowest bid, however, a well-written document distinguished by clear and reasonable criteria for evaluating proposals is of critical importance.

PLANNING FOR THE PROCESS

Librarians who have never issued an RFP ought to seek out people at their institutions who have. For newcomers, it is a foreign process fraught with red tape. Librarians should seek out sample proposal documents from their own institution to serve as a model for their efforts and learn if there are support or administrative staff who know the proposal process and are willing to shepherd a first-timer through it. Librarians will find that procurement officers have a tendency to quibble at length over the wording of proposals, prolonging rather than expediting the preliminary step of writing a proposal draft. While this can be frustrating, such concerns are grounded in professional experience and motivated by a genuine desire to protect the library's interests. After all, great pitfalls exist in poorly worded contracts. For this reason, librarians should exercise patience with solicitation administrators while standing up for the library's goals and values so that these do not get lost in the editorial process.

ESSENTIAL ELEMENTS OF AN RFP FOR
LIBRARY DIGITIZATION

A clearly worded RFP document will help establish the type of healthy transparency that ought to exist between a library and its digitization vendor. Lack of specificity in the RFP only ends up creating more work for the library. With a poorly worded call, vendors will submit multiple questions trying to understand what exactly the proposal means. If there is confusion on key points in the RFP among multiple vendors, their official responses will be skewed and difficult to judge fairly. To ensure mutual understanding between the library and prospective vendors, a solicitation for library digitization ought to consist of the following elements, to be elaborated on in the pages to follow:

1. Statement of need
2. Technical specifications

3. Care and handling requirements
4. Transfer of items
5. Quality requirements
6. Pricing
7. Evaluation

Statement of Need

A procurement proposal should begin with a clear statement of what kind of items shall be digitally reformatted, in what volume, and for what period of time. Is the library seeking a vendor to digitize books, newspapers, manuscripts, or audiovisual media? Are the items in paper, microfilm, or a time-based media format? The proposal should be specific about the range of sizes of the materials and the physical carriers on which they reside. If books, are they primarily brittle materials? If microfilm, are they on polyester-based stock that has been maintained under favorable storage conditions? Material type, size, and physical condition all make a difference to costs incurred by digitization vendors and ought to be spelled out clearly. For example, following is the statement of need from a proposal for the digitization of brittle books bound for the HathiTrust Digital Library:

> Vendor will produce high quality digital images of bound and loose papers, including journals and books, whether printed or typescript. All digitized books and book-like materials must meet ingest requirements (http://www.hathitrust.org/ingest) for the HathiTrust Digital Library (http://www.hathitrust.org/), a preservation and access repository for digitized public domain and in copyright works owned by libraries. Original print materials may be brittle. While some print materials will be supplied disbound as indicated in shipping lists, others will need to be scanned with bindings intact.

To strengthen an opening statement like the previous one, the library may also wish to provide a bulleted list of its needs for easy reading and comprehensibility:

The vendor shall:

- digitize books, often in brittle condition, and will retain them in bound format or disbind them according to library instructions;
- return all materials to the library post digitization;
- deliver digitized files to the library post digitization either via secure web download or via shipped hard drive. Vendor will be responsible for media costs (hard drive/DVDs);
- digitize paper at the following maximum sizes:

  ○ Unbound documents—up to 34" (w) × 44" (h)

- ○ Bound documents—up to 15" (w) × 21.5" (h)
- ○ Large documents (sheet fed)—42" (w) with unlimited length

- • crop and de-skew all images necessary to best represent the original materials. The process for cropping and de-skewing images will include the following steps:

  - ○ De-skew images with a skew of greater than 3 degrees.
  - ○ Crop to include visible edge of paper, retaining up to 1/4" inch beyond edge.
  - ○ Provide digital image files with color, gray scale, or bitonal color values as specified by the library in shipping lists.
  - ○ Provide digital image files within the JPEG 2000 format as specified by library shipping lists, as well as supplementary files prepared according to the file format specifications outlined to include plain text and XML formats.

Next, the library should state the scope and timeline for its project. Is it a grant-funded effort to digitize a predetermined number of items, say 2,000 audio cassette tapes over a two-year period? Or is this to meet an operational need, such as the ongoing digitization of brittle books from the general collections at a rate of approximately 50 per month?

Technical Specifications

Technical specifications describe the technical qualities of the files to be delivered to the library. What file format should the vendor use? What metadata, if any, should the vendor embed in them? How should the vendor name and package the files? Is the library simply seeking preservation quality files or preservation masters and access derivatives? Given the great flexibility in the way people and systems may interpret the same file standard (De Vorsey and McKinney 2010), is there an independent tool for verifying compliant files?

For those not technically inclined, writing these specifications is a tall order. Unfortunately, the space considerations of this paper prohibit the compilation of sample technical specifications for the full gamut of library digitization formats and project types. In lieu of such a resource, librarians who lack technical expertise should seek out colleagues within their library or professional community who are qualified to advise on these details. In writing their specifications, they should keep in mind that digitized files usually have a destination repository or repositories for preservation and access and that digitization requirements should be crafted in order to ease smooth deposit into these systems. For example, in a proposal to digitize microfilmed newspapers for ingest into a locally managed newspaper repository, the library may rely on best practices already established by the Library of Congress's Chronicling America project, with some modifications for local needs. The following example is lengthy, but is provided to demonstrate the high level of detail often necessary in contractual technical specifications:

The library bases its packaging and file format specifications for digitized newspapers on the National Digital Newspaper Program's (NDNP) Technical Specifications Profiles and Schemas for 2015–2017 Awards (http://www.loc .gov/ndnp/guidelines/NDNP_201517TechNotes.pdf). Please note that some specifications will differ from NDNP. The vendor shall:

- provide digitized page master images in the TIFF format scanned at a maximum possible resolution, with a minimum of 300 dpi and a maximum of 400 dpi, relative to the original paper material;
- provide digitized page images in three formats: uncompressed TIFF 6.0 files, JPEG 2000, and PDF. The contractor shall produce master files in the TIFF format and derive JPEG 2000 and PDF page image files from the TIFF masters;
- package files related to each library item in a folder named according to a unique identifier provided by the library. Content within this folder shall be structured as indicated next, where each package contains a folder named after the digitized issue with a four-digit year, two-digit month, two-digit date, and a two-digit edition to reflect the date of its publication: yyyymmddee:
  - The package shall contain a Metadata Encoding and Transmission Standard (METS) XML document describing the issue's structure named yyyymmddee.xml.
  - The package shall contain a PDF file containing page images of the entire issue named yyyymmddee.pdf.
  - The folder shall contain digitized page images in the TIFF, JPEG 2000, and PDF formats, as well as an Analyzed Layout and Text Object (ALTO) XML OCR file named with a four-digit number padded with leading zeros—for example, 0001.tif.
- produce master page images as 8 bit gray scale uncompressed TIFF 6.0 files;
- provide compressed JPEG 2000 page images derived from the TIFF master files;
- derive PDF page images either from the compressed JPEG 2000 files or from the master page images;
- bundle page PDFs and Optical Character Recognition (OCR) data for each individual issue in a single-issue text-searchable PDF file;
- provide the contractor with metadata related to newspaper volume, issue, edition, and date in its shipping lists. The contractor shall include this

metadata in the descriptive metadata section of an issue-level METS file, along with information on page numbers for individual pages in the issue:

- ○ The METS file shall follow the "Issue XML Metadata Template" in Appendix C, page 47–57 of the NDNP's Technical Specifications— Profiles and Schemas for 2015–2017 Awards (http://www.loc.gov/ndnp/guidelines/NDNP_201517TechNotes.pdf).

- provide ALTO OCR formatting. Vendor shall:

  - ○ provide one OCR text file per page image in ALTO XML format;
  - ○ produce discrete files for each page, rather than for a multipage issue or entire title;
  - ○ have each OCR text file name correspond to the page image it represents;
  - ○ save text in the UTF-8 character set;
  - ○ not save graphic elements with the OCR text;
  - ○ produce OCR text ordered column-by-column (i.e., in a natural reading order);
  - ○ produce OCR text file with bounding-box coordinate data at the word level; and
  - ○ have OCR files conform to the ALTO XML schema, Version 2.0 or greater.

- For an example of the file packaging specified here, see next:

  {unique identifier}/
  1905112901/
  1905112901.xml
  1905112901.pdf
  0001.tif
  0001.jp2
  0001.pdf
  0001.xml

Note that the file package outlined previously for a digitized newspaper will differ significantly from that of a digitized book bound for HathiTrust, or a digitized manuscript bound for a library's local instance of DSpace, or an audio file for a digitized oral history cassette. Each type of content, the use to which the digital files will be put, the files' destination system or systems, and local requirements for file naming and management will affect the way the library structures its technical requirements.

Care and Handling Requirements

In this section, the library ought to provide clear instruction on how vendors should handle its items. This will allow vendors to determine if they have the proper equipment and staff expertise to manage the library's needs, which comes into play especially when considering that many vendors offer both "destructive" and "nondestructive" methods of creating digital surrogates. When digitizing books, the tight bindings and narrow inner gutters often force digitization operators to use time-consuming, expensive techniques to capture a representative page image. In this case, would the library be comfortable with the vendor cutting the binding to allow for a better image, and either rebinding the book using a commercial process or, for those materials that are not robust enough to be subjected to commercial rebinding, relegating the disbound leaves and covers to storage in a box? This latter solution is sometimes applied to items of perceived low value from circulating general collections, usually because other copies exist in abundance, but is of course not a recommended practice for rare books.

In both the cases of destructive or nondestructive digitization, it is important to convey the condition of the materials. If a proposal is explicitly for brittle manuscript materials that will require attentive, time-consuming handling and page-by-page copy-stand imaging, to include specialized treatment for fold-out illustrations, the library's needs are more expensive than those of a peer institution with a collection of historical registers with supple pages, whose curator is comfortable allowing them to be imaged using a dual-camera book cradle imaging system. Similarly, microfilmed newspaper filmed according to U.S. Newspaper Program standards (Library of Congress 2010) on polyester-based film and stored under advantageous conditions will cause fewer problems than a box of assorted films produced haphazardly in, say, the days of Soviet Russia, and stored in a basement next to a hot water pipe, causing the film to warp and requiring a high level of professional acumen and patience to digitize.

Such examples abound for every format there is, but the vendors who cast their proposals into the pool do not know the library's collections as well as its librarians. Vendors will only be able to provide an accurate response to a library's call for proposals if that library is specific about the condition of its materials, and their subsequent care and handling requirements.

Transfer of Items

The library should spell out how items will be transferred from its facilities to those of the vendor, how both parties will track the items, and what an acceptable turnaround time is for the digitization work. For circulating items, barcodes are the most reliable, readily available unique identifier at hand. At the very least, the library should provide a shipping list of barcodes for each batch sent to the vendor to be verified on return of the items. Many libraries provide additional identifying metadata from bibliographic records to accompany barcodes to simplify identification of items by vendors once the books are transferred off-site.

Some vendors will propose to take a library's items and outsource one or more steps in their digital processing offshore, most frequently to India. This is common in the digitization of microfilm and the processing of digital files to derive searchable text from the pages of digitized books. The library ought to state whether or not it approves its materials, in original or digital format, leaving the country for treatment abroad.

Critically, the library must state its requirement on turnaround time for the accomplishment of digitization work. Given the fact that vendors juggle multiple projects from a variety of clients at any given time, they cannot always commit to completing work promptly. The author has had vendors drop out of bidding pools where a 60-day turnaround time was required, suggesting that 90 or 120 days would be more reasonable. While turnaround times will vary based on the fragility and format of the originals, the library should set reasonable time limits in its call for proposals in order to indicate its expectations.

Quality Requirements

The Project Management Institute defines "quality" as "the degree to which a set of inherent characteristics fulfills requirements" (2004, 371). The designation of quality as something measurable is useful in writing vendor specifications for digitization work. It provides the library with the language necessary to state how it intends to review the work returned to it, what measures will be used to assess said work, and what rate of failure to meet its requirements is acceptable.

For example,

> Within 30 days of the receipt of materials from the vendor, the Library will complete a quality assurance review of the materials for purposes of acceptance and request correction of any failures to meet specifications. Errors in deliverables shall be corrected by the vendor at no cost to the Library within 14 days after the Library identifies the errors to the vendor. The vendor's exceeding a 3% monthly error rate (calculated as the percentage of the total number of files produced for initial submission over the course of a month that fail to meet specifications) in any two (2) months in any six (6) month period may be deemed to be grounds for contract termination, at the sole discretion of the University. Vendor and the University may review vendor's performance monthly. This basis for termination is in addition to any other basis for which the contract may provide. (University of Illinois at Urbana Champaign 2011, 2015)

Librarians should check with the rules and regulations of their business office to determine appropriate disciplinary language and possible actions that can result from breach of contract, but in the example cited above, the proposal's authors essentially state that the full body of technical specifications is to be respected in work submitted to the library, and that failures to meet these specifications will constitute a rejection of files that evince these problems. Armed with such language, the library positions itself to receive high quality work, or to have an exit route should a vendor fail to consistently meet expectations.

Pricing

In its call for proposals, the library should provide a single worksheet for vendors to fill out pricing details. This may be formatted as a table (see Table 11.1) with the specific type of item to be digitized in the first column, the quantity in the next, followed by cost per item, and a total or extended cost based on the previous two column values:

Table 11.1 Pricing

Bound Color Scanning (Sizes Are Closed Books)	Estimated # of Pages per Year	Cost per Page	Extended Cost (Estimated # of Pages per Year × Cost per Page)
Up to 8.5" × 11"	100,000	–	–
Up to 11" × 17"	10,000	–	–
Up to 15" × 21.5"	500	–	–
Larger than 15" × 21.5"	500	–	–

Vendors should know whether shipping costs should figure into these numbers. Shipping is not a negligible cost, especially for heavy items like books, and geographic proximity to the vendor will affect the cost to transport boxes. Many libraries find it best to place at least some of the onus for shipping costs on the vendor to protect themselves from a seemingly inexpensive contract that ends up costing large sums in item transport.

In a brittle books proposal, the library could include language like, "The Library will be responsible for the shipping of original materials to Vendor as well as for securing transit insurance for such shipments when necessary. Vendor will be responsible for shipping of those materials back to Library, for bearing the risk of loss or damage to the materials in transit, and for ensuring that materials are tracked on a box level, including all cost for the foregoing. The Library will advise the vendor in advance of shipment of the value of any given item having a replacement value in excess of the Library's standard replacement value of $250.

"Per page pricing must include costs of shipping from vendor to the University, including the shipping of file packages (where applicable) and the return shipping of original material with insurance necessary to protect against loss in transit. Based upon the estimated quantities stated above and recent usage, shipping is estimated to be 25 20lb boxes (5184 cubic inches each) for books. Additional expenses are not allowed."

If massive numbers of digital files, or even a small number of very large files, will change hands between vendor and library, the library ought to consider the best way to accomplish efficient file transfer. In the author's experience, arranging to ship external hard drives back and forth using postal mail is often easier and more cost- and time-efficient, and less prone to data loss and error, than exchanging files via the web using a file sharing or transfer service.

Evaluation

The library should state clearly what criteria it will use to evaluate vendor proposals. These should be clearly listed in the RFP, along with how they will be weighted. Once vendors submit their responses to a library's call for proposals, the evaluation process is typically run like a hiring committee, with a small number of critical stakeholders examining submissions and ranking them in as objective a manner as possible. It is recommended to create an evaluation matrix in spreadsheet form, with columns representing requirements, and librarians assigning numerical values on a predetermined scale on each vendor's ability, based on their individual responses, to meet said requirements. For a simplified version of an evaluation matrix, see the example in Table 11.2:

Table 11.2 Evaluation Matrix

	Ability to Meet Technical Specifications	Care and Handling of Materials	Pricing	Total
Points assigned	500	100	100	700
Vendor 1	500	95	75	670
Vendor 2	300	80	90	470

An actual matrix will feature many more rows to represent each requirement. However, the example in this table does demonstrate the library's ability to grant certain requirements greater weight than others by assigning greater points values to them. In it, the library has decided that a vendor's ability to meet technical specifications is of greater importance than pricing, and Vendor 1, who is strong in its ability to meet technical specifications and care and handling requirements, wins more points than Vendor 2, who offers its services at a lower price.

Most important, the library should require vendors to submit digital files that conform to the standards stated in the call itself, thus indicating that they are capable of meeting said requirements on an ongoing basis.

CONCLUSION

When embarking on a project to solicit competitive pricing from vendors for library digitization services, libraries should first determine whether a formal process is necessary, and if so, whether an RFP or a call for competitive bids is best. Whether issuing an RFP or a call for bids, however, stakeholders should prepare a solicitation document that consists of the following parts:

1. Statement of need
   - Specifies format, condition, and volume of materials to be digitized, as well as the span of time this service is desired
2. Technical specifications
   - Specify required file format(s) and file format specifications for the digital files
   - Describe the desired file packaging structure for the digital files
   - If the files are bound for a specific preservation or access repository or repositories, provide information on the deposit requirements of said system(s)
3. Care and handling requirements
   - Describe how materials should be handled by vendor, that is, with great care, and nondestructive methods in the case of high-value materials, or utilizing destructive digitization techniques for items of low perceived value
4. Transfer of items
   - Describes how items will be tracked (e.g., using barcodes and spreadsheets) and transported back and forth between library and vendor
5. Quality requirements
   - Describe how the library intends to verify the quality of submitted work
   - Define a threshold for failure to meet quality standards to result in breach of contract

6. Pricing
   - ○ Specifies who will pay for shipping, and whether shipping costs should be built into per-item pricing
   - ○ To ensure fairness, provides a single worksheet for vendors to submit pricing information
7. Evaluation
   - ○ Evaluates vendors' abilities to fulfill requirements using a matrix where each requirement is weighted based on its importance to the library

Clarity in an RFP is always important but is critical when soliciting digitization services. Vended digitization is a complex process involving the shipping of materials between library and vendor, the mutual management of identifying metadata for items to be digitized, the safe care and handling of original materials, the creation of digital files according to strict technical specifications, quality assurance, and payment for work accomplished. Successful call documents spell these details out clearly, expressing the library's need in terms all vendors will understand. By following these principles and the steps outlined in this chapter, libraries improve their chances for establishing satisfying professional relationships with digitization vendors.

REFERENCES

De Vorsey, Kevin, and Peter McKinney. 2010. "Digital Preservation in Capable Hands: Taking Control of Risk Assessment at the National Library of New Zealand." *Information Standards Quarterly* 22 (2): 41–44.

Library of Congress. 2010. "USNP Preservation Microfilm Guidelines." https://www.loc .gov/rr/news/usnp/usnpguidelinesp.html.

Lopatin, Laurie. 2006. "Library Digitization Projects, Issues and Guidelines: A Survey of the Literature." *Library Hi Tech* 24 (2): 273–89. doi:10.1108/07378830610669637.

Project Management Institute, ed. 2004. *A Guide to the Project Management Body of Knowledge (PMBOK Guide)*. 3rd ed. Newtown Square, PA: Project Management Institute, Inc.

University of Illinois at Urbana-Champaign. 2011. "Request for Proposal No. 1NRC1105: Digital Imaging Services for Library Material." University of Illinois Purchasing Division.

University of Illinois at Urbana-Champaign. 2015. "Invitation to Bid 1JWS1605: Provide Digital Imaging Services." State of Illinois Public Institutions of Higher Education.

University of Illinois Office of Business and Financial Services. 2016. "Small Purchase Limits and Competitive Solicitation Thresholds . . ." https://www.obfs.uillinois.edu/ purchases/procedures-rules/bid-limits/.

12

SERVICES FOR EMERGENCY/DISASTER RECOVERY

Edward Castillo-Padilla

To be Prepared is Half the Victory.

—Miguel de Cervantes

INTRODUCTION

Library disasters strike academic, public, and school libraries when least expected. Emergencies range from relatively minor situations such as a water leak to major disasters related to fires, floods, weather (hurricanes, tornadoes, heavy rain, and snowfall), earthquakes, construction-related accidents, terrorism, and utility outages that prevent the library from maintaining normal services.

Many librarians hope that a disaster will not occur in their library, but wishful thinking is not a substitute for planning (Miller 2008). Failure to seriously consider the possibility is a costly oversight that poses a danger not only to staff and patrons but also to library collections, and all other contents in the library.

Library administrators want to protect and preserve their collections and library facilities in the most efficient and cost-effective way possible, and developing a comprehensive and frequently updated disaster preparedness, response, and recovery plan is an important step. A key element of the plan is contracting for emergency and disaster recovery services before a disaster happens. Using the request for proposal (RFP) process to select a vendor(s) to provide these services is a sensible, preventive step toward mitigating response time and recovery costs. In addition, insurance providers look favorably on such proactive steps.

THE DISASTER RECOVERY PLAN

Awareness that disasters can and do occur in libraries has increased since the devastation of Hurricane Katrina (Thomas 2009, 3). Based on a review of the Federal Emergency Management Agency (FEMA) website (https://www .fema.gov/), it is clear that not only is awareness increasing, but the number of actual disasters, especially due to hurricanes and fires, is also increasing. These factors underscore that a disaster preparedness and recovery plan should be an integral part of every library's overall safety plan. This plan will include, among other things, the names and contact information of both small local vendors and major emergency and disaster recovery vendors, noting if any of these vendors has a precontract arrangement with the library or its parent organization (Wilkinson, Lewis, and Dennis 2010, 19).

Why Have a Contract in Place?

Contracting with a disaster recovery vendor is different from other kinds of library contracts. In all the other cases, libraries purchase a specific product or service, with a fairly well-defined cost, for a period specified in the contract. Contracting with a disaster recovery vendor is like buying insurance. One hopes never to have to use it, but one needs to make sure it is there if/ when the occasion arises. It is also impossible to predict the exact cost and scope of the occurrence, because the library needs to be prepared for coverage of small and less costly contingencies to the largest and most disastrous incidents. These factors make the RFP for a disaster recovery vendor different in terms of the level of the product and service needed, as well as the timeline. But the major criteria for issuing a good quality RFP still apply.

Having a comprehensive contract in place with a disaster recovery specialist before an emergency or disaster happens can ensure that emergency and disaster recovery professionals will respond to the library's call for assistance to help minimize extensive damages, and to help ease the anxiety and stress in an already very stressful situation. It cannot be emphasized enough that to respond effectively to emergencies and disasters, library personnel will need help from professionals who have a proven track record mitigating minor emergencies and major disaster response and recovery. This includes a broad range of successful experience in remediation work with trained and certified support staff, and the availability of equipment and supplies that are necessary when responding to emergency/disaster situations.

Without a contract(s) in place, the library will not have the assurance or peace of mind in knowing that either the local vendor or a larger, more comprehensive vendor will be available when they are needed most. Depending on where in the country the library is located, this could be an important and critical issue. With a contract in place, the library will have the information and resources needed to immediately initiate response and recovery efforts. The time to start thinking about emergency and disaster response is not when you are knee-deep in water or you have a room or building on fire. Be prepared!

Two Contracts for Your Library?

Emergencies and disasters vary in scope and size, and libraries may want to consider two contracts for services. This would include a contract for minor emergencies that can be effectively resolved by a local restoration and cleaning company and a separate contract for major disasters requiring a vendor that can respond to large-scale emergencies and disasters. Also, major disasters will often necessitate a local vendor to assist immediately with mitigation and recovery efforts, while a vendor with major disaster experience, who may not be available locally, can mobilize personnel and equipment for their on-site recovery work. With two contracts in place, the library will have the confidence in knowing that a local vendor will be on hand to address smaller emergency situations or the initial work for large-scale disasters, and there is also a contract in place that will provide services for large-scale disasters. When deciding vendor options for emergency and disaster recovery, it is worth considering pre-contracting with two vendors.

THE RFP

Upon undertaking the assignment of preparing an RFP for vendor(s) services for library emergency/disaster recovery, an initial step is to review all pertinent policies, procedures, and plans of the parent institution and to understand the library's scope of authority to contract for vendor services as well as what services it is permitted to contract. Most parent institutions' plans will address overarching organizational priorities but may not include more granular details regarding individual entities such as the library.

Assuming that the library administration is authorized to prepare an RFP and award an emergency/disaster recovery contract to a vendor(s), the librarian(s) writing the RFP will need to understand what the contract can cover. Is it only library collections (books, journals, media, etc.), or does it also include library furnishings, computers, and the building? Typically, the library's emergency/disaster recovery services RFP covers collections and sometimes furniture or minor/initial building mitigation and repairs (e.g., removing standing water from carpets, setting up dehumidification, mold prevention or remediation, initial treatment of fire damaged areas) while infrastructure and major building repairs may be handled by contracts put in place with other vendors by the parent institution.

If the library's RFP covers all aspects of the recovery, contracting with an emergency/disaster recovery vendor is multifaceted, and the skills and actions needed to address the disaster can be quite different. For example, the expertise and equipment needed to rescue a collection from damage will be very different from the expertise and equipment required to fully repair damaged walls, flooring, ceilings, or water lines, and yet the disaster recovery vendor with which you contract will need to be able to address both, either separately or at once.

Once the scope of work to be covered is known, take the time needed to carefully consider the required elements of the RFP. This work is best undertaken when not under the pressure of dealing with a dire emergency because sometimes making ad hoc decisions when under severe stress and deadlines of disaster recovery could lead to inadequate or even wrong choices. Writing the RFP creates the perfect opportunity to think each situation through in a non-emergency, and therefore, non-stressful atmosphere. It also allows for consultation with experts to address questions for which there would not be time if dealt with in the middle of the crisis.

PREPARING THE RFP

Who is included in writing the RFP will depend on the size and administrative organization of each library, but even the smaller public library will require assistance from city or county personnel. School libraries will need assistance from their school administrations. Academic libraries will typically include administrative and facilities personnel from the library as well as representatives from the campus Physical Plant (which may include construction, electrical, mechanical, and remodel personnel and also the campus architect's office), the university purchasing department, and possibly a representative from the university's emergency response team. Keep in mind that firsthand experience counts for a lot, and library personnel with hands-on emergency and disaster recovery experience can be vitally important when preparing the RFP. Experienced staff will have learned many important and detailed lessons from their experiences that can not only save the library time and expense, but they will also know how to respond to many of the unforeseen details or circumstances that may not be included in the contract.

Before embarking on writing the RFP, the team or committee should have thoroughly discussed why the contract is needed and what criteria and outcomes are expected and consider funding options to augment potential losses not included in insurance claim coverages. They must understand clearly the scope of work expected from the vendor; how the vendor's work will affect the library, staff, and patrons; and the potential costs to the library, or its parent institution. This can only occur with in-depth discussions by all key participants involved with writing the RFP. With a clear understanding in place of what you want included in the RFP scope of work, it will make writing the RFP easier and enhance efficiency and comprehensiveness.

Speak up! Participants writing an RFP must speak up when their expertise is needed, or when they can determine that there may be problems or difficulties that could be offset or resolved by considering other potential options.

Vendor Requirements

The requirements of the service providers are extremely important and will establish the standards for all the work that will be completed in the scope of work. The requirements to be evaluated should be agreed upon in advance by all participants writing the RFP and evaluating the vendor proposals.

Choose a vendor with a proven track record! The following considerations can help determine if the vendor is qualified and can meet your expectations. This list includes requirements and questions pertaining to both vendors that handle collections recovery and those that handle broader recovery, including buildings.

Sample Requirements

- The vendor must have proof of certification and current contractor's license to provide services in the state where the work will be completed.
- The vendor, and all subcontractors, including engineers, must have demonstrated experience in emergency and disaster response and recovery.
- The vendor and subcontractors must be able to provide the highest level of emergency and disaster recovery services at preplanning stages, response and recovery stages, and post recovery stages with follow-up on emergency or disaster-related work that needs attention (punch list items).
- The vendor must have the finances to complete all services required for the successful completion of the scope of work.
- The vendor must have knowledge of regulations, laws, and policies that are utilized by the FEMA Public Assistance Program.
- The vendor must maintain a daily clean and safe workplace.
- To avoid work overloads due to other commitments, the vendor and all hired contractors must outline current workloads that might impact the requirements of the contract. (Are they taking on more than they can effectively handle?)
- The vendor must affirm no current or potential conflict of interest by their company or any subcontractor hired to complete the scope of work.

Sample Questions

- If located outside the city/state where the emergency or disaster is located, how long will it take the vendor to mobilize and be on-site for an emergency or disaster?
- Does the vendor have the necessary equipment, staff, and transportation capabilities to respond to large emergency situations and disasters?
- Does the vendor specialize in fire, flood, and/or other natural disasters?
- Can the vendor respond to mold damage to book collections, including special collections, and other building components such as heating, ventilation, and air-conditioning (HVAC) that can be affected by mold?

Vendor Background and Experience Questions

Questions addressed to the vendor are intended to determine their background information, overall experience, and qualifications to provide services for emergency disaster recovery. Some sample questions to consider include the following:

Vendor Background

- What are their qualifications for emergency and disaster response and recovery, both large- and small?
- What experience does the vendor have working with a library of your size?
- How long has the vendor been in service?
- Describe the vendor's quality control policies and procedures.
- Does the vendor have safety and code personnel?
- Does the vendor have a warehouse facility (to store collections and/or equipment and furnishings that must be removed from the library), and if so, what is the capacity?
- Does the vendor have a remediation facility that can address water and smoke damage for both large and small library collections? Elaborate on how they handle and treat special collections and artwork.
- What is the vendor's mission statement?
- How large is the company, and how is its management setup for on-site emergency services?
- What type of insurance does the vendor have?
- Does the vendor have a safety and security plan?
- What certifications does the company have?
- Is the vendor licensed and bonded? Is there an on-site project manager?

Vendor Expertise and Specialization

- Does the vendor's service include HVAC and total surface cleaning?
- Does the vendor provide water and flood cleanup services that include water removal, extraction, drying, dehumidification, and decontamination? Odor and smoke removal? 24/7 on call service?
- What type of quality control does the vendor adhere to?
- Does the vendor offer air quality testing by a certified industrial hygienist, including mold and other potential inflammation causing substances?
- Can the vendor coordinate with certified, licensed, and bonded contractors for rebuilding damages, and does this include small- and large-scale damages?
- Does the vendor offer pack-out and storage and pack-in services?
- Can the vendor provide references? Can they provide references similar to your library in type and size?

- Can the vendor accommodate large volumes of damaged collections, equipment, and furnishings for remediation work?
- What methodologies are used for repairing collection damages due to water, fire, or mold?
- What type of warranty or guarantees for work accomplished do they provide?
- Can the vendor provide letters of recommendation?

CATEGORIES AND EVALUATION CRITERIA FOR SERVICES

Consider which categories are needed to meet the standards necessary for the services required. The categories you select should be based on the questions you ask the vendors and the requirements that you state in the RFP. A clear scoring methodology for evaluating categories should be utilized to rate each vendor. There are a variety of categories and scoring methods to choose from. One method is to define the categories you want to score, and assign each category a score from 1 to 10, with 1 the lowest and 10 the highest. One category may include experience, another cost, and another customer service. It is important to take the necessary time to carefully consider criteria, categories, and scoring because your final selection will be based on these considerations.

Evaluating the Proposal

After the deadline date for the submission of the RFP proposals, the team who wrote the RFP or a designated evaluation committee will review and evaluate each proposal. The evaluation process should be based on the criteria the team has formulated. Evaluation criteria can differ markedly depending on organizational and facility priorities within each library. The following is an example of specific categories with scoring that can be used when evaluating RFPs.

A. Qualifications, experience, and past performance—40 points. The qualifications, experience, and past performance of the vendor, and all subcontractors, must be capable of fully and successfully completing the scope of work in the RFP, and including, when appropriate, the ability for the handling of fine arts and special collections materials.

B. The system and methods (methodology) used to complete scope of work—20 points. The RFP will be evaluated on the vendor's approach for completing the scope of work, which will include a project plan demonstrating a complete and thorough knowledge of all requirements outlined in the RFP.

C. Workloads—10 points. The vendor must be able to demonstrate that it can maintain the workloads required by the RFP while still committing to other current and anticipated workload demands.
D. Finances—10 points. The vendor must be able to meet all anticipated costs in the RFP scope of work.
E. Cost—20 points. This includes all anticipated costs for both personnel, including subcontractors, and equipment that will be used to successfully complete the scope of work in the RFP, and for other potential emergency or disaster-related tasks that may be required, but not specifically noted, in the scope of work. Include hourly or daily rates for personnel, including subcontractors, and equipment and fuel costs for equipment. The vendor with the lowest total cost will receive 20 points for the cost category. Total points—100.

Unanticipated Costs

Remember that final cost figures for emergency/disaster services can only be ascertained when an evaluation of the size and scope of damages has been carefully examined and determined, and all response and recovery work have been completed and expenses tabulated. Additionally, there may be hidden conditions that could affect final cost figures. Hidden conditions can include minor or major problems. Examples of hidden conditions include books that have undetected water damage that cause mold to grow, contaminating other materials, as well as instances when a contractor working in a building finds an unknown problem or difficulty, perhaps because it was located behind a wall, between walls, above a ceiling grid, below flooring, or possibly a problem below grade, and not discovered until the wall or other obstruction has been removed to allow a full view of the problem.

Specialized Personnel and Expertise Could Increase Costs

Note that criteria may change or be altered depending on the needs, physical environment, or availability of personnel and equipment at the home institution. For example, personnel working for vendors can include, but not be limited to, a project manager, project coordinator, assistant project manager, health and safety staff, restoration supervisor, project auditor, clerical support, emergency responder, labor staff, equipment technician, environmental expert, carpenter, electrician, mechanical (HVAC) technician, painter, plumber, glazer, roofer, grounds worker, and roofing inspector. Equipment can and will vary depending on the scale of the emergency or disaster and should include dehumidifiers, fans, scrubbers, equipment decontamination, desiccant dehumidification and dehumidifiers, cooling equipment that will include air conditioners, generators, portable lighting equipment, air ducting cleaning equipment, extraction units, foggers, infrared thermos camera, ozone machine, pallet jack, dollies, electric pumps, gas pumps, trash cans (30 gal), vacuums, high-pressure washers, wheel barrels, front-end loader, backhoe, forklift, dump truck, van truck, portable compressor, pickup truck, elevated platform, truck crane, scaffolding, construction hoist, loading/off-loading ramp, conveyor (for movement of sublevel materials), shipping pallets and boxes, and tractor/trailers.

AWARDING THE CONTRACT

Once the vendor proposals are evaluated and the scoring is completed, the library RFP team or committee will select and recommend the award of the contract to the vendor that receives the highest score based on the evaluation criteria. Depending on the organizational structure, the final contract will be negotiated by either the library administration or an entity within the parent organization. The library should maintain a copy of the contract and include it in its disaster preparedness and recovery plan.

LESSONS LEARNED

When all emergency or disaster recovery work has concluded, and all reme-diation work has been successfully completed, library administrators should consider arranging open and frank discussions with library employees who participated in the recovery efforts. One of the positive outcomes of post-emergency/disaster discussion includes sharing the "lessons learned" during the response and recovery period. The lessons learned can be invaluable to library personnel when addressing future small or large emergencies or disas-ters, and for colleagues in other libraries who may benefit from the informa-tion. It would be useful to create a document that lists these lessons, which can be included in the library's disaster preparedness plan.

Some lessons learned may include:

- Have an emergency and disaster preparedness plan available that includes current, updated information, including emergency contact information for library personnel and restoration and recovery services. Your plan should be available online and in paper format off-site with library and other emergency responders.
- If possible have an emergency contingency budget in place for initial costs for emergencies/disasters.
- Review insurance coverage before an emergency or disaster. Does the library have emergency/disaster insurance, including flood insurance, or does the parent institution have the necessary coverage? How will the insurance adjuster work with the contracted vendor?

- Have experienced leadership on the library's emergency/disaster team with direction and oversight from a designated project leader who will communicate with the contracted vendor.
- The library's project leader(s) should be prepared for overnight stays at or near the emergency or disaster location, and this includes having extra clothing and overnight necessities available.
- Create an online message board for all parties to communicate.
- Anticipate that large major disaster recovery services may not arrive from 48 to 72 hours.
- Anticipate the potential need for triage of library services while recovery and restoration are ongoing. Coordinate with the recovery vendor as needed.
- Remember that emergencies and disasters affect not only work but home life as well for both library personnel and contracted recovery vendors and their subcontractors.
- Decisions can be impaired by emergency/disaster workloads, timelines, and deadlines. Follow your emergency and disaster preparedness plan, and coordinate with your contracted recovery vendor.
- Prioritize "must save" collections, equipment, or other library materials, and communicate the priorities to your contracted recovery vendor.
- Have library personnel who are cross-trained, competent, reliable, and sensible enough to work in a disaster/emergency environment, and this includes working with emergency responders and restoration specialists. Library personnel should have respirator and fire extinguisher training and emergency kits on hand.
- Maintain documentation, including photographs, on all significant emergency and disaster recovery efforts by both library personnel and contracted recovery vendors. This will be invaluable later when post-response and recovery efforts have been concluded, and post-recovery reports are due to the parent institution and/or insurance adjustors.
- Address building safety for library personnel and contracted recovery vendors. Be sure that all emergency exits in the library have unobstructed access to emergency exit doors and all exit lights are functional, including at night.
- Train and cross-train key library personnel who will have leadership responsibilities. You will want to ensure that you will always have library personnel available who can respond to the emergency or disaster and work with contracted recovery vendors as needed, including nights, weekends, and holidays.
- When loading library collections for pack-out and pack-in, be sure to sort correctly by call number order, and do not use the cutter number for sorting collections (a situation that actually occurred in the author's library). This requires staff at pack-out and pack-in who understand the library classification call number system to direct contracted recovery vendors.

- Review your disaster and recovery plan to be sure all information is still current, especially important contact information, key library contacts, and support service contacts, including emergency and disaster services vendors' contact information.

CONCLUSION

Emergency and disaster experiences are thoroughly unpleasant, emotionally and physically draining, require long and exhausting working hours, disrupt home life, reduce or sever services to patrons, and can take very long periods of time to completely resolve. Having professional services in place for emergency and disaster recovery can help alleviate some of these drawbacks. They can also be a vitally important step the library can take to help mitigate damages to their collections and facilities and can aid in safeguarding the well-being of all library staff and patrons.

Librarians are noted for their meticulousness and attention to detail. Use the RFP process to select one or more vendors to provide the best emergency/disaster recovery services at a reasonable cost. Consider contracting with two vendors: one contract for small emergency situations, which a local vendor can readily address, and one contract for a large vendor, national or global in scope, who can respond to major disasters. Often, the major vendors will have local affiliates that can be the first responders, until the heavy equipment and personnel can be brought in to deal with a major disaster. Also, during a major disaster two contracts will provide the services of a local vendor for immediate assistance, while the large vendor is mobilizing to be on-site at your library. These vendors will partner with the library to provide the guidance, assistance, and peace of mind to help the library successfully recover.

REFERENCES

Miller, William. 2008. "Natural Disaster in the Academic Library." *Library Issues* 28 (3) 1–2.

Thomas, Marcia, ed. 2009. *Emergency Response Planning in College Libraries.* Chicago: American Library Association.

Wilkinson, Frances C., Linda K. Lewis, and Nancy K. Dennis. 2010. *Comprehensive Guide to Emergency Preparedness and Disaster Recovery.* Chicago: Association of College and Research Libraries (a division of the American Library Association).

13

WORDS THAT BIND: USING THE RFP PROCESS TO SELECT A BINDER

Laura Kohl

INTRODUCTION

A primary duty of the library is to preserve and prolong the life of all materials housed within its walls. While technology continues to evolve and the means by which library users obtain information has changed rapidly, many of the methods for preserving library print collections have changed very little. While librarians continue to face shrinking budgets and embrace a reality in which they have to do more with less, there are still some areas of preservation that are necessary for maintaining a functional print collection. Binding of printed material, which can include everything from periodicals to paperbacks that are heavily used, can drastically prolong the use-life of these items and remains a much-needed service in the library world.

HISTORY OF BINDING

Binding of books has a long and rich history dating back to the Roman Empire (Thomson 1969). Once a craft that was prohibitively expensive and affordable only to the wealthy, the introduction of machinery in the 18th century reduced the costs of binding and made it more easily affordable to a broader market. The reduction in cost, along with new binding processes, such as oversewing that was developed in the 20th century, made a once-timely process more efficient. Additional methods such as computerized measuring, computer-driven stamping, and notched double-fan adhesive binding further reduced the cost making binding well within the reach of most libraries (Merrill-Oldham 1995).

BINDING AND PRESERVATION

Traditionally binding has been the primary technique for preserving materials within the library. Given specialized training and costly machinery involved in binding, most libraries choose to contract with a commercial binder in order to meet all of their needs. Historically the relationship between libraries and binders was mutually beneficial. By contracting for bindery services, libraries gained the ability to preserve large portions of their print collections at a reduced cost while binders were guaranteed a stable partner that enabled their continued survival.

Though technology has progressed and libraries continue to experience a shift away from print materials in favor of electronic access, the means to manage a large print collection is still incredibly important. Binding serves a vital function for libraries by protecting newly acquired material from deterioration, mutilation, and theft while also extending the use-life of older, more heavily used items (Benaud and Bordeianu 1998). For periodicals, binding is important to maintain complete volumes, because with time, individual issues may be lost. While most libraries choose to outsource the binding of their monographs and periodicals, binding services can also be used for specialized material requiring routine conservation. In addition to the standard fare, most commercial binders are able to offer conservation services at a reasonable cost.

Binding Standards

In order to avoid vendors of poor quality, it is recommended that a library first review the current standards within the binding profession. Specialized associations, such as the Book Manufactures' Institute (BMI), are dedicated to upholding the highest standards for printing and bookbinding, and offer a certification process to their members that meet their criteria. With roots dating back to the early 1900s in New York City and the goal of employing bookbinders, BMI was incorporated in 1933 and has since grown to include several divisions within its organization. In 2014 BMI merged with the Hardcover Binders International (HBI) and the Library Binding Institute (LBI) (Book Manufactures' Institute n.d.). Most seasoned librarians will be at least slightly familiar with the LBI, which dates back to 1935 and boasts a long tradition of working with librarians in order to establish the standards for prebinding and binding of monographs and periodicals. The work between the LBI and libraries resulted in a certification program developed by the LBI and helped to create the most current library binding standard, ANSI/NISO LBI, Z39.78–2000. Recognizing that changes were taking place in the industry and building upon the fact that its members were evolving to include services beyond the scope of what a typical library required, LBI reorganized in 2008 to include the HBI whose primary focus was on the printing and binding of books. To date the

BMI has grown significantly to include 80 members representing all aspects of the book manufacturing industry, with BMI's member companies publishing more than 85 percent of books in the United States (Book Manufactures' Institute n.d.). Those libraries searching for a reputable binder are encouraged to visit the BMI's website for information on its certification program and to peruse the list of members currently certified with the BMI.

GOING OUT FOR BID

The process for selecting a commercial binder varies depending upon the type of library involved. The procurement method used in the purchase of a new product or service is dictated by the governing structure under which the library operates. Generally, states mandate the process while private institutions have more flexibility. Using a request for information (RFI), request for quotation (RFQ), or request for proposal (RFP) are three of the most common methods. (Wilkinson and Bordeianu 1997).

RFI

The RFI is a valuable tool for libraries that are simply trying to learn what general services a binder offers. Vendors are able to make a sales pitch without investing much in the way of time or resources. Because the RFI process is informal, the library is also not obligated to abide by strict and structured evaluation criteria that would be required with an RFP.

RFQ

The RFQ is also informal and is used to gather general information about the binder that will assist with determining deviations in prices among vendors. Libraries that are bound by price alone commonly use this method because it helps to quickly identify those commercial binders with the lowest pricing structure. The RFQ does not allow for the consideration of other factors, such as service or quality, and therefore, it is recommended that institutions that desire a higher degree of choice in selecting a binder should choose another method.

RFP

The RFP is by far the most formal means of engaging in this process and requires official documentation that outlines in detail the services and products that an institution is looking to acquire. Though costly in staff time, the RFP process is beneficial in that it forces the library undertaking it to perform an in-depth analysis of its actual needs. A high degree of care and examination is recommended during this process so as to best capture the library's priorities within the RFP and so that time is not wasted on describing "pipe dreams" rather than concrete needs. In addition, the RFP can pose challenging questions to the vendors asked to participate and even allows for a library to find solutions to problems dealing with services, workflow, and effectiveness (Breeding 2016).

Questions drafted within the RFP document will be used by vendors to measure their responses and therefore should also be tailored to the library requesting the service. There are many sample drafts of RFP documents available via the Internet, and though it may be tempting to copy and paste, it is not recommended. An added benefit to the RFP process is that it places the relationship between the library and the vendor within an official legal framework, making expectations and responsibilities clear and giving each party a means of enforcing their rights (Wilkinson and Bordeianu 1997).

The RFP process can be time-consuming for staff, but when done well, it can help a library to obtain meaningful information in order to make the best purchase decision. When not done well, the RFP can yield "canned responses brimming with sale-speak" (Breeding 2016, 15). It is important to recognize that both the library undertaking the process and the vendor responding to the RFP have much at stake. Responding to an RFP entails a significant cost in both time and money should the vendor fail to comply with the strict requirements, invalidating their reply. Vendors that perceive their chances of being selected as low may be reluctant to submit a response at all. The library issuing the RFP must carefully monitor all its communication with each vendor in order to avoid the appearance of favoritism that may lead to one vendor challenging the legality of the process (Breeding 2016).

PLANNING YOUR RFP

Prior to drafting the RFP, the library needs to appoint a team to work on the RFP. This team will consist of functional experts from various areas of the library who have knowledge and expertise in collection management, serials, book processing, and binding. In addition, there needs to be a public services voice on the committee. The chair or cochairs of the committee will ensure that all voices are heard and all opinions are considered, and they will be responsible for creating a cohesive and clear RFP document. Unclear documents confuse vendors and create extra unnecessary work for all involved and may discourage vendors from replying to the RFP.

RFP Timeline and Tasks

One of the primary responsibilities of the RFP committee is to develop a timeline that will lay out the specifics for each phase of the process. Some of the tasks of the committee typically will include providing a description of the library and the regulations that govern the procurement process, the value and duration of the contract, a description of any confidential aspects involved, the format preferred for responses, and the evaluation criteria that will be used to weigh vendor responses. An RFP committee should meet with the institution's purchasing officer at the start of the process in order to ascertain the answers to the above. In many instances the purchasing officer will have access to a list of binders with interest in doing business with the institution. As stated previously, it is recommended that a library researching potential binders check whether those on their list are BMI certified. A library may choose to invite the binders to present samples of their work and to give a short presentation. On-site visits, while certainly not mandatory, will allow for both the library and the vendor presenting to ask valuable questions.

WRITING THE RFP

The first important step in ensuring a successful RFP process is to establish the criteria and methodology for evaluating each vendor's proposal. A good plan will include an explanation of how your criteria are weighted, a description of your methodology, an explanation of the selection process, a complete list of the library's conditions, and any requirements for on-site visits or contacts with a vendor's current customers (Breeding 2016). It is during this time that the library can highlight its most important needs, and therefore, the criteria should be crafted with care. The library should make sure to thoroughly explain how responses will be assessed whether using essay-style or open-ended questions. It is generally best to avoid ambiguity, focus on needs rather than wants, and remove the use of all-or-nothing terms such as "must" that are rigid and carry legal ramifications. Generally, the RFP author should try to resist his or her "inner Charlton Heston" (Breeding 2016, 20) by steering clear of statements that sound at all biblical or remind one of the phrase "thou shall not." Above all, the library staff should manage expectations with the understanding that it is very unlikely any vendor will meet 100 percent of the library's needs or wants (Benaud and Bordeianu 1998).

Cover Letter

The RFP may include a cover letter that should be clear and to the point, summarizing the library's priorities and communicating what services will be required of the vendor. The cover letter must include the following:

- A summary describing the library, its parent institution, and the consortium if the contract is for a larger partnership
- Description of the library's current automated system used for binding
- Names and contact information of staff involved in the RFP process and to whom questions may be directed to

- Estimated dollar amount of the contract
- Period of time the contract will cover and the date by which the contract will start
- Any requirements, such as samples of catalogs, that are required of the binder
- Format by which the vendor's response should be submitted
- Criteria by which vendor responses will be evaluated
- Deadline by which vendor responses must be submitted

Specifications

The RFP will generally be subdivided into four areas that should consist of general specifications, binding specifications, manual or computer-based services, and pricing (Wilkinson and Bordeianu 1997). Structure and detail will vary depending upon the type of library. When deciding what to include, the author recommends that a library undertaking the RFP process consult the BMI website to purchase or download a PDF copy of the *Library Binding Standard* developed by the National Information Standards Organization and the LBI.

General Specifications

The general specifications portion of the RFP should contain various points of important information for the vendor. Some general specifications might include a binder's general financial stability, requirement that the binder use the most up-to-date equipment, a quality control program, a full inventory of binder's supplies, insurance and security protocols to protect library materials, guarantees of contract compliance, a responsive customer service program, and invoicing requirements. The library should be very clear as to which of these requests is required, meaning the binder must satisfy the request to be considered for the RFP, and which requests are simply desired. It is also recommended that binders provide at least three references of libraries currently using the binder, which are comparable in size and type to the library requesting the proposal. Furthermore, if the library requires samples from the binder, this should be made clear in the general specifications portion of the document.

Binding Specifications

Binding specifications are generally taken from the LBI standards. More technical specifications may include "examination and collation, spine preparation, leaf attachment, stubbing, endpaper construction and attachment, trimming, cover making, casing-in, lettering, pockets for supplementary materials, and inspections" (Wilkinson and Bordeianu 1997, 40). If overall a binder complies with the LBI standards, a general statement indicating this should be all that is required. Any deviation from the standard, as well as additional statements regarding material specifications, should be communicated in this portion of the RFP document.

Most binding specifications can be applied to libraries across the board. However, there may be some variance in local practices, and these should be noted within the RFP. For example, libraries can vary in their collation requirements, with some libraries choosing to include or remove advertisements from periodicals. For requests that fall outside the scope of the contract, binders can often accommodate them for an additional fee. In order to avoid confusion, the library should devote separate sections of the RFP for different types of binding. This might include a section on monographs, periodicals, paperbacks, and so forth. Any specialized requests—for example, conservation services—should be clearly described within its own section.

Computer-Based Services

In our current market it is fairly common for the library seeking a bindery contract to have an integrated library system (ILS), with many of these systems equipped with a binding module that produces binding slips for periodicals, as well as instructions for binding monographs. Libraries that wish to use their own ILS binding module should make this clear within the RFP document.

Many commercial binders will have their own automated system, and in many instances, use of the binder's system will be an option. Some advantages to using these proprietary systems are ease of use when searching for or adding new titles to the database, complete elimination of binding slips, reduction in errors, and the ability to generate statistical reports. Having the ability to run reports is something that most libraries find very useful as reports can reveal the number of items bound during a specific period, current costs, and projections, and the history for each item sent to the bindery.

Libraries with ILSs that have a dedicated serials or a bindery module may want to request seamless compatibility between the ILS and the binder's system. This would improve productivity and reduce the probability of introducing errors. However, libraries need to be open-minded and not make this a make-or-break proposition, because stand-alone vendor systems may be just as easy to use and provide additional benefits that do not exist in the local ILS. As the market is changing, fewer ILS vendors are developing powerful serials modules with dedicated bindery components, so it may be unrealistic to expect this functionality from all vendors.

Pricing

With library budgets around the country continuing to shrink, the pricing of services remains to be an issue for most administrators. The price of the binding contract will often be a major factor in deciding which vendor to select during the RFP process. With that in mind, the author recommends that a unit price sheet for the binding of all materials, call number application, and freight charges be established. Depending upon the library's needs, the price sheet can include:

- shipping, including rush shipments;
- tattle taping;
- collating;
- cover and spine stamping;
- sewing;
- pockets and stubbing for maps;
- imitation leather;
- special housing; and
- conservation services for special collection items.

EVALUATING RESPONSES AND AWARDING THE RFP

The evaluation of the responses and awarding of the final contract are the most important steps in the RFP process. Selecting the right vendor, one that understands and supports the library, will ensure a good partnership, and in many cases the relationship can last for years. Therefore, the reputation and financial stability of the vendor need to be taken into consideration.

Once all of the RFP responses are received, the library's RFP committee can begin evaluating each vendor. The first step in this process is generally to contact the vendor's references. The RFP committee should have a list of questions developed that will be asked during each conversation with the binder's references. Reponses should be carefully noted and shared with the entire committee regardless of which member makes the call. Depending on the laws or the library's practice, confidentiality during this process is usually expected.

Development of a price sheet that allows for the committee to easily compare each vendor is highly recommended. Using past statistics for each type of material, the library can estimate how much the annual charges will be. The use of this method may help a library in making their final decision, especially so if budget restriction is an issue, as even a small price variation can sometimes make a large difference to the library.

Evaluations of vendor responses are based upon the criteria developed within the RFP document. A percentage value is usually assigned to each section (general requirements, binding requirements, system requirements, and references), but evaluations can be expressed using numerical or non-numerical systems. The author recommends using an evaluation form that can be given to each committee member and that contains an explanation of the point system used in addition to a section for explanation for committee members where they can explain how they assigned the score. Each member of the committee will fill out the forms independently of the group and for each vendor. Once the results have been tabulated and averaged, the committee can begin to discuss the results with the final goal of selecting and recommending a vendor.

Once the committee has made its final recommendation, the library's purchasing office can award the contract. The RFP document and the vendor's responses generally form the bulk of the contract, but additional documentation may be needed and is normally done by the library's purchasing officer. When the RFP is complete, all vendors that submitted a response should be notified of the outcome. This final step helps to ensure future participation of vendors not selected should the library ever require another RFP.

CONCLUSION

Even though the content of library collections is shifting form print to electronic, libraries are still essentially collections of books and journals. Binding is the primary way of preserving print materials, and libraries rely on commercial binders to perform this task. Traditionally binders have made most of their income from binding journals. Libraries were eager to protect their investment in journals by binding as soon as the volumes were complete, in order to prevent losing individual issues that would be difficult to replace. As journal publishing and usage have shifted from print to electronic, the need to bind print journals has become less urgent. Libraries, in order to save money, space, and processing time, increasingly choose to cancel print subscriptions in favor of electronic access, or in the case where they still acquire print, to stop binding if the journal is available online. This shift has affected the financial well-being of commercial binders, as a large source of revenue disappeared. As a result, the industry has seen a lot of consolidation, as many binders went out of business. Another sign that journal binding is becoming less prominent is that the new ILS systems no longer provide serials modules with dedicated claiming and binding functions. In that sense, journal binding is becoming a legacy activity that continues to diminish but will probably never totally disappear.

Binders will continue to be a valuable partner for libraries, especially in the area of conservation and restoration of books. The true expertise, including special equipment and materials, as well as developing the standards for binding, is maintained by the bindery community. What it means is that there is a shift in binding activities from the old, in which journal binding formed a significant portion of the business, to binding books in order to increase their shelf life. For preserving the heavily used monographic materials in a library's collection, this is a great advantage since the budget freed up by the decrease in journal binding can now be spent on monographs. And in this scenario, a good binder is crucial. The RFP process will enable libraries to identify the best qualified binder for their binding needs.

REFERENCES

Benaud, Claire-Lise, and Sever Bordeianu. 1998. *Outsourcing Library Operations in Academic Libraries: An Overview of Issues and Outcomes.* Englewood, CO: Libraries Unlimited.

Book Manufactures' Institute. n.d. "BMI History." Accessed October 9, 2017. https://bomi.memberclicks.net/bmi-history.

Breeding, Marshall, ed. 2016. *Library Technology Buying Strategies.* Chicago: ALA Editions, an imprint of the American Library Association.

Merrill-Oldham, P. 1995. "Bindery Preparation Software: The Electronic Link between a Library and Its Binder." *Technicalities* 15 (12): 4–7.

Thomson, Lawrence S. 1969. "Binding." *The Encyclopedia of Library and Information Science* 2: 486–509.

Wilkinson, Frances C, and Sever Bordeianu. 1997. "In Search of the Perfect Cover: Using the RFP Process to Select a Commercial Binder." *Serials Review* 23 (3): 37–47. doi:10.1080/00987913.1997.10764391.

PART III

Vendor Perspectives and Ethics

14

VENDORS' PERSPECTIVES ON COLLECTIONS RFPS

Justin D. Clarke and Patricia M. Rodgers

INTRODUCTION

Since the first edition of this book, the marketplace has seen several losses and consolidation of vendors, limiting the number of options available to assist libraries in acquiring their content. Librarians are constantly challenged to manage their budgets against the spiraling costs of materials for their collections, and the loss of vendor options caused by the acquisitions/mergers or bankruptcy of companies has not helped. Additional pressure often comes from local purchasing agents to cut costs or prove the libraries are getting the best value for the money they are spending. If the library chooses to issue a request for proposal (RFP) as a way of trying to save their institution's financial resources and/or to substantiate to purchasing departments that costs are in line with the marketplace, one should realize that issuing an RFP can be a complicated, lengthy, and time-consuming process not only to the library but to the vendors as well.

To produce a well-written document takes much time and thought on the library's part. So too does the vendor's response. Meetings at conferences, with sales representatives, or even a small survey sent to vendors with the library's questions might provide the information a library needs. Bids, requests for information (RFIs), and requests for quotations (RFQs) are other options to gather information in a more structured way.

If the library is purely interested in making a decision based on price, they may want to consider having a simple bidding process. This is sometimes referred to as the "office supplies" approach, because the goal is to get a price per unit. However, instead of getting a cost per piece, such as paper clips or pencils, the goal is to get the service charge or charges the vendor would bill for its services. All of the vendors are treated on an equal playing field and service level, but expertise and reputation, among others, do not play into the decision-making process. This is often the preferred method used by purchasing agents, though it needs to be clear that it is the service charge itself that agencies are bidding on, not the cost per subscription. It can be misleading to treat subscriptions as a commodity such as keyboards, given their pricing models are far from transparent and prices range from the negligible into the thousands. It is Kitty Henderson's (EBSCO) opinion that "if the decision is solely based on price, please say so in the opening and do not require responding to . . . pages of questions about [vendor] personnel and services that will have no bearing on the final decision."

When the library's goal is to find out what new, emerging, or even existing services are available from their current vendor(s) and other companies, the RFI is a good way to discover what is available in the market. Vendors are constantly evolving and developing products and service lines to address existing and new challenges presented to libraries in the acquisition of materials. The RFI is a casual yet structured way to survey the market and get detailed responses to questions from multiple vendors. There is no obligation to "award" a vendor with a certain amount of business, and there are no binding contracts as a result.

Another option is to release an RFQ. In this case the library can still not only perform its environmental scan but also request pricing to be included. The detailed service component may or may not be included in the RFQ process, and generally RFQs are not expected to be binding in the same way as an RFP.

An RFP is the most formal approach to soliciting proposals from the vendor community and generally combines a variety of questions concerning services needed as well as financial questions. RFPs frequently employ a point system that is used to evaluate responses with certain factors weighing more heavily depending on the library's needs. It is expected that at the end of the RFP process, a formal contract will be instated with the winner. The resulting contract may or may not be the RFP document itself.

RFPs inherently imply that the library is interested in a full and fair evaluation of the market and what is available to them. Depending on the size and scope of the RFP, an award could result in significant changes for the library and vendors involved. Rick Anderson says, "Resist the temptation simply to create a list of requirements based on the 'wouldn't it be nice if . . .' criterion. If you have no plans to implement, say, online ordering or electronic invoicing, there is no point in insisting that vendors responding to the RFP be able to provide those services" (2004, 22). In fact, the vendors interviewed and queried all agreed that they will often not respond to an RFP if they can't meet the requirements or they think the requirements are written for the incumbent or for a specific vendor.

Please note that no matter whether a library chooses to issue a bid, RFI, RFQ, or RFP, vendors discourage asking for title-by-title quotes for serials subscriptions. Compiling a title-by-title quote is extremely laborious on the vendor side, and in the end the library is focused on the resulting service

charge. All vendors should be charging the publishers' list prices, or prices negotiated by the library or consortium. When multiple vendors are requesting
multiple prices from publishers, this can result in confusion at the publisher's
end and has even interfered with libraries' existing subscriptions and access.
Some publishers only issue quotes to the incumbent vendor, and depending
on which subscription year the vendor is quoting, the library could end up
comparing different data sets. The entire process of compiling a title-by-title
quote is lengthy and complicated, and all vendors ask that for periodical subscriptions, the library focus purely on the services provided and service charge
to cover such work. If the library absolutely insists on a title-by-title quote,
please provide a statement from the library permitting publishers to release to
all agencies the library's prices.

The authors interviewed and surveyed book and serials vendors in order to
garner opinions from the marketplace. Those who were interviewed or submitted comments are:

Kitty Henderson—EBSCO Information Services
Mary Sue Hoyle—EBSCO Information Services
Carol Seiler—EBSCO Information Services
John Elliott—GOBI Library Services and Subscription Services Division/
  EBSCO Information Services
Kim Stewart—Prenax US/Basch Subscriptions
Maria Hatfield—WT Cox Information Services
Deb Knox—WT Cox Information Services

COMMUNICATION AND TIMELINE

Once the library has determined to issue an RFP, a designated contact at the
institution should reach out to the vendors under consideration to alert them
that an RFP will be forthcoming and ask who the correct contact at the vendor
is. Once the process has started, it is important to clearly state to the vendors
what communication is possible and with whom. This is especially important
if the vendor has existing business with the institution and must correspond
directly with the library regarding day-to-day business matters. Also include
the contact for receipt of the RFP response and physical shipping address, if
applicable.

The time granted for responding to an RFP is critical to the vendor. The
response time depends upon the number and type of questions and if a priced
title list is required. Kitty Henderson said, "As a rule of thumb, at least 45 to
60 days." John Elliott from YBP says for a book RFP, "a very minimum of
two weeks should be provided to allow the vendor to gather all the appropriate information to complete the RFP. Three to four weeks seems more typical,
particularly for large RFPs, and this allows the vendor to ensure they have
provided the best information in their answers to the questions on the RFP."

All vendors agreed that a minimum of six weeks is desired for responding with a period of two weeks at the beginning to ask questions. The library must be responsive with answers to the questions, as this could also result in time lost. Often the answer to questions asked by vendors could result in whether the vendor responds or not, so the vendor might not actually be working on the response until all questions are answered. Ideally the library will respond to questions as they are received rather than holding answers until the end of the allotted time period. The vendor generally has multiple people working on the RFP response and needs to coordinate the process of responding internally. Some responses require customization whereas others do not, so vendors need to coordinate internal communication with sales managers, customer service managers, and senior management to get the best response for the library. Just as it takes the library time to compile the RFP document, it takes time on the vendor side to organize appropriate responses for each institution.

If the RFP includes on-site presentations, this should be made clear when the RFP is released. There is no consensus among vendors whether presentations should be made before issuing the RFP or after the written response has been submitted, and arguments can be made for the value of each. Deb Knox from WT Cox Information Services says, "Vendors could better negotiate with librarians if an opportunity to present services BEFORE [the] RFP process was given. Often the questions are vague and we find ourselves coming up short because we don't answer the question correctly." Other vendors see the benefit of a presentation after the response has been submitted, so the library can clarify any responses and possibly view a vendor demo of their system, if needed. Whether the library chooses to have a pre- or postmeeting, specific questions should be provided to the vendors a week prior to the scheduled presentation. Generally, it is recommended to allow two to three hours for the presentation. Rick Anderson states, "Insofar as it is possible, you should limit your invitations to those vendors whom you are considering seriously" (2004, 23). Also remember that on-site presentations are costly to vendors in terms of travel, housing, and staff time. Anderson continues, "They will spend quite a bit of time preparing their presentation, and will bring handouts and other materials for distribution. To ask a vendor to do this kind of effort when you have already decided against giving that vendor your business is far worse for the vendor than simply having its RFP rejected early on" (2004, 23). If the library is not truly interested in hearing vendor presentations, please avoid requiring them and follow industry expectations as outlined previously.

For RFPs related to subscriptions, the committee should aim to have an award made no later than June for January start dates. For some state institutions, the legislature or institutional board may need to review and sign off on the contract, adding additional time before the award can be formalized. If the award is given to multiple vendors, the work is compounded and timing must be budgeted accordingly. The library should also build in time for transition meetings and planning, possible training by vendor representatives and data uploads into vendor and library systems.

THE RFP DOCUMENT

The RFP should contain these core components: Purpose, Communication, Timeline, Services Required, Evaluation Process, Award, and Follow-Up. This chapter aims to offer guidance on these steps as well as the vendor's perspective thereof.

As a guiding principle, the RFP document itself should be as brief and concise as possible. Begin with a simple introduction stating the purpose and intent of the RFP. The terms and conditions should be clearly stated and delineate those that are required versus those that are only desirable. For RFPs related to collections, the focus of the RFP should be the services required for the library to acquire and maintain content. The length of the resulting contract is also critical, along with any possibilities for any annual renewals thereafter. Vendors can be skeptical of locking in terms longer than five years, given the unpredictability of the market. The document should also clearly state if the award is expected to be made to a single entity, or the possibility of being awarded to more than one vendor. An overview of the library and institution is helpful, but details unrelated to the library market should be excluded. Vendors are keen to know about full-time equivalent (FTE) counts, site definitions, consortial memberships, and affiliated institutions. If the intent is to include other institutions within the state or sister institutions, please state so up front. A full summary of the expected annual expenditure should also be listed as this helps the vendors see the full financial intent of the proposal.

As mentioned earlier, a clear and generous timeline is crucial for vendors to be able to provide professional and customized responses to libraries. This timeline should be stated in the RFP along with as many fixed dates as possible, allowing vendors to better plan and coordinate in-house efforts to issue responses. It is agreed among vendors that an inadequate timeline to respond to an RFP is a top reason for not responding. Vendors do agree that six weeks is a reasonable minimum to allow for written responses to be submitted. Presentations would be held outside of this window. Any extensions to the timeline need to be communicated as quickly as possible to all vendors notified of the initial proposal. When developing the timeline, please be cognizant of industry conferences and conflicts that might preclude the vendor community from adhering to deadlines. The best time of the year for subscriptions vendors to receive and respond to RFPs is the spring before the renewal season begins.

The format of the RFP document and requested response can greatly contribute to or hinder the ease of submitting the response. John Elliott from YBP says:

> The format of the RFP document itself can sometimes pose challenges for both vendors completing the document as well as librarians reading and evaluating the response. Even though the RFP document format may be prescribed by a Purchasing Department, it is important that the format itself not contribute to a lack of clarity in the questions themselves and/or the evaluation of the answers provided.

In general, vendors prefer to see an RFP issued as a Word document in which responses can be inserted where they make the most sense. The vendors feel this may help the evaluation process because the responses align with the questions. Furthermore, responses are in a format that is easier to include in the resulting contract if it is one document. There should be clear instructions on how to format the response, such as one document or two separate ones: technical response and financial offer. Instructions for packaging and shipping the response should also be clearly stated: shipped in one package or packaged and shipped separately?

The RFP document should include all requirements for submitting the proposal itself. Multiple paper copies are discouraged as they are expensive in terms of materials and shipping. If electronic copies are submitted by e-mail, confirmation of receipt is preferred, as well as confirmation that files are able to be opened. Some RFP responses, particularly if in PDF format, can result in extremely large file sizes, and vendors should be made aware if the institution didn't receive a message due to e-mail size limits, or another reason.

A recent trend is the use of RFP software to submit a response to a proposal. These software products seem to be made for commodities rather than services and frequently hinder the ability of a vendor to answer complex questions about workflows and services rendered, among others. Data fields are often limited in the amount of text that can be entered, so questions requiring extensive responses cannot be adequately entered. There are sometimes only yes/no options for questions that require narrative responses or additional clarification. Pricing can also be difficult when using such software, as vendors are not quoting a price per piece, but for periodical subscriptions, service charges that may apply to the entire title list, or a portion. Knowing any limitations to data fields ahead of time is helpful to vendors for formulating responses quickly.

SERVICES REQUIRED

The Services Required section of the RFP, sometimes called the Scope of Work, is the portion of the RFP used by the library to outline their needs and expectations. This is also the best place for the vendor to supply a detailed written explanation of services provided to meet the library's requirements. The library should take the opportunity to phrase questions that meet their specific needs in order to determine which vendor will be the best fit. Deb Knox (WT Cox) warns not to "include specifications that are written for just one vendor, typically the incumbent. Librarians and purchasing staff should know that other vendors cannot provide specific services proprietary to the vendor. The other common mistake is asking for services that you truly do not require."

It is very important to clearly define the library's requirements versus what are only desirables. A vendor may choose not to respond to an RFP if the desirables seem to be requirements and the vendor cannot fulfill all requirements. Another reason not to respond is if it looks like a proposal is written for a specific vendor based on the requirements. The vendors were unanimous in this. Keep in mind if the vendor is agreeing to all requirements, their pricing has to cover all of these services. The result is that the library could end up with a higher price quote because the vendor interpreted that the library wants everything and has included everything in their cost proposal.

Another concern from the vendor's perspective is receiving an RFP document that is simply a boilerplate or exact copy used by another institution, which contains expectations that are not really requirements of the issuing library. The vendors receive enough RFPs to recognize these types of documents, and the result is that the vendor may not consider it a serious request or will only be able to return boilerplate responses. Vendors want to respond to the library's specific requirements and propose solutions to meet their current needs.

The library should be careful to avoid unrealistic requirements or stating that the vendor must "guarantee" something out of the vendor's control. For example, when subscriptions are drop-shipped to the library by the publisher, a vendor cannot guarantee 100 percent delivery rate for all issues of all titles, or that 12 months of uninterrupted access to online content will be provided. The library could instead consider services that would fulfill such requirements, such as a consolidation service that could then be included as a requirement.

The vendors unanimously and strongly encourage a consistent voice throughout the entire RFP document. Some RFPs arrive that are clearly comprised of multiple contributions by different people with different perspectives and wishes. This can lead to a confusing and sometimes even conflicting final document if not edited and harmonized across the entire RFP document. Requirements should be stated once and not reworded and included in other parts of the document, thus making the document and response excessively long. It is not the goal of the RFP process to have to read the same answer from the vendor over and over again. Before issuing the final document, the vendors suggest carefully double-checking that numbering is complete and chronological, everything referenced elsewhere in the document is in the proper place, and that appendices and attachments are sequentially listed as well as actually included. Nicole Waller explains that "although several staff members will contribute to the contents of the RFP, the library's purchase team should appoint one person to write the first draft and final document. Working with a lone writer ensures that the staff's varying specifications will be translated into a consistent format and language throughout the document" (2003, 31).

FINANCIAL OFFER

The resulting financial offer of an RFP for subscription services should be the service charge to cover the services outlined in the Services Required. As referenced earlier, asking for and trying to compare priced title lists for subscriptions can result in comparing apples to oranges. Mark Kendall says, "Full service vendors prefer to have the opportunity to be evaluated on their ability to offer solutions and services that address the library's needs rather than to be evaluated primarily on price" (2002, 83). The individual subscription prices are set by the publishers as list prices or prices negotiated by the library or purchasing groups, and will be the same for all vendors. Kitty Henderson suggests, "Instead, ask to break out all costs and fees associated with ordering from the vendor." If the library must have a title-by-title quote, please submit a letter of permission, which the vendor can submit to the publisher along with the price request. There is a large corpus of titles that require negotiated prices by publishers. Requesting price quotes from multiple vendors frequently raises questions at the publisher, which can result in confusion as well as adding significant time to the entire response process. Maria Lopes from Springer Nature notes, "One has to make sure the pricing and model being quoted is correct, that title lists do not differ between agents and that the information being used for the quote is checked and double checked for accuracy. A full understanding of the RFP and the process is necessary to make sure both the agent and the end customer do get the most transparent and customized quote."

It is, however, important to provide a complete title list along with the RFP document for evaluation purposes. The list should be submitted in Excel format and include title, ISSN, publisher, and format. Along with the list, information about FTE counts, IP ranges, and site definitions are important in evaluating service charge(s) for periodical subscriptions.

The most important criteria that go into establishing a service charge for managing subscriptions are mix of titles and services required. A clean title list in Excel allows the vendor to analyze the title list and establish what the average subscription price is, operational costs needed to supply service, and average publisher commission. All of these factors go into establishing a service charge that will cover operational costs while allowing reasonable and fair profits to maintain healthy financial viability in the market. Most vendors are willing to offer an average service charge across all titles, recognizing that some higher priced titles will subsidize lower cost titles with low average publisher commission. If the RFP includes multiple libraries and would like individual quotes per list, please state so in the financial requirements section.

An overall description of the annual dollar spend, which will be the award from the RFP, is also encouraged. It is also extremely helpful if the library can parse out large package deals and describe them separately in terms of annual spend, publisher name, and if the negotiation is through a consortium. Any major upcoming cancelations or renegotiations are also helpful in determining the financial offer.

Vendors find it challenging to make good faith pricing offers if the final outcome or award terms are not clearly defined. Volume alone is not a factor in determining a lower service charge. For example, extending contracts to the entire state or university system leaves the vendor vulnerable to applying pricing not applicable to a stated subscription list. These situations usually result in the vendor offering a price range from which they could make an offer if a title list is presented in the future. If the goal is for a large group purchase without all title lists presented, perhaps an RFP for an approved vendor list would be more applicable. Likewise, when the RFP states that the award could be made to multiple vendors, it is not clear what the final mix of titles will be that is placed with the vendor, and consequently impossible to price.

EVALUATION PROCESS

Perhaps the most critical stage of issuing an RFP is evaluating the vendor responses. A carefully crafted RFP should allow the committee to compare vendor responses in a fair and organized way. It is useful for vendors to know when the RFP is issued what point system or evaluation criteria will be used in determining the award. It is likely that several factors will go into the evaluation process, including the written response, references, vendor's online system, company's financial viability, offer, and on-site presentation. The result should be an award offered to the vendor that not only fulfills all the requirements but is also the best fit for the institution. This will ensure a good future working relationship and ultimate partnership between vendor and library for the life of the contract.

AWARD AND FOLLOW-UP

If the award cannot be announced by the original date in the RFP proposed timeline, a courtesy message should be provided to all vendors who responded with a revised award date. Once the RFP has been officially awarded, all participating vendors should be alerted of the results. Vendors appreciate an opportunity to receive feedback should they not be awarded a contract. Kendall says, "While the end result invariably leaves some vendors disappointed, if they are provided notification that they are not selected, with some explanation as to the factor(s) that led to the selection of another vendor, they at least gain a better understanding of where they might have fallen short and how they can be more competitive in future RFP response situations" (2002, 83). Rick Anderson says, "Do the same for the winning vendor, making it clear that you expect the promises it made to be fulfilled, and that you will be monitoring the vendor's performance carefully to see that they are" (2004, 25).

BEST PRACTICES

The mark of a model document should include the following best practices:

- Clear, concise narrative
- Explicit requirements for the issuing institution
- Title list included in Excel format
- Annual spend of Big Deal packages if applicable
- No title-by-title quotes
- Adequate time for response and implementation
- Timely responses to vendor questions
- Clear evaluation criteria
- Make sure RFP is right tool versus bid, RFI, or RFQ
- State what is required versus what is desired
- Friendly formatting
- Presentations preferred
- Understanding complexity of pricing

REASONS FOR NOT RESPONDING

The vendors interviewed and comments gathered from the literature suggest that the following are one or more reasons their company would not respond to an RFQ, RFI, or RFP.

- Services fall outside scope of what vendor provides
- Inadequate time to respond
- Poorly written, confusing, or redundant document
- Unrealistic expectations
- Title list not provided
- Uneven playing field/slanted toward single vendor; biased
- RFP solely based on price
- Total expenditures
- Previous experiences with library
- Contract is only for one year or longer than five

CONCLUSION

The RFP process can be stressful and time-consuming for all parties: library, vendors, and publishers. Writing, responding to, and evaluating a detailed document of services required for managing subscriptions, in particular, is an investment of time and resources for everyone. The ultimate goal is not only to determine the vendor that will provide the best suite of services at an appropriate price but also to forge a lasting and mutually beneficial working relationship. A clear description of services needed, as well as an awareness of vendor margins and capabilities, will ensure a smooth start to any library–vendor partnership.

Kitty Henderson says that "going into the discussion with a win-win attitude, with the objective to meet in the middle" sets the tone for a successful RFP process. The library learns more about the marketplace and the vendor's capabilities, while the vendor understands the library's workflow and its service requirements. Henderson goes on to say that the process requires "mutual respect and trust. Ours is a symbiotic relationship, a partnership. The vendor provides the services the library needs to in turn provide services to library users. In return for these services, the vendor receives compensation." Treating the RFP process as the first step in a business relationship that could last for years will ensure a successful process, outcome, and delivery of services agreed upon.

REFERENCES

Anderson, Rick. 2004. *Buying and Contracting for Resources and Services: A How-to-Do-It Manual for Librarians*. New York: Neal-Schuman Publishers.

Kendall, Mark. 2002. "Issues in Vendor/Library Relations—The RFP Process . . . A Book Vendor's Musings." *Against the Grain* 14 (6).

Waller, Nicole. 2003, July/August. "Model RFP for Integrated Library Systems Products." *Library Technology Reports* 39 (4).

15

THE LIBRARIAN–VENDOR RELATIONSHIP

Stephen Bosch

"Vendor" is a general, all-inclusive term used to refer to another party, outside the library, from whom library materials or services are purchased. Distinctions are made between vendors based on the range of products and services they make available to libraries. Most vendors focus on content such as books, serials, and databases; services including software or library service platforms; or supplies, shelving, binding, and barcodes among others. Some large vendors provide a wide variety of goods and services from all of the categories mentioned here. Librarians may draw distinctions between vendors and publishers, but since digital distribution of content has blurred that line, for this discussion they are interchangeable. If the provider is selling directly to libraries, they are considered a vendor.

WHY SHOULD A RELATIONSHIP EXIST IN THE FIRST PLACE?

A basic driver of these relationships is simply libraries need the goods and services that are provided by vendors in order to support the services and content they provide patrons. Vendors need the revenues from these sales to continue in business. This mix of nonprofit libraries with profit-making suppliers may seem like a bad match, but there is the common goal of providing quality information services to users that bonds the two together. The library–vendor relationship is a very important investment on both sides and does require effort and nurturing to be successful.

One critical aspect of this relationship is the provision of many to one and one to many relationships by vendors. This allows for the creation of economies of scale that support cost efficiencies in the supply chain. It is far cheaper for a vendor to take products from multiple producers and supply these to multiple libraries than it would be for the producers to build the infrastructure to supply their products directly to libraries. Never underestimate the cost of building this infrastructure. With the shift to digital, many small producers simply do not have the resources to build systems that can deliver metadata, invoicing, and other products across the myriad platforms present in libraries. Their customer base is not large enough to support the costs. A vendor can spread these development costs among more customers enabling them to provide these services at a manageable cost. Large publishers do have the resources necessary to develop some of this infrastructure, and this enables them to market directly to libraries.

For most libraries, the many to one relationship is especially true when using vendors to purchase serials. Libraries subscribe to thousands of periodical titles, and managing subscriptions on a title-by-title basis is not feasible. Serial vendors traditionally have performed well on both sides of aggregating many publishers' business for a library and, conversely, many libraries for a publisher. Libraries use subscription agents to save staff time and combine the important functions related to subscriptions, including the placement of new orders, payment of invoices and billing, and maintaining records of what was bought and when it was bought. In the world of electronic journals, verifying access rights based on the purchase history as journals move from package to package has supplanted claiming as important work provided by vendors. By using a serials vendor for their subscriptions, librarians can turn to the vendor when problems arise. It is also important for the library to remember that a vendor, in this case a third party and not the actual publisher/supplier, cannot remedy certain problems that arise. In the one to many and many to one relationship, the problem may track back to original supplier, and in that case the vendor can act as your agent, but the final resolution depends on the original supplier.

COMMUNICATIONS ARE ESSENTIAL TO RELATIONSHIPS

Communications are extremely important in the relationship between a library and a vendor. This is especially true in the request for proposal (RFP) or request for information (RFI) process. Communication is a complex process and is far more than a simple activity. An activity, like talking, e-mailing, or other social media, can occur without a true exchange of information. Good relationships are dependent on good communications, and good communications are based on an exchange of true information. A vendor is not going to be able to provide the goods and services that will enable a library to provide high-quality content and services to their patrons if the library does not clearly articulate their needs and desires to the vendor. This starts from libraries freely sharing their identified needs as well as results from performance assessments and improvement suggestions with vendors. This includes any direct feedback that libraries receive from their patrons, both the good and the bad. This exchange of information may result in specific improvements in products and services that could lead to improvements in the ability for libraries to meet their patrons' needs. In addition, if there is a problem or issue with a vendor's services, vendors will want to know about it so it can be resolved. Vendors cannot fix what they do not know about. Libraries also need to be able to articulate clearly their vision and plans for the future so that the vendor can determine how their company can help the library achieve their goals.

Good communications are a two-way street and apply equally to vendors and their ability to communicate clearly with libraries. Again, true communication is needed, not simply meeting and talking up the company story and giving the standard sales pitch for current products. Most libraries are very different from other libraries, and these differences do matter. Vendors need to understand the needs of the libraries they serve and have a good understanding of how the vendor's offerings can help the library achieve their mission. In addition, vendors need to be able to communicate their company's strategies and goals and how these could align with the library's strategies. Vendors need to do their homework and learn about their libraries. This includes asking questions to determine library needs and, most important, listening to the answers. Librarians generally do not respond well to straight on sales pitches. Good communications help build trusting relationships with libraries, and by promoting only those goods and services that are a good fit with the library's needs, a vendor can avoid wasting their time and the customer's time.

The RFP/RFI process is essentially a complex exercise of communication and exchange of information. The quality of the process directly correlates with the quality of the information exchange. Outcomes, even for vendors that are not selected, can have a major impact on future relationships. Libraries should consider the RFP as a marketing tool since vendors will remember good RFPs and that will raise the stock of the library and that creates a foundation for future relations. Poorly written RFPs will have the opposite effect. Same for vendors, a good response, even if not selected, creates an opportunity for building future relationships, and a poor response on the RFP will make future relationships more difficult.

The ability of the vendor and library to communicate with each other is a vital aspect of the relationship. Communication is a key component to the service relationship between a library and a vendor. It is important to establish clear expectations of the roles of the library and the vendor. Each party must communicate effectively with the other in order for everything to operate efficiently. Vendors need to have multiple options available for customer service with knowledgeable personnel available, and likewise libraries need to have staff who can easily work with vendors so that transactions can be successfully completed.

HONESTY IS THE BEST POLICY

Honesty is extremely important in building good library–vendor relations. If there is not an honest exchange of information, it will be difficult to establish good working relationships. It is far better to disappoint with an honest answer than it is to be caught in a lie. If an invoice was misplaced and was not paid, it is better to let the vendor know that the invoice has been received and is being expedited for payment as opposed to bluffing with the standard statement, "The check is in the mail." If it is unlikely that a current offering will result in a sale, it is better to let the vendor know that is the situation. Do not lead them on. Disappointing the vendor with the negative news early in a process saves everyone time and effort. The vendor will not continue to try to sell you something you do not want, and you will not have to hear pitches for something that the library staff are not interested in. Explain the reasons for this decision. It may be simply that there are no funds available, or the product may not be a good fit for the library. Clear, honest information about why a product will not be bought can help the vendor improve the product. The vendor may learn that the content is not a good fit for the targeted market segment. Was the price point not in line with the perceived value? Are there technical issues? Clear, honest feedback may seem negative in the short term but in the long term can have benefits for both vendors and libraries.

Vendors also need to be open and honest with libraries. The information marketplace in which vendors and librarians work is tightly woven. Librarians get information from many sources including vendors, peers in the industry, listservs, and blogs, among others. Word gets around. Again, it should be stressed that it is far better to disappoint with an honest answer than it is to be caught in a lie. If a software upgrade went wrong, be clear about the problem, and discuss the corrective measures that will fix the problems. Trying to sugarcoat the situation will only hurt the trust customers have with vendors. In some situations, the spin on problems comes from high up in a company, but a good field representative will know that after delivering the official stand, it is best to be honest with the customer. In the long run, it is easier to maintain a trust relationship than it is to repair one damaged by a lack of honesty. Also, the rep may be working with another company at some point in the future, and they will want to maintain a good relationship, which, again, is supported by honest dealings.

BUILDING MUTUAL SELF-INTEREST IS IMPORTANT FOR RELATIONSHIPS

Library–vendor relationships exist in order to advance their mutual self-interests, and these relationships grow from a foundation of mutually beneficial goals. The strength of relationships between libraries and vendors depends on how successful each party is at aligning these goals with each other. A basic factor for good library–vendor relationships is the development of clarity concerning what each part of the relationship is bringing to the table as well as what each gains from the relationship. Mutual self-interest can be a powerful motivator. Each participant should develop a good understanding of what is desired from the relationship; this starts with defining the basic needs as well as goals. Financial considerations are important, but other less tangible aspects like service, development plans, and organizational culture can be equally important.

The library needs to outline exactly what is required from the vendor. Depending on what the RFP concerns or any other aspect of the relationship, this could be a large variety of items. Not all products and services are equal in importance across the different parts of a library. Decisions concerning what is most important need to be discussed with those parts of the organization that could be impacted by the service or product. Horizontal and vertical communication must occur to ensure all stakeholders are part of decisions. Decisions should focus on the core vendor products that meet the identified needs. The core services required by a library may be hard to isolate from the overall suite of packaged services readily available from vendors, but it is important for libraries to define their core needs.

When communicating needs, be realistic. Understand the difference between desired products and services versus those that are needed. Asking a vendor to supply anything and everything leads to unrealistic expectations, and, bottom line, the more services requested, the higher the costs. Avoid creating unnecessary work, both for the library and for the vendor, and clearly outline those products and services that are truly required to meet the current and future needs.

In addition, the library needs to communicate clearly information about how their organization operates, the corporate culture, the decision-making process, tolerance for risk, as well as the current vision that drives the library's mission. Vendors should also clearly communicate this type of information. Aligning these types of intangibles will allow for the development of mutual self-interest as each part of the relationship pursues their stated goals, but there is alignment and synergy in those goals. If a library has a conservative organization and is risk adverse, a vendor may not want to try to sell them out of the box products and services. If a library wants to develop new ways of providing services to users, they probably do not want to try to convince a more conservative, risk-adverse vendor to collaborate with them on the development. If the corporate cultures are not in alignment, building a solid relationship becomes more difficult.

ASSESSMENT: YOU DO WHAT IS MEASURED

Vendor-supplied products and services help shape the future of the library. These relationships are very important investments on both sides and require effort to be successful. Vendor evaluation is an important part of this process, as assessments will indicate the resources needed to strengthen and improve the relationship. Evaluations help librarians make objective judgments about vendors' ability to meet their needs in supplying resources and services accurately, economically, and efficiently. The evaluation process can be simple or quite extensive depending on the amount of business involved and the drivers for the assessment. An RFP is essentially an extensive vendor assessment, but that type of evaluation is not required in all situations. Keeping a simple e-mail log of interactions and reviewing the log to see if there are problems surfacing or recurring themes may be sufficient in many situations. Use common sense in developing evaluation tools. It is possible to spend a good deal of time and resources on assessments, so be sure to match outcomes to effort. Unless there is an RFP/RFI process in place, formal evaluations are needed only when problems are identified, and a study that is more rigorous is needed to provide data about the problem. Because procedures and service needs vary widely from library to library, exercise caution in sharing results of vendor assessments with colleagues or in accepting the results of others' assessments as appropriate for one's own library.

A well-conducted evaluation can be useful both for compiling information and as a communication tool between library and vendor. Because a vendor's performance can change over time, it is important to let a vendor know if there are problems and to allow sufficient time for improvement. At the core of the evaluation lie the products and services supplied by vendors to a library. A good starting point for evaluations is determining if there are defined performance standards and if those standards are being met. Performance standards may have been established by an RFP or license. If there are defined standards, that should be the core of the evaluation.

When looking at serial vendor assessment, an important consideration would be the mix of serials subscriptions handled by the vendor. This is of major significance in determining a vendor's performance. A serials vendor should have no trouble servicing a list of titles from large commercial publishers whose discounts and responsiveness would allow that vendor to offer a library account prompt delivery and competitive pricing. Most of that content is probably electronic, so costs are lower. On the other hand, if a library has gone direct or through a consortium for content from the large publishers, this will impact the library's title list. If the list that goes to a serials vendor is from obscure publishers that have irregular publication schedules and small or no available discounts, by nature of that list, a vendor would have more fulfillment issues and would have to assess higher charges to cover its costs of obtaining such material, if, indeed, the material was ever obtained.

Many of the business relations established between vendors and libraries are determined by a contract or a memorandum of understanding (MOU). These may have been generated through an RFP or similar process. Services and products like approval plans/demand-driven acquisitions (DDA) plans, serials management, integrated library systems, outsourcing, and document delivery could be governed by various forms of purchase agreements or contracts. These may be less formal letters of agreement or very formal contracts depending on the needs of the transactions and the local business rules. If an

RFP is used as the acquisition process, a good rule to follow is to be sure to use the RFP as the basis for a contract that outlines expected performance of the vendor.

COMMON TOOLS USED TO FOSTER RELATIONSHIPS

Vendor Representatives, Staffing

Library–vendor interactions occur most frequently on the front lines. It is critical that staff on both sides of the relationship are well trained and knowledgeable. Taking care that the first lines of communication are working well will go a long way in creating a solid relationship. In this area, perceptions are important. When questions are posed about performance, the last thing that went wrong tends to be what is remembered, not what went right. There are many important considerations for both libraries and vendors. Staff must be helpful. They may not be able to solve a problem themselves, but they should be sure that a process is in place with someone to get the issue resolved. Training is an important factor for good service in both libraries and vendors. Response time is another important factor. The lack of a response in a timely manner reflects poorly on an organization. Even a simple acknowledgment that the message was received is important. It will forestall future inquiries trying to determine if the message got through.

Vendor representatives are also important in fostering good relationships. It is important for representatives in the field to get to know their accounts. Libraries will have different needs, and reps should tailor their interactions based on those needs. Library visits may not result in sales but can still be productive if the budget situation or library priorities are clarified. A good vendor rep will ensure that the library is served well and does not perceive the library merely as a source for making a quarterly sales target.

Communications Ladders

Vendors and libraries should provide a list of names in escalating order of importance that enables interactions to be targeted to appropriate levels. As problems or issues become more complex or pressing, each party will know whom to contact in succession. There is nothing more frustrating than not being able to identify and communicate with the appropriate level of staff. Use of such a communications ladder can reduce the occurrence of complaints as both the library and the vendor can target messages to the appropriate people.

Advisory Boards

Creating library advisory boards is another tool for communication between vendors and libraries. Advisory boards promote communication that is more general and do not address the relationship between specific libraries and vendors. These boards consist of librarians identified by the vendor as being able to provide quality feedback. Advisory boards provide advice, guidance, and insight on initiatives being considered by a vendor. Boards can also provide input on a vendor's policies as well as overall approach to business. Some vendors have established multiple boards to cover different products/areas. Some vendors just use a single board, and they work at a high level. By the nature of their work, board members have access to information that may be confidential. In some cases, nondisclosure agreements may be in place to protect a vendor's confidential information. Advisory boards provide the initial sounding boards for new ideas, and these boards communicate with vendors through multiple channels that include face-to-face meetings, video conferences, e-mail, and conference calls.

E-mail Applications

E-mail is a very powerful tool in library–vendor communications and helps develop good relationships, but e-mail can also have a negative impact on relationships. E-mail is now used to communicate new product announcements, stay in touch with customers, conduct surveys, as well as practically anything else that comes to mind. E-mail also supports the development of communities of interest (listservs) and vendor-supported groups that can act like quasi-advisory boards. A well-crafted and thoughtful e-mail message sent to its proper audience can be a very effective communications tool. If soliciting feedback or a survey response, again it can be a very good tool. A downside does exist; a poorly done e-mail and e-mails to the wrong groups will generate negative responses. Negative e-mails on listservs also must be monitored and responded to quickly. Vendor bashing on listservs is all too common. If legitimate issues are raised, it is appropriate to bring those issues to light. However, it is best to be careful and be sure of data before sending information out to listservs as often the molehill turns into a mountain. Thus, e-mail can be a powerful tool, but it is a double-edged sword.

FINANCIAL STABILITY

Quantitative analysis can and should be used to analyze company date in order to determine their financial health. The financial health of a vendor should be an important consideration when building relationships. There have been too many situations where failure to do this analysis has been very detrimental to libraries and the industry as a whole. Normally, the financial health of small, external vendors is not a huge concern for libraries. However, for those vendors that are prepaid by libraries or those vendors that libraries do considerable business with and have customized their processes to align with, the financial health of the company is of critical importance. The financial collapse of large serials vendors and the difficulty that many libraries had recouping funds after the bankruptcies are good examples of why libraries need to be aware of the financial strength of the companies they are working with. The main areas used to examine financial stability include bond and credit rating, valuation, sales, earnings growth trends, and overall financial strength. These considerations apply mostly to publicly held companies. Privately owned corporations are a different matter, and, normally, the same depth of financial data is harder to obtain. For companies that are publicly held, the value of a company is usually established through the price-to-earnings ratio. Another quantitative measure is the price-to-earnings growth (PEG) ratio, which compares the current fiscal-year price earnings (P/E) ratio to the long-term growth rate. Debt is not necessarily a negative factor, but it is important to watch a company's debt very carefully. These ratios compare total liabilities, debt, to the total equity, debt and book value equity. A ratio of below 1.0 means that there are more debts than assets available to cover them. Too much debt can cause a company's credit rating to drop. This makes the cost of borrowing funds higher. Libraries can use this information to compare a vendor's financial stability with other vendors in the library industry. Many suppliers and publishers are privately held businesses, and the best way to determine financial stability is to ask for a statement. Normally, privately held companies can produce statements from banks and bonding agencies that will attest to the companies' credit worthiness. If large prepayment deposits are made, it is good practice to ask for financial statements before sending a check.

CONCLUSION

Library–vendor relationships are a key component of the information marketplace. Libraries need the goods and services provided by vendors in order to support the services and content provided to library patrons. Library vendors are in business to sell these goods and services to libraries in order to generate the revenue that helps them maintain their business and develop new products for the industry. The common goal of providing quality information services to users links nonprofit libraries with profit-making suppliers and bonds the two together. The library–vendor relationship is an important investment and requires effort and nurturing to be successful. Communication, honesty, creating mutual self-interest, and assessment are important to the development of quality library–vendor relationships.

16

VENDORS' PERSPECTIVES ON LIBRARY SYSTEM RFPS

Andrew K. Pace

Let's start with a not-so-radical notion. No one loves an RFP. They are hard to write. They are hard to answer. They are hard to analyze and judge. For the winner, the RFP represents a necessary rite of passage—a painstaking process that allows one vendor to nose out the competition and take home the library's business. For the loser, the RFP reminds its authors of a grueling process in a race whose loss now seems predestined. While any library that has created an RFP can tell you about the hours and hours spent in preparation, analysis, and judgment, little attention is given to the vendor or service provider and their own investment in the process. Libraries likely think of this as the "cost of doing business" for vendors, but it's important to make the syllogistic step of determining who pays those costs in the long run.

What follows will be a mixture of candor and seeming truisms regarding RFPs from someone who has been on both sides of the process. No one person can speak for all vendors or all libraries, so the greater the bluntness, the more caution the reader should take in applying it in all situations. There is a lot of room for improvement in the library RFP process, especially as it pertains to an integrated library system (ILS) (if such a thing even still exists!). Even the smallest changes can have tremendous impact for both the writer and the responder.

WHITHER THE ILS

First things first. The ILS isn't what it used to be. Or more precisely, if a library is considering an RFP for what is now most definitely a legacy system, that library should think again. There is no sense trading in a 2005 Honda Accord for a 2006 Toyota Camry. Well-known library systems consultant, Marshall Breeding, has dubbed the next generation of systems as the "Library Service Platform" (LSP) and has already written extensively about this technological sea change in *Smart Libraries Newsletter* and *American Libraries*. While it might not be the perfect name, its importance is in differentiating next-generation platform services from their predecessors, the ILS, the electronic resource management system, and the digital access management system. Think of it this way: the LSP is to the ILS as the very first ILS was to the card catalog. In both cases, the former replaces the latter but is a completely different beast.

This is not simply marketing copy from someone who spent five years building and launching the first-to-market LSP. There are distinct differences between an ILS and an LSP that libraries should consider when creating an RFP. Moreover, those distinctions have a significant impact on a vendor's ability to accurately answer RFP questions. If the questions describe a legacy system when the offering is an LSP, the vendor spends cycles trying to force a square peg through a round hole at the risk of being noncompliant to the requirements as stated.

Breeding has spent a lot of energy documenting the characteristics of an LSP, but they are worth summarizing here because, as he notes, the LSP "describes a set of products that each embody a somewhat different set of conceptual, technical, and functional characteristics."[1] Libraries need to stay mindful of the differences between what they are shopping for and the wares that are currently on the market. If a library is tempted to use its last RFP and it was written before 2011, they should throw it away. It is most likely not a useful template for the following characteristics:

- Management of both print and electronic materials
- Extensive and expanded metadata management: MARC, Dublin Core, and emerging standards
- Multiple procurement workflows for purchased, licensed, and open-access materials
- A robust knowledge base of electronic resources
- Built-in collection analytics
- Next-gen discovery services
- Replacement for disparate library management system platforms

Moreover, technically, libraries can expect a multitenant, cloud-hosted, web-based suite of services. Wikipedia defines "multitenancy" as a software architecture in which a single instance of software runs on a server and serves multiple tenants. A tenant is a group of users who share a common access with specific privileges to the software instance. This is a far cry from the days of the client-server architecture and locally deployed (and isolated) relational database management system (RDBMS) that dominated the ILS market from the late 1990s through the first decade of this century. It's also important to note that multitenancy along with cloud-based services distinguish an LSP from the old model of software-as-a-service, or simply hosting a stand-alone ILS in a remote data center.

Library systems staff will undoubtedly have high expectations from an LSP. These include a service-oriented architecture (SOA). Think of this as the 21st-century replacement for asking about RDBMS and locally deployed systems. While this is essentially a checkbox question, a high-level diagram of the system architecture should help satisfy inquisitive IT staff. Where a systems librarian of the 1990s might ask about Structured Query Language (SQL) and database accessibility, his or her 21st-century equivalent will want to know about application programming interfaces (APIs) and system interoperability. APIs allow libraries with technical prowess or financial means to contract for it to create local applications and middleware that can interact, often in real time, with the LSP. Good vendors will have well-documented APIs, including whether the API has full create, read, update, and delete (CRUD) capabilities.

The final characteristic that might come as a shock to libraries is subscription pricing. For decades, most library systems have been sold on a license plus maintenance model. Transitioning to subscription pricing can provide significant savings, especially up front. If your library has not completely amortized the up-front licensing cost of the current system, the transition to subscription pricing can seem more jarring. Regardless, the transition to LSP and its new pricing model should be seen as a renewed investment in new technology.

The bottom line is that nothing is more frustrating to the vendor than to open an RFP and see a 10- to 20-year-old description of functionality, technical architecture, and local deployment requirements that handcuff the responder. The vendor will likely view the library as not quite ready to shop and might not even respond. Before venturing into an RFP, make sure to conduct a thorough environmental scan of the marketplace—often accomplished through a request for information (RFI)—to identify the products that fit your specific need and the vendors who offer them.

TIME IS MONEY

It might be useful to think of sending out an RFP like an author submitting a manuscript to multiple publishers. The author hopes that one will respond with the answer he or she wants, and there is little incremental cost to the author to send the manuscript to more publishers. The writer gives little thought to the costs involved for each publisher. Nor does the writer consider the hundreds of other writers who have followed a similar model. The publisher in this analogy faces the difficult decision of which manuscripts to read, which to respond to, and which to publish.

Beyond this analogy, library vendors face additional time constraints and financial commitments: requests for clarifications, online demonstrations, site visits, printing and shipping costs, best and final offers, and the valuable time of product managers, engineers, and systems staff required to answer more complex questions. Every vendor has boilerplate answers to RFP requirements. There are even several RFP management systems on the market to help manage the workflow and standard answers. But RFP responses are part art and part science—qualitative questions appear as frequently as quantitative ones—and it would be the most unusual of circumstances that allowed a vendor to use the exact same responses twice for two different customers, even in circumstances where the exact same RFP was used.

A company called Ringold tried to solve this problem in the early 2000s by providing a standardized template for creating RFPs in which vendors could place their standard answers. The plan backfired, however, allowing even the smallest library to employ the template and produce 100-page-plus RFPs. What was meant to lighten the burden on libraries and vendors simply shifted the burden (i.e., costs) to the vendor.

THE TARGETED TENDER

A joke in the world of RFPs borders on truism. A vendor will say that the only RFP it can surely win is the one that it wrote. It's not unheard of for vendors to provide templates that steer answers in more favorable directions. This practice is hardly unique to library vendors. And while an even playing field might be the intent, small nuances of language in the RFP are not lost on the vendor. On occasion, the language isn't even nuanced, mentioning specific product names and using wording straight from marketing copy on the company's website or PowerPoint presentations.

When faced with such a situation, the vendor has a few choices. The vendor can "phone in" a response, giving little effort to what appears to be a losing battle. A riskier gamble would be to not respond at all. This is where the library should be careful. Most RFP rules require a minimum number of respondents. A vendor sensing a foregone conclusion could decide not to respond; if more than one vendor does this, the library could be faced with a stalemate and might need to start the process over entirely. But even a freshly minted RFP might not warm respondents.

If process and bureaucracy demand a formal procurement process but the library has already made up its mind about a vendor, one could argue that it's ethically imperative to do whatever it takes to avoid the RFP process. Most institutions have a sole-source justification process that could save the library and several vendors time and effort. While every salesperson worth his or her salt wants to make that sale, the vendor will be more respectful in the long run for not having participated in a no-win scenario.

If the RFP is unavoidable, there is frankly still no reason for a library to tip the scale in the process, even if a clear path for the library is already apparent,

The RFP can be written with enough qualitative questions and judged with enough subjectivity that the library can have the winner it wants. And who knows? Answers from the other vendors might just surprise the library.

PRICES MAY VARY

No answer is more frustrating in an RFP process than "it depends." Truth be told, vendors hate giving the answer as much as libraries hate reading it. And no answer makes the vendor more anxious than the ones about pricing. When a library asks, "How much does it cost?" the answer the vendor *really* wants to give is "How much have you got?" But that would be impolite. Pricing models—simultaneous users, library size, Carnegie class, library type, library region—will vary, even between products from the same vendor, so it behooves libraries to provide as much information as possible. Conversely, the vendor needs to be clear about not only the price but also the pricing model itself, and the library should ask for it. These formulas are hardly magic, and it's unnecessary to obfuscate the model that leads to the final price. Failure to do so makes the pricing look arbitrary. Also keep in mind that RFP prices often equate to sticker prices. Libraries should weight the pricing score accordingly and stick a pin in the pricing proposal pending the negotiation or "best and final offer" phase of the process.

Libraries should also endeavor to provide the most accurate print collection and licensed collection sizes. In addition, staff size, number of patrons or population served, full-time equivalent (FTE), and so forth should be accurately portrayed. Frugality will tempt libraries to lower these numbers to attain a better price. Beware. This kind of fudging is best done during final negotiations when there is always a little room to haggle. Since a lot of the demographic information is available publicly or is aggregated by third parties, vendors will be wary of numbers that don't make sense. Libraries' numbers related to collection sizes and population served should match the ones on brag sheets used with provosts and library boards.

Scoring the pricing section makes vendors nervous, so your library might sense anxiety. Objectively scoring what might be apples-to-pears comparisons with other vendors generates all kinds of footnotes and asterisks in pricing tables. For example, a library might list a certain service as optional, for example, electronic resource management, but if that functionality is included in the basic pricing from the vendor, an apples-to-pears situation is created when another vendor charges extra for that same service. While no scientific model exists, libraries should try to attain pricing information in a way that allows them to create apples-to-apples comparisons. Assuring vendors of this model will result in more honest and accurate answers.

In addition, libraries need to make sure the pricing section aligns with the functionality section. On occasion, services listed as optional in the pricing section have the related functionality as "required" in the functional checklist.

This causes a quandary for the vendor whether to associate pricing with required functionality as included or optional.

THE APPROACH

Clarity is the name of the game. The more the vendor understands the evaluation factors the library uses to make a decision, the more accurate the answers; moreover, the vendor will have a clearer picture of where to spend its valuable time on the response. This section will focus on tangible advice that will increase the quality of vendor responses.

Checklists in RFPs are hard to avoid. To help with scoring and weighting replies, libraries might consider the Must, Should, Could, Would (MoSCoW) model that software providers use in creating functional requirements. If a library creates too many Must requirements, it creates functional inflation and hurts the overall scoring.

Without a "MoSCoW" approach to desired functionality, checklists can take the shape of unrealistic and unattainable moon shots. A library should be realistic about the potential costs (sunk, opportunity, and investment) to the organization itself to implement what it says it must have. Without sounding patronizing, if the words "should," "could," or "would" slip out in the explanation of your "must" functionality, consider reprioritizing the need.

Questions come in many forms: yes and no, high and low level, multipart, and essay. The burden on the vendor to answer and on the library to score is reduced if questions are grouped accordingly. To ensure accurate answers, libraries should avoid multipart questions altogether. While it might appear to shorten the RFP, it will not shorten responses. Multipart questions only invite "Yes, but . . ." and "No, however . . ." responses especially if used with a checklist format, making it harder for libraries to score the answers. Essay questions are fine, but seeing them in a spreadsheet or checklist gives vendors heartburn. If the question begs a lengthy response, it's better to template a format that allows easy writing and reading of the response.

The RFP and sales process is not like a library reference desk interview, with its iterative nursing out of more and more information from the client. Ask everything you can think of, and don't place the onus on the vendor to ask questions that the library has not thought of. It's well established that no vendor will ask a question if the answer might jeopardize the sale.

Please *deduplicate* questions. It sometimes takes a village to write an RFP. When the division of labor in creating questions is by department or delegated by organizational charts, duplicate questions are inevitable. It's not uncommon to see patron discovery questions from a reference librarian duplicated by cataloging questions from technical services staff. If by some intricate design this is a test to see if the answers will match, the return on that investment of time can hardly be worth the trick.

Standard functionality questions often plunge libraries back into the 20th-century RFP model. "Can your system check out a book to a patron?" Really? Should libraries be asking questions to which they will receive the same universal answer from every vendor? Asking "Does the system do 'x'?" is not nearly as meaningful as letting the vendor explain how its system works.

Long lists of basic functionality questions introduce the "new system irony"—after weeks or months deciding to shop for a new system out of frustration with the current one, librarians and staff spend weeks describing exactly how that existing system works and asking whether a replacement can replicate its capabilities. As noted in the section about LSPs, libraries would be better positioned to ask questions about new functionality and features missing from their current systems.

Corporate philosophy matters. Twenty years ago, it was taught in master of library science (MLS) programs that the life of an automated library system averages 7 years. More recent numbers would probably push that figure to 10 years. And it's too early to tell how much easier switching cloud providers will be in a new LSP environment. Regardless, the RFP represents the embarkation point for a long relationship between a library and a vendor. It's likely that the value of a strong library–vendor relationship (assuming such strength exists) is greater than the functionality distinctions between two competing library systems.

In this vein, questions about corporate ownership, financial position, product operations (implementation, training, documentation, and help desk) staffing, research and development (R&D) investment, community engagement efforts, product planning procedures, and overall corporate mission far outweigh the number of loan rules allowed or the order of facet displays in discovery services. It's more prevalent in European tenders, but vendors jump at the chance to include professional profiles of product managers, analysts, developers, and product operations support staff. This team will provide core support in the library–vendor relationship, and gathering that information should play a part in choosing a system.

Also, vendors are looking at library mission statements for potential customers. Are libraries looking at vendors? In short, the RFP should include open-ended questions that allow libraries to make a subjective appraisal of the organization based on its executive management, target markets, future prospects, longevity, and overall corporate strategy.

If open-ended questions aren't considered, the library might consider asking the vendor to align its corporate philosophy with the library's own mission. Instead of "tell us your future vision" or "describe all the stuff you do that we didn't ask," libraries could be open with their own vision and the problems the current system will not solve. That gives the vendor an opportunity to frame its solution in the context of the library's challenges and opportunities.

VENDORS ARE PEOPLE, TOO

Recall the analogy of the book publisher with a lot of manuscripts to read. It's likely that a vendor has as many as 10–12 RFPs in its pipeline, and more if its product offerings are more varied than a traditional ILS. There are several niceties to consider when interacting with vendor staff. A library's style of doing business in the RFP process is an indicator of how it will do business as a customer. Vendors making hard business decisions about capacity—for both RFPs and customers in general—will judge a library on how professionally it handles the RFP process.

Regardless of what the library might think, business process staff at a vendor are not unlimited, and the people doing most of the heavy lifting are not typically highly placed in the organization. Their size, capacity, and expertise are usually in direct proportion to the vendor organization's win rate and the size of their sales pipeline. Libraries should be respectful when designing timelines and deadlines. This includes being mindful of holidays, weekends, and a volume of work that includes responding to many other libraries.

Short response times are also indicators of a library's seriousness in considering a vendor, especially when combined with targeted RFP templates as noted previously. Failure to give enough time for a serious response may lead the vendor not to reply at all. Like librarians themselves, library vendors might prefer no answer at all to an insufficient or incomplete one.

When it comes to travel, vendors need plenty of lead time for planning and scheduling. A lot of vendor budgeting for these activities is indeed the cost of doing business, but that doesn't rule out courtesy for busy schedules for people who practically live in airports and hotels. Libraries should consider that giving vendors a one- to two-week lead time does two things: first, it dramatically increases the cost of travel for the vendors (which must ultimately be passed on to libraries), and second, it puts a strain on vendors' finite staff who are likely already booked for other visits and demonstrations that another library properly scheduled weeks in advance.

While it might be tempting to test a vendor's perseverance when they arrive, leaving them on their own for hotels, parking, meeting logistics, and equipment would not serve the library well in the long run. Waiting until the last minute to alert vendors to remote participants or inadequate technical infrastructure will frustrate all parties. Some libraries also go to great lengths to make the best use of library staff time during demonstrations and vendor presentations. For example, they may have a rotating group of staff come in and out, but they can be neglectful of providing breaks for the presenters and demonstrators. It seems like it would be common practice to provide breaks and agendas that allow vendors to share responsibility for presenting. But agendas that expect a vendor to be on for four to six hours straight are not unheard of; some draconian agendas include staggering meals for staff while the vendor is expected to continue presenting.

It takes a village to run a library, and the same can be said of on-site library visits. Library vendors are not trained monkeys exchanging tasks (product management, marketing, sales, sales engineering/demos, and project management) at will. They are no more a Borg of collective knowledge than the staff in a library are. Great pains are taken, greater than any library would imagine, to determine whom and how many to send on a library visit. Of course, once the vendor is there, the library should maximize the time and expertise of those present. If an executive is there, quiz them on corporate philosophy and direction. If a product manager is there, talk about road maps. If project managers are there, ask about implementation timelines and training methods. If appropriate, start talking negotiations and timelines with sales staff.

THE CONSULTANT

After all this advice and numerous observations, one elephant remains in the room. It's no secret that libraries lean heavily on library consultants to recommend, distribute, and even evaluate RFP responses. Another industry secret revealed: vendors can see the fingerprints of consultants on RFPs even when the consultative relationship is not disclosed. Again, be mindful of the sea change that has occurred in library automation. Has your consultant changed his or her templates to keep up with the times? Is the library spending inordinate amounts of time writing its own requirements that the consultant is contracted to provide?

This should not be interpreted as an admonition against using consultants. On the contrary, most of them provide valuable service, capacity, and business procedures to a complicated and complex process. They can also serve to ensure compliance with the rules of procurement offices, most of whom lack any industry knowledge of libraries and on whom most nuances of this niche industry are lost.

PARTING THOUGHTS

This chapter opened with a nonradical notion, so let's close with a radical one. Library vendors are not in the software business. They are in the relationship business. And like any personal relationship, libraries and vendors both need to consider important partnerships before adventuring together. Library systems don't yet represent a "try it and see" kind of platform like so many apps on a smartphone. Library systems are complex software applications that mean months of procurement process, migration, training, and implementation.

It's also a general rule of product management that customers don't make large cost purchase decisions based solely on discrete pieces of functionality. It's rare that a library or a salesperson could name the single piece of functionality (or lack thereof) that will win or lose a sale. While it's unlikely that functional checklists in RFPs will end, libraries could lead a shift in the RFP process that emphasizes relationship, professional ethos, and shared outcomes over simplified functional descriptions. In the end, the library should feel good not only about the system they have chosen but also about the organization with whom they have chosen to do business.

NOTE

1. Marshall Breeding, "Library Services Platforms: A Maturing Genre of Products," *American Library Association Library Technology Reports* 51, no. 4 (2015): 1–38, doi: http://dx.doi.org/10.5860/ltr.51n4, https://journals.ala.org/index.php/ltr/article/view/5686/7063.

17

ETHICS FOR
THE RFP PROCESS

Sever Bordeianu and Frances C. Wilkinson

ETHICS: THE TWO SIDES

The American Library Association (ALA) Code of Ethics contains the statement: "Ethical dilemmas occur when values are in conflict."[1] Indeed, thinkers throughout the ages have struggled with these dilemmas. Finks, in 1989, summarized the importance of ethics in a succinct statement: "The Value of values . . . is that they point us toward what is important and worth in the long run."[2] There is a philosophical aspect to ethics, and there is a practical aspect. Philosophy has an entire branch of study dedicated to ethics, and some of the most famous philosophers have written about it and attempted to live by it.[3] Philosophy defines "ethics" and explains the importance of applying ethics to daily life in the personal, public, social, and political spheres. The practical side of ethics deals with specific behavioral norms in the same areas of human activity, such as social interactions, politics, or business relations by defining codes of ethics to a specific area of activity. Professions generally have well-defined codes of ethics, which are developed and enforced by the professional organizations that govern the profession, by which their members are expected to behave. Complete codes of ethics encompass the entirety of professional behavior, which in the case of librarianship is strongly slanted toward public services, copyright compliance, freedom of information, equal access to resources, and fighting censorship.[4] Literature on these aspects is abundant. This chapter will focus on ethics that apply to the acquisitions process and the business transactions between the library and the vendors of library products and services.

CODES OF ETHICS

The ALA Code of Ethics provides broad guidelines for librarians as a profession. The Association of Library Collections and Technical Services

(ALCTS), a division of ALA, has issued its own guidelines, which address specific ethical consideration for technical services librarians. Other library associations have issued their own codes of ethics. Here are some examples: the American Association of Law Libraries;[5] the American Society for Information Science and Technology;[6] the Society of American Archivists;[7] and the International Federation of Library Associations and Institutions.[8]

Business and commercial entities also have codes of ethics developed by their professional organizations, in the same spirit of defining and creating a fair and equitable climate for conducting business. A simple online search will discover the code of ethics for any professional or business association. One such example is the code of ethics of the Antiquarian Booksellers Association of America.[9]

Codes of ethics are developed by professions in order to give its members guidance regarding proper behavior in the conduct of their profession. As it struggled with defining its professional identity, librarianship also began to develop its code of ethics, even though admittedly, this was a slow start.[10] It has also been pointed out in the literature that for a long time, library budgets were not perceived as large enough to warrant unethical behavior since there simply was not enough money involved to pose temptation for fraud.[11] The situation has changed dramatically beginning in the middle of the 20th century. Library budgets are no longer insignificant, and the argument that not enough is at stake to reward unethical behavior no longer holds. Moreover, in the past couple of decades, the management of academic institutions has moved toward the corporate model, with university presidents and even library directors acting more like corporate CEOs than academic administrators. While this model makes sense from a purely business and fiscal point of view, it has caused considerable unhappiness with academics who perceive it as a loss of idealism and putting profits before intellectual inquiry and exploration. Still, today's large library budgets, often entailing millions of dollars, and the price of products or services such as approval plans, integrated library systems (ILSs), or digitization services, necessitate clear ethical guidelines for behavior and practice when a library needs to acquire one of these products. The request for proposal (RFP) process is one such safeguard. Ethical considerations are built into this process.

Ethical behavior is an important component of professional behavior, and it is during business transactions when two or more professions interact that ethics apply. In the case of RFPs issued by libraries, one party is obviously librarians. The other parties vary with the type of product or service that the library is purchasing. It could be a book vendor, a computer services vendor, an architectural firm, a commercial binder, or a mail and package delivery firm. Each of these businesses has its own rules of conduct, and ethics creates the common behavioral expectations that ensure that despite a large variation of activities, every party is treated fairly, every party treats its partners fairly, all parties behave ethically and legally toward their partners and competitors, and the partners have a common belief system that they can confidently rely on to trust each other.

ETHICS AND LIBRARIANSHIP

Each profession has a professional code of ethics developed and maintained by its accrediting organization. In 2011, Kendrik and Leaver provided a fascinating and detailed history of the development of librarians' code of ethics, which was first introduced in a speech by Mary Wright Plummer at the 1903 Illinois Library Association's meeting.[12] While warmly received, the code was not implemented. Six years later, in 1909, Charles Knowles Bolton published *The Librarian's Canons of Ethics*, but it was not until 1938 that the ALA adopted an official code of ethics.[13] Unexpectedly, the profession reacted with lots of criticism, pointing out the lack of authority for ALA to enforce its code of ethics on the profession and lamenting specific weaknesses of the code, such as being too broad or too specific and unrealistic to implement. Major revisions, accompanied by equally "biting" criticism—one author referring to such a revision as "one of the worst codes of occupational ethics in existence"—occurred in 1975, 1995, and finally 2008.[14] The current code produced significantly less negative feedback, and it seems that the profession has finally managed to produce a solid, acceptable code by which librarians feel comfortable to abide. The ALA Code of Ethics focuses primarily on the provision of information, protecting intellectual freedom, user's privacy, and respect. None of the provisions deals directly with financial or business transactions, but number VI—"We do not advance private interests at the expense of library users, colleagues, or our employing institution"—can be interpreted to extend to ethical business behavior.

The ALCTS, a division of ALA, has two other documents relating to ethics, which are specifically developed for technical services librarians. The ALCTS Guidelines, issued in 1994, are general principles, more theoretical in nature, such as developing collections within the collection priorities of the institution; providing unbiased access to information; preserving and conserving materials; developing and applying standards; establishing a secure and safe environment for users; fostering fair, ethical, and legal trade and business practices; maintaining equitable treatment and confidentiality in competitive relations and manuscript grant reviews; and supporting and abiding by the contractual agreements made by the library.

Also in 1994, the Acquisitions Section of the ALCTS issued a Statement of Principles and Standards of Acquisitions Practice. These standards are the most detailed statements yet by the profession regarding ethical behavior in business transactions and purchases. The statement is reproduced next in its entirety.[15]

In all acquisitions transactions, a librarian:

1. gives first consideration to the objectives and policies of his or her institution;
2. strives to obtain the maximum ultimate value of each dollar of expenditure;
3. grants all competing vendors equal consideration insofar as the established policies of his or her library permit, and regards each transaction on its own merits;
4. subscribes to and works for honesty, truth, and fairness in buying and selling, and denounces all forms and manifestations of bribery;
5. declines personal gifts and gratuities;
6. uses only by consent original ideas and designs devised by one vendor for competitive purchasing purposes;
7. accords a prompt and courteous reception insofar as conditions permit to all who call on legitimate business missions;
8. fosters and promotes fair, ethical, and legal trade practices;
9. avoids sharp practice;
10. strives consistently for knowledge of the publishing and bookselling industry;
11. strives to establish practical and efficient methods for the conduct of his/her office;
12. counsels and assists fellow acquisitions librarians in the performance of their duties, whenever occasion permits.

By applying these principles, librarians can ensure not only that the institution's money is spent responsibly but also that the right products are purchased. It also creates a fair, even playing field for vendors.

The first two statements make it clear that the librarian's foremost responsibility is to purchase good value for its institution. For example, statement #2 exhorts librarians to obtain the maximum value for each dollar of expenditure. Statements #3–#10 deal with fair business practices and the treatment of vendors, whose financial well-being is vital to a vibrant marketplace, by giving all vendors equal consideration (#3), using proprietary vendor ideas only by consent (#6), and avoiding "sharp practices" (#9), a powerful term that makes buyers aware that asking for excessive discounts or unreasonable services could jeopardize the vendor's financial stability. Finally, the last two statements relate to the librarian's responsibility to create an internal culture of ethics, both by establishing practical, and one presumes, ethical methods in the office (#11) and to counsel and assist colleagues in the performance of their duties (#12). Studying and applying these principles at each step of the RFP process, no matter what product is being purchased, ensures the highest level of ethical behavior.

ETHICS AND THE RFP PROCESS

RFPs are generally issued to purchase an expensive product consisting of significant sums of money being expended. While the RFP process itself is designed to minimize favoritism and ensure equal treatment of each respondent, it is important for all parties concerned to abide by ethical and legal standards. Public as well as private institutions have explicit rules of conduct codified in laws and procedures. Awarding a large contract on behalf of a large public institution, especially a state entity, is governed by state and possibly federal laws not only to ensure fairness in the treatment of vendors but also to foster the responsible stewardship of public moneys. Despite the legal frameworks in which business is conducted, abiding by ethical standards is important to ensure a fair and honest outcome that will benefit all parties involved. This extends not only to the library and the eventual winner of the bid but to all the other vendors that responded to the bid as members of a robust marketplace, which can only thrive if there is healthy and fair competition. It is only such an environment, governed by ethical behaviors, that allows companies to develop innovative quality products and services for libraries at fair and competitive prices.

Ethical behavior in business practices ensures that all parties operate in an even playing field, all are treated with the same respect, and all are given the same opportunity and consideration to present their product or service, to be evaluated by the same criteria, and to have the same level of access to the purchasing institution. Unethical behavior is not only illegal and can lead to costly litigation, or worse, but it can also negatively affect the marketplace by stifling competition, causing financial harm to vendors or the library, and ultimately having a negative effect on the development and support of new products and services.

PROCUREMENT OR PURCHASING OFFICE

Most organizations to which academic, public, and school libraries report have a procurement or purchasing office that monitors and oversees business transactions. This office will provide training, guidance, and support to the RFP team and teach them the dos and don'ts of proper behavior. At the beginning of the RFP process, there should be an orientation session during which the procurement officer will explain the legal and ethical behavior requirements of the process. They will share proper documentation that details both practices and behaviors and any legal document that members need to be aware of. The procurement officer or designate will also be the point person to field any questions from vendors once the bid process is on the way. This will ensure consistent and equitable treatment for each vendor. A centralized point of contact will guarantee that all parties are apprised of problems or delays and that each party gets the same level of attention to their specific questions. The procurement office, not having any bias toward a specific product or service that the library would purchase, will act as a neutral communicator between vendors and the library when questions arise. They can provide the objectivity of the outsider in the discussions between the library and the vendors.

CONFIDENTIALITY

It is important that vendor information is treated confidentially. Vendors' description of their products, technical specifications, and any proprietary information about the company must be kept confidential and not shared with competitors. Such practices are common in the business world, and breaches of these rules often make the news. It is not just technical specifications or proprietary products that have to be kept confidential, but financial and pricing information also has to be dealt with discretion because one of the most powerful tools a vendor has for selling its product is negotiating a price. Finding out about a competitor's price allows one vendor to submit an artificially lower bid just to secure a contract, but the library may not benefit from the lower price if the vendor is unable to provide an acceptable product or level of service. Equally damaging, it would create an uneven playing field for the innocent competitor who is submitting a good faith, realistic quote for its product.

TRANSPARENCY

One of the best ways to ensure ethical behavior is transparency. All communications with the vendors need to be handled transparently, so all parties know at all times when communication is being exchanged and between whom. The same documents need to be shared with all the vendors. If changes, additions, or clarifications are made, all members need to be informed at the same time. Communication between the vendor and the library has to go through the designated official channel, which provides answers to each vendor in a timely manner. This is typically the university's procurement officer or designate, and ideally, the same individual should be in charge of communication for the entire RFP process. If individual committee members receive questions from vendors, they will need to refer all the questions to the procurement officer. Transparency has a double benefit: it ensures fair, legal, and ethical behavior among all parties, and it creates an atmosphere of trust.

CONFLICT OF INTEREST

Hand in hand with personal responsibility is avoiding a conflict of interest situation. Only the individual members of the committee will know with certainty when they have a conflict of interest and they need to disclose it. If there is a conflict of interest, members will need to recuse themselves. Conflict of interest is a very sensitive issue. Even the appearance of conflict of interest can create doubts about the integrity and fairness of a process, so team members need to make every effort avoid it. Certainly, going into a situation knowing that there is a conflict of interest and taking advantage of it would constitute a serious ethical breach. The system has built-in mechanisms for allowing people to identify and disclose conflicts of interest, but just like in the case of personal responsibility, it is up to each individual to act responsibly.

INTEGRITY

In many situations it is possible to act unethically and not be discovered. Despite the strong safeguards in place to ensure ethical behavior, there are opportunities when these safeguards can be circumvented. It is therefore incumbent on each committee member to use his or her personal integrity and act ethically, especially in situations that could be ambiguous or not transparent. Individual integrity is the only factor that can prevent unethical behavior in situations where the monitoring tools do not reach, such as informal or secret meetings. It is hoped that committee members would keep in mind that the RFP system is designed specifically to benefit all parties involved, and it works best when each party behaves ethically. Breaking the rules might benefit an individual, but it will hurt the organization and the competitors. It will create an uneven playing field for the honest players. It might also result in acquiring a product or service that does not serve the library as well as that of a competitor. Clearly, the disadvantages are many and are obvious, and so are the advantages.

PERSONAL RESPONSIBILITY

Ultimately it is the responsibility of each individual to behave ethically in all interactions, both public and private, and to make every effort to abide by the rules. The system has built-in mechanisms for dealing with every kind of situation by defining official channels of communication, with a designated individual responsible for handling all communication in an open, transparent way. There is no reason for secret communication and sharing of information between members of the RFP committee and vendors, which may disclose a competitor's proprietary information and thus give another vendor an unfair advantage. RFP committee members need to be aware of what constitutes a breach of protocol and not engage in any of these unethical behaviors. They also have a duty to report inappropriate behavior by vendors, should it occur. That is why the procurement officer is part of the team.

There are many venues for learning about proper ethical conduct while conducting business. Most public institutions provide, even require, extensive training in ethical behavior. For example, the University of New Mexico offers a course titled "Ethics: A Framework for Ethical Decision Making" through the University's Learning Central portal. The University of Illinois and the University of Washington offer similar courses.[16] Undoubtedly, so do most other universities. There is no reason for any individual in a position to conduct business on behalf of the university to be ignorant, or worse, ignore, the ethical rules of conduct. As the saying goes, it is not only wrong, but it is also illegal.

CONCLUSION

Behaving ethically benefits all parties involved. The legal framework in which libraries and businesses operate is guided by strong ethical guidelines designed to provide the optimum environment for fair business transactions and the responsible expenditure of an institution's money. While ethics is a universal value, how one behaves ethically varies depending on the specific situation in which one finds oneself. People need to be aware if there are additional ethical requirements depending on what product or service is purchased, which may not apply to other situations. Each of the chapter contributors discusses ethical behavior either directly or indirectly, and all acknowledge its importance. The authors make it clear that ethical behavior is a paramount consideration in the proper conduct of business and the responsible exercise of professional duty. Stephen Bosch's statement, "Honesty is the best policy," summarizes in the most succinct way the attitude of the other contributors. Engaging in ethical behavior creates a win-win situation for all parties involved and ensures that the library gets the best product for its money. Ethics should be the underlying motivation driving these business transactions. When followed, every participant will end up a winner.

NOTES

1. American Library Association, "Professional Ethics," Text, ALA Code of Ethics, May 19, 2017, http://www.ala.org/tools/ethics.

2. Lee W. Finks, "What Do We Stand for? Values without Shame," *American Libraries*, no. 4 (1989): 352.

3. Richard Kraut, "Aristotle's Ethics," in *The Stanford Encyclopedia of Philosophy*, ed. Edward N. Zalta (Stanford, CA: Metaphysics Research Lab, Stanford University, Summer 2017), https://plato.stanford.edu/archives/sum2017/entries/aristotle-ethics/.

4 American Library Association, "Professional Ethics."

5. "AALL Ethical Principles," accessed November 17, 2017, https://www.aallnet.org/mm/Leadership-Governance/policies/PublicPolicies/policy-ethics.html.

6. "ASIS&T Professional Guidelines," *ASIS&T* (blog), October 20, 2017, https://www.asist.org/about/asist-professional-guidelines/.

7. "SAA Core Values Statement and Code of Ethics | Society of American Archivists," accessed November 17, 2017, https://www2.archivists.org/statements/saa-core-values-statement-and-code-of-ethics.

8. "IFLA—Professional Codes of Ethics for Librarian," accessed November 17, 2017, https://www.ifla.org/faife/professional-codes-of-ethics-for-librarians.

9. Antiquarian Booksellers Association of America, "Code of Ethics and Standards," accessed November 17, 2017, https://www.abaa.org/about-abaa/code-of-ethics.

10. Kaetrena Davis Kendrick and Echo Leaver, "Impact of the Code of Ethics on Workplace Behavior in Academic Libraries," *Journal of Information Ethics* 20, no. 1 (April 1, 2011): 86–112, https://doi.org/10.3172/JIE.20.1.86.

11. Frances C. Wilkinson, Linda K. Lewis, and Rebecca L. Lubas, *The Complete Guide to Acquisitions Management*, Library and Information Science Text Series (Santa Barbara, CA: Libraries Unlimited, an Imprint of ABC-CLIO, LLC, 2015), 155.

12. Kendrick and Leaver, "Impact of the Code of Ethics on Workplace Behavior in Academic Libraries," 88.

13. Ibid., 89.

14. Ibid., 90.

15. ALCTS Acquisitions Section Ethics Task Force, "Statement on Principles and Standards of Acquisitions Practice," Text, Tools, Publications & Resources, August 22, 2017, accessed November 15, 2017, http://www.ala.org/tools/ethics/statement-principles-and-standards-acquisitions-practice.

16. "Illinois Mandatory Ethics Training—University of Illinois . . .," accessed November 29, 2017, https://www.ethics.uillinois.edu/training/illinois_mandatory_ethics_training; University of Washington Internal Audit, "Ethics Training," accessed November 29, 2017, https://fa.uw.edu/audit/ethics-training.

GLOSSARY

Definitions in this glossary are not meant to be all-inclusive definitions, but rather the terms and phrases are defined in the context of the RFP process described in this book.

Other sources of definitions include *Serials Acquisitions Glossary* (Serials Section, Acquisitions Committee, Association for Library Collections & Technical Services, third edition, revised (2005) [http://www.ala.org/alcts/sites/ ala.org.alcts/files/content/resources/collect/serials/acqglossary/05seracq_glo .pdf]), the American Library Association, Association for Library Collections & Technical Services, Publications & Resources (www.ala.org), and *ODLIS: Online Dictionary for Library and Information Science* by Joan M. Reitz (ABC CLIO: http://www.abc-clio.com/ODLIS/odlis_A.aspx).

Adhesive binding   A method of binding that uses glue instead of sewing to keep the pages together.

Agent   A person or company retained by many publishers to represent their business interests to libraries and other clients. *See also* **dealer** and **vendor.**

Aggregator   A company providing electronic databases that include both indexing and full-text content that may have been originally published in a wide range of sources.

Alkaline paper   Paper with little or no acid content and intended to last indefinitely. Also known as acid-free paper.

American National Standards Institute (ANSI)   It oversees the creation, promulgation, and use of thousands of norms and guidelines that directly impact businesses in nearly every sector. *See* http://www.ansi.org/.

Approval plan   A plan that selects books for a library by a vendor using a profile that identifies types of books wanted by the library. Some vendors may offer to process the materials for an added cost; *see* **shelf-ready materials**. The vendor may also provide notification of other books the librarians may want to consider. Libraries receive shipments of books or notifications at predetermined intervals, generally weekly.

ARL   *See* **Association of Research Libraries**.

Association of Research Libraries (ARL)   Currently consists of the 125 largest academic and research libraries in the United States and Canada. The association focuses on collection rankings and deals with timely issues such as copyright and scholarly publishing. *See* http://www.arl.org.

Barcode   A machine-readable code made of vertical lines printed on books or other materials, used for circulation.

Bibliographers   A term rarely used in recent years. *See* **collection development librarians, selectors, subject liaisons**, or **subject-matter specialists**.

Bibliographic data   The information found in the cataloging record describing a book or serial that includes publication information. These data are the basis for the cataloging record.

Bid   An offer to sell goods and services at a specific price, within a specific time frame. The term "bid" is also used in the vernacular to refer to a vendor's response to an RFP, including the full scope of goods and services, beyond merely price considerations.

Blanket order plan   A vendor plan that does not provide for the return of unwanted titles by the library. The library must keep every title selected for and sent to it. Blanket order plans are designed to encompass numerous broad subject or geographical areas.

Boilerplate   Standardized wording used by the library or purchasing office to provide the vendor with clear information regarding response to an **RFP** including such information as the type of materials that the RFP covers, the services the library seeks from the vendor, the estimated dollar value of the contract, the time frame in which the vendor has to respond, the format in which it should respond, a description of the library and its parent organization, contact names, proposal deadlines, and the criteria to be used to evaluate the vendor's proposal.

Bookseller   A person or company that sells books. Booksellers are known by various names, including vendor and agent. Booksellers range in size and may include the independent corner bookstore, large international corporations, or companies that only have an Internet presence.

Cataloging records   The permanent record for any publication, regardless of format. It includes information about the author or authors, the title, the publisher, the physical description, the edition, the subjects addressed in the publication, and any other facts perceived as important for a specific item.

Cessation   The demise of a publication. A vendor or periodical materials should notify its customers when titles have ceased publication so that the library may adjust its records accordingly.

Claim   A report generated by the library and sent to the vendor or publisher when an item ordered is not received by the library. Some **ILS**s generate claims automatically after a specified time has passed.

Claim reports   Documentation relating to claims, either recording the claims generated or reports supplied by a vendor responding to claims sent by the library.

Classification systems   Systems such as the Dewey decimal system or the Library of Congress Classification System that locates books and serials on library shelves.

Collection development librarians   Librarians who are responsible for managing and building collections for the library. They may also perform outreach or reference duties; most often found in large research, academic, or public libraries. *See also* **bibliographers, selectors, subject liaisons**, or **subject-matter specialists**.

Collection Development Policy Statement   A statement describing the library's collecting philosophy and defining the relative importance of specific subjects, including the depth and strength of the collection.

Comes-with title   A title that comes at no additional charge as a result of purchasing another title. For example, some societies and associations will supply a newsletter with a subscription to their journal.

Competitive procurement process   An often state-mandated process that affords vendors an equal opportunity to submit proposals or bids stating their ability to supply goods or services. In this process the rules and requirements are the same for all vendors, with no vendor being given special advantage. Competitive procurement is most often accomplished via the **RFP, RFQ, RFI**, or bid process.

Conflict of interest   When an individual has multiple interests in a situation where the interests could be opposing. For example, if an individual on an RFP committee has a financial interest in a company bidding on the contract, there could be a bias that could be improper.

Conservation   Repairing or treating materials in order to maintain or restore the physical item. *See also* **preservation**.

Consortium   A group of libraries that work together to accomplish a common goal. Consortia often negotiate **contracts** on behalf of their members for various library goods or services at reduced prices.

Contract   A legal, written agreement between the library or institution and the publisher or **vendor** clearly stating the requirements and specifications of the agreement. The person or persons authorized to sign contracts (librarian, purchasing officer, or institution attorney) will vary among institutions; check before signing any contract. For libraries using the **RFP** process, the contract may consist of a copy of the RFP and the vendor's proposal along with the award letter and conditions of the award.

Contract compliance   The specification that both the library and the publisher or **vendor** must act in accordance with the terms of the contract. Noncompliance is usually grounds for canceling the contract.

Copublished material   An item that is published jointly by more than one entity. Art exhibition catalogs are examples of materials that are often copublished because one institution cannot bear the costs alone. Such copublishing can be a problem in an approval plan if the **vendor** does not have adequate ways of guarding against **duplication**.

Copyright holder   The individual author, publisher, or developer who legally has the right to publish, reprint, or reproduce copyrighted material. The holder may or may not be the vendor of the material. Most states allow for the purchase of materials from the copyright holder without bid, regardless of the cost of the item.

Copyright royalties   A sum paid to a copyright holder. Royalties must be paid to publishers for more than the minimal use of copyrighted material; nonpayment can result in prosecution.

Cost projections   Forecasts, estimates, or best guesses made by vendors using information on current trends and gathered from publishers and other sources to determine the rate of inflation for various categories of materials. Such projects can help librarians in their budgeting process.

Country of origin   The country where an item is published. When determining how to divide its business, a library may prefer to purchase materials from a **vendor** in the country of origin.

Coverage   The types of materials supplied by **vendors**, which may include specific formats, publishers, geographic areas, subjects, or languages.

Credit   A surplus assigned to a library's account when a payment has been made and the item is not supplied, when an item is defective, or when a **prepayment** discount is given.

Customer-driven-acquisitions   See **patron-driven-acquisitions**.

Customer service   Assistance provided to the library by the **vendor**. Such service may include customer service representatives who answer questions about orders, invoices, or services; a **sales representative** who visits the library; and any other service that will make for the efficient acquisition of materials.

Customized reports   *See* **management reports**.

Deacidification   A process that neutralizes the acid content in paper to prevent further deterioration of the paper.

Dealer   A **vendor** of library materials. *See also* **agent**.

Debarment   The exclusion of a **vendor** from consideration for a contract for a valid reason.

Demand-driven-acquisitions   See **patron-driven-acquisitions**.

Deposit account   Money kept in an account with the publisher or vendor for the library. This practice may result in a larger discount or deposit credit to the library.

Digital object identifier (doi)   An identification system for exchanging and locating digital items. The unique number assigned to each item functions as a permanent electronic link. *See* http://www.doi.org/.

Digital preservation   A method that ensures access to reformatted and born-digital content regardless of the challenges of media failure and technological change.

Digital publishing   *See* **electronic publishing**.

Digital rights management (DRM)   Methods used for controlling the use of digital content.

Digitization   The conversion of text, images, videos, or sound into a digital form that can be processed by a computer.

Disaster plan   A plan that includes procedures to be followed by library staff to prevent or minimize the risk of a disaster occurring. The plan describes the response when a disaster happens and includes personnel contact information, building plans, locations and types of emergency supplies, salvage priorities, and contact information for emergency recovery vendors.

Disaster recovery   The process of recovering and rebuilding after a disaster including steps to identify the extent to the damage, potential losses, and resumption and continuity of services.

Discount or discount rate   A reduction in the list price of materials. Although discounts to the library will depend upon the discounts offered to the vendors by the publishers, such discounts are often established at a set rate for the library's purchases if the range of materials being purchased is fairly broad.

Discussion list   An electronic mailing list for individuals who have subscribed to it. Generally devoted to a particular topic such as SERIALST-L for serials, such lists are used to discuss information and problems. Such professional lists are usually moderated.

Domain name   An alphabetic representation of an **Internet** site's **IP address** number.

Download   For libraries, to download a record is to transfer that record from a bibliographic utility, **vendor**, or other source to a local database or online catalog system.

Download   For library patrons, the ability to save a file on their personal computing device.

Dublin Core   A way of describing electronic resources using standards agreed upon in a meeting held in Dublin, Ohio. *See* http://dublincore.org/.

Duplication   The receipt of more copies of a title than the library ordered. **Vendors** of **approval plans** must be able to monitor possible causes of duplication such as **copublished materials**, materials published simultaneously in multiple formats or countries, or items received on a library's **STO**s from titles supplied on the approval plan in order to prevent unwanted duplication.

eBooks   Books published in electronic format; they may or may not also be published in paper.

EDI   Electronic data interchange. The computer-to-computer exchange of data for business transactions using standard formats.

Electronic publishing   Publishing items in electronic or digital **formats**.

Encryption   The process of encoding or locking information before transmission to provide data security.

Ephemera   Printed materials that are intended to have short-lived interest or usefulness. These materials may be collected to support a research library's comprehensive collection.

Fair use   The right to make a copy of a portion of a work for personal use or for interlibrary loan without requiring permission of the copyright holder.

Fire suppression systems   Systems used to prevent or extinguish the spread of a fire in a building. The automated systems include sprinkler systems, gas-based fire suppression, and aerosol-based fire suppression.

Firm order   A book ordered on a **title-by-title selection** basis; it is normally not returnable.

Format   The physical rendition of information, whether print, electronic, or media.

Fulfillment rate   The time period that the vendor takes to fill orders and the number of orders filled.

Fund codes   Codes used in **ILS**s to represent accounts of money devoted to different purchasing areas such as subjects or formats. Fund codes define the budget line an item will be charged against in an ILS. The codes can be supplied to **vendors** to add to their records. They are also used to produce **management reports**.

General terms and conditions   Stipulations in a **contract** used to define those issues that affect the award, fulfillment, and possible longevity of the contract. Such provisions may include but are not limited to insurance, penalties, warranties, affirmative action, information regarding acceptance and rejection of goods and services, addresses for notices, assignment of the contract, multiple awards, cancelation, changes and alternations after the award, discounts, governing law, conflict of interest, and indemnification.

ICOLC   *See* **International Coalition of Library Consortia.**

IFLA   *See* **International Federation of Library Associations.**

ILL   *See* **interlibrary loan.**

ILS   Integrated library system. An integrated library system, also referred to as a **library management system**, or **library services platform**, is one in which components or modules work together to perform library functions such as ordering, receiving, claiming, cataloging, circulation, reserves, online public access catalog, and database access. It provides onsite and remote use.

Integrated library system   *See* **ILS.**

Interlibrary loan   A process in which libraries lend materials to other libraries, or borrow materials from other libraries, at the request of their patrons.

International Coalition of Library Consortia   An organization that facilitates discussion among library consortia on shared interests. *See* http://icolc.net/.

International Federation of Library Associations   The leading international organization representing the interests of libraries and their users. *See* www.ifla.org.

International Organization for Standards (ISO)   The developer of international standards and specifications for products and services. *See* http://www.iso.org/iso/home.htm.

Invoice data element   A unit of information displayed or pertaining to an invoice. It may include information such as the library addresses, title of the item, **ISBN**, and cost.

IP address   Internet protocol address. A unique identifier composed of four sets of numbers separated by periods that indicates how to reach an Internet computer. IP addresses are used to determine the path to a computer's physical location via interconnected wide area networks and local area networks.

ISBN   International Standard Book Number. A unique 10-digit or 13-digit number assigned to books. It can be used for ordering, invoicing, and finding a title in a database.

ISSN   International Standard Serial Number. A unique eight-digit number assigned to a **serial** publication. It can be used for ordering, invoicing, searching, or linking a serial title in a database.

Levels of access   Password levels, determined by the system administrators, that can provide or deny access and show reduced or enhanced information to an individual user in an ILS or other electronic system or database. For example, while patrons need access to the catalog, they do not need access to the program that actually places an order. *See also* authentication.

Library management system (LMS)   *See* **ILS**.

Library services platform (LSP)   *See* **ILS**.

Licensing agreement   A written contract between the library or institution and the publisher or vendor allowing access to electronic materials or databases. Institutional policies vary concerning which individuals can negotiate and sign such agreements. *See also* **contract** and **general terms and conditions.**

LMS   *See* **ILS**.

Long-range plan   A formulated, systematic plan for predicting future trends and directing future activities to achieve expected results for an organization for periods longer than one year. *See also* **strategic planning**.

LSP   *See* **ILS**.

Machine-readable cataloging *See* **MARC**.

Management reports Reports that are made to order or modified according to individual library requirements. They include reports such as current expenditures, historical expenditures, fulfillment time, or use of electronic resources. Reports can often be generated online via access to computer-based services provided by the **vendor**.

MARC Machine-readable cataloging. A standard file format for storing bibliographic data.

Membership A library may become an institutional member of an association or group either to support the goals of the group or to obtain its published materials. Memberships may be the only way to acquire materials of some groups.

Metadata Data about data; records describing items using standards such as the **Dublin Core** or **MARC** records.

Microform The photographic image of a document reproduced on film. Microfiche and microfilm are common types of microform.

Migration The act of transferring a product or service from one vendor to another. The term can apply to transferring subscriptions, approval plans, or ILS services. It generally involves the preparation and transfer of large sets of data from the old vendor's system into the new vendor's system.

Mix The mix is the percentage of titles that fall into a given subject category (e.g., science, fine arts, humanities, or social sciences) for **serials** or **approval plans**. The **vendor** receives varying levels of **discount** from publishers, with some subject areas tending to generate higher discounts than others. The discount rate that the vendor receives affects the discount the library receives from the vendor for books or the service charge that the library pays to the vendor for serials.

Monograph An item that is complete in one part, or has a finite number of parts, as compared to a serial that has no specific end or number of parts.

Monographic series A group of items related by theme or subject. Each item has an individual title and also has the title of the overall series.

Music score A record of a musical work in which all the parts are written so that the individual parts are all shown.

National Information Standards Organization (NISO) An organization where content publishers, libraries, and software developers work together to create information industry standards. *See* https://www.niso.org/

Nonreturnable Materials that cannot be sent back to the **vendor** or publisher from which they were obtained by the library for a refund, exchange, or **credit**. Some publishers, particularly small ones or professional organizations, will sell to a vendor only when there is an agreement that no titles can be returned.

OCLC A **bibliographic utility** that provides bibliographic records, databases, and other library services, including ILSs throughout the world.

Open access Open access allows unrestricted access via the Internet to scholarly research. This may include scholarly articles, theses, scholarly monographs, book chapters, and other research. *See* https://sparcopen.org/open-access/.

Open archive A database containing full-text articles, preprints, or documents that are available without fees or restrictions on access. *See* http://www.openarchives.org/.

Open Source Software Integrated Library Systems (OSS ILS) Software that is widely available and is not part of a proprietary product.

Out-of-print materials Items no longer available from the publisher and for which there are no plans to print more copies by that publisher. Librarians may locate copies by working with used book dealers or searching on the **Internet**.

Outsourcing The contracting out of library functions such as cataloging to a private enterprise.

Packages Combinations of publications, possibly including journals, books, or databases, sold as a group.

Password A code required to access a computer system or electronic resource.

Patron-driven-acquisition *See* **PDA**.

PDA **Patron-driven-acquisition** is a method of acquiring items for the library based on requests from patrons.

Periodical *See* **serial**.

POD *See also* **patron-driven-acquisition (PDA)**. Purchase-on-demand gives libraries the option to purchase an item when it is requested either directly by a patron or via an interlibrary loan/ILL.

POD **Print-on-demand** is a printing technology as well as a business model in which books and other documents are not printed until the vendor or company receives an order for them. POD is most often done for prints of singular or small quantities and typically reduces costs.

Prepayment A payment made for materials before they are supplied to the library. This practice is especially common for **nonreturnable** or expensive materials. Many publishers require prepayment for selected titles, while most **vendors** of monographs do not require prepayment.

Prepayment credit A percentage of the total library expenditure prepaid to periodical **vendors** who offer libraries a prepayment discount for early payment of the annual renewal invoice.

Preprint A preliminary version of research or presentation made available prior to its formal publication.

Preservation The slowing or prevention of the deterioration of materials by a number of methods including **conservation**, binding, microfilming, or scanning.

Print-on-demand *See* **POD**.

Print run   The number of copies of a book or serial that are printed by the publisher.

Procurement code   A set of legal rules or statutes for acquiring goods or services.

Procurement officer   *See also* **purchasing officer**.

Professional association or society   A group or body of individuals united by a common interest, principle, or purpose pertaining to a specific profession. Such a group may publish materials of special interest to its members. It often makes its materials available to libraries only through institutional membership in the organization. *See also* **membership**.

Profile   The document that tells a **vendor** which materials to supply or not to supply on an **approval** or **blanket order plan**. The library and the vendor must work together closely to create the profile, as it is the instrument that determines the success or failure of any plan. The profile must be monitored continuously and modified as needed for the plan to function optimally.

Property stamping   The act of stamping an item with the name of the library to indicate the library's ownership of the material. A label or tag identification can be used instead of a property stamp.

Purchase-on-demand   *See* **POD**.

Purchase order number   A unique number assigned by the library to identify an order.

Purchasing department   The department in an institution charged with overseeing the purchase of materials. Such departments do not usually involve themselves in the purchase of individual titles for the library but do generally oversee the **RFP** process. They may also be responsible for reviewing, negotiating, and signing **contracts** for electronic resources.

Purchasing officer   An employee of a university or other organization, responsible for buying or approving the purchase of goods and/or services.

Radio-frequency identification   *See* **RFID**.

RDA   Resource Description and Access, the standard for formulating bibliographic data. RDA was released in 2010.

Reformat   To transfer information from one **format** to another as in microfilming or digitizing a print title.

Regional and local publications   Materials published by small local and regional publishers, often in very small print runs. Because most large **vendors** are not able to supply such materials, libraries should arrange with local vendors to acquire these items or work with the publishers directly.

Regional library network   Any nonprofit, multistate organization that promotes, develops, and supports programs related to access to information services for its members, such as Amigos Library Services, PALNI, or Lyrasis.

Request for information   *See* **RFI**.

Request for proposal   *See* **RFP**.

Request for quotation   *See* **RFQ**.

Resource Description and Access   *See* **RDA**.

RFI   Request for information. The RFI requests general information from a publisher or vendor regarding its goods and services. It does not state library requirements or desired elements. RFIs are often valuable tools for a library to determine what it requires prior to writing RFP or RFQ.

RFID   **Radio-frequency identification** is a technology that uses micro-sized computer chips to track items, such as library books and other materials, at a distance.

RFP   **Request for proposal**. The RFP can be viewed as a process as well as a document. As a process, it provides a clear, impartial method for a library to state its needs, evaluate vendor proposals, and justify its vendor selection and contract award, based on objective decisions regarding those proposals rather than solely on emotional reactions either for or against a particular vendor. As a document, it can be used to monitor vendor compliance and performance. In the document, the library's requirements and desired elements for vendor services are clearly articulated as are the steps to be followed for vendors that wish to submit proposals to handle the library's account.

RFQ   **Request for quotation**. When using an RFQ, awards are based on the lowest-price bid for a good or service. No other factors are taken into consideration in a true RFQ although in some modified versions of the RFQ they may be considered to a lesser degree. This process is best suited to the purchase of goods rather than services.

Rush orders   Orders that are placed with a **vendor** or publisher with instructions that they will be supplied to the library on a priority basis.

Sales representative   An **agent** for the **vendor**, representing its products and services to libraries. The sales representative visits the library one or more times per year as needed to consult about the library's needs, check on the library's satisfaction with the vendor's service, discuss trends in the market place, and apprise the library of new developments or services available through the vendor.

Security strips   Magnetic strips placed in an item or affixed to nonprint media. The strips are sensitized so that an alarm will sound if someone attempts to take the materials out of the building or area without checking them out and properly desensitizing them.

Selectors   Generally found in academic or large public libraries, librarians who determine which materials to purchase for particular subject areas, monitor budget allocations and expenditures, and monitor approval plans. They may also be responsible for working closely with academic departments and other constituents and for managing and evaluating the collections in their areas. *See also* **bibliographers, collection development librarians, subject liaisons**, or **subject-matter specialists**.

Serial   A publication in any **format**, issued in parts with numerical or chronological designations, intended to continue indefinitely, such as magazines, newspapers, yearbooks, and so forth.

Serials check-in   A control system that records the receipt of print **serials**. The system may be manual or part of an **ILS**.

Serials holdings (statement or data) standard   The standard for serials holdings that sets the rules for creating consistent records of the print serials located at a particular institution. It outlines the data elements, prescribed punctuation, and specification for displaying the data. The volumes or years of a **serial** a library owns are accessible to patrons and staff in the holdings data, which also includes location. Included in the ANSI/NISO Z39.71–2006 Holdings Statement for Bibliographic Items. *See* https://www.niso.org/publications/z3971-2006-r2011.

Serials price increase   The amount or percentage that the price of a **serial** or category of serials has increased from one year or period to another. Because the cost of serials has grown at such a rapid rate, many libraries, especially large academic and research libraries, have experienced difficulty subscribing to all the titles needed by their patrons. Prices have increased faster than the consumer price index over the past decades. Total annual serials expenditures vary with the type and size of the library but generally range from a few hundred dollars for school and small public libraries to millions of dollars for medium to large academic and research libraries and can comprise half the of the library's total material budget.

Serials vendor   *See* **subscription services**.

Service charge   A charge above the cost of the titles managed by the **vendor** for the assistance or service provided to the library. The amount of the service charge generally depends on the size and **mix** of the library's account. Service charges are usually associated with serials accounts due to limited or no publisher discounts.

Service representative   The person at the **vendor**'s office who is assigned to assist the library with all areas of its account, ranging from answering simple questions to solving complex problems.

Shelf-ready materials   Items that are supplied by a **vendor** that are already processed and ready to be shelved by the library, for an added charge. They are cataloged, have labels with call numbers, are marked with the library's property stamp, and are ready for circulating. Various other services, such as affixing **security strips** and **serials check-in** from a remote site, may be available; services vary by vendor.

Simultaneous publication   Books that are published at the same time in two or more countries or in two or more formats. **Vendors** of **approval plans** providing materials from multiple countries or in multiple formats need mechanisms to know which format the library prefers and avoid unwanted **duplication**.

Site licenses   *See* **licensing agreement**.

Societies, associations, research institutes   *See* **professional association or society**.

Sole source   The only source that can supply an item or a service.

Split a contract   To award segments of a contract to two or more vendors.

Standard   A measure that serves as a nationally or internationally agreed upon basis or example to conform to, ensuring consistency. The major organizations concerned with library standards are **ANSI**, **NISO**, and **ISO**.

Standing order   *See* **STO**.

Statement of financial solvency   A statement supplied on behalf of a **vendor** by a reputable financial institution or auditor attesting to its financial strength and indicating its capacity to meet its liabilities. This document provides important information to a library that is deciding which vendor to do business with.

STO. Standing order   An instruction to a **vendor** to supply a specified title regularly. Standing orders are generally placed for nonperiodical **serials** such as annuals, yearbooks, and series. These titles are generally not paid for until the library receives them. Some libraries, however, opt to prepay for them as part of their serials renewals even though the price may be an estimate.

Strategic planning   A formulated, detailed plan in which an organization identifies and develops its long-range goals and selects activities for achieving them. *See also* **long-range plan**.

SUB   An abbreviation for **subscription**. Subscriptions are a regular method of procurement for publications such as periodicals, journals, magazines, newspapers, and items generally issued more than once a year. These are generally paid for in advance of receipt by the library.

Subject liaisons   *See* **collection development librarians** or **selectors**.

Subject-matter specialists.   *See* **collection development librarians or selectors.**

Subject parameters   The part of the **approval plan** profile that specifies which subjects should be sent to the library, which should be provided as bibliographic notifications, and which should not be sent at all. They are used in combination with nonsubject parameters to form the library's total approval profile.

Subscription   *See* **SUB**.

Subscription agency or agent   *See* **subscription services**.

Subscription services   A commercial agency that processes **serials** orders for all types of libraries. It provides a variety of services for the library including placing orders with the publishers, processing renewals, consolidating many publisher invoices into one or several **vendor**-generated invoices, processing claims, and providing a variety of **management reports** and specialized **computer-based services**. Vendors maintain detailed records for titles that the library has on order with them.

Technical services   Library-wide units, often found in medium or large libraries, which handle acquisitions (procurement, receipt, and payment approval) and cataloging of materials in all formats and languages. These operations may include binding, marking, and in some cases stacks maintenance and collection development.

Title-by-title selection   Items that are selected one at a time instead of being received through **approval plans**, **STO**s, or **SUB**s. These titles may be ordered on the basis of librarians' decisions or patron requests. *See also* **firm orders** and **patron-driven-acquisitions**.

Title change   The action of a publisher of a serial to change the title of that serial from one name to another. It is imperative that a **vendor** has mechanisms in place to notify libraries of such changes so that receipt can continue without interruption.

Transfer assistance allowance   A onetime allowance granted by a **vendor** to the library, usually in the form of a credit percentage or a reduced **service charge**, to defray the cost to the library of transferring its titles to one vendor from another vendor.

Transfer process   The transfer of titles in a given category (e.g., **serials**) from one or more vendors to different vendors. Also known as the transition process.

Transition process   *See* **transfer process**.

Trial electronic resources request   A request by the library asking the publisher or **vendor** to supply free access to an electronic resource for a limited period. The library generally uses such a trial to decide whether to add the resource to its collection.

University press   A press that is the publishing arm of a university. University presses range in size from large, publishing more than 200 books a year, to small, producing very small **print runs**. Supported and controlled by their universities, they are known for publishing scholarly research for specialized audiences, but they may also publish some trade books intended for general readership as well as scholarly journals. Their publishing programs often reflect local or regional interests. Many presses, especially smaller ones, exist primarily on subsidies from their universities, and others make a profit.

URL   Uniform resource locator. The Internet address that represents a web server and its documents. It is usually preceded by "http://" for websites and often, but not always, includes "www." For example, the URL for the American Library Association is http://www.ala.org.

User ID   An assigned user name for accessing a product. Used in conjunction with a password to provide full authentication of the user. *See also* **password**.

Value-added service   A service offered by a vendor that enhances a basic product thus adding value to it, such as adding table of contents notes to a cataloging record.

Vanity publishers   A publisher that requires authors to pay for some or all of the costs of producing their books.

Vendor   The seller or provider of materials to libraries, regardless of format. May be used interchangeably with **agent** and **dealer**.

Vendor evaluation project   A plan designed to appraise or judge vendor performance—how well the vendor met the conditions of its contract with the library. Such factors as vendor turnaround time for orders, invoices, and **claims**, as well as other performance data elements can be quantitatively measured. More subjective, qualitative measures regarding the vendor's service may also be considered in the evaluation.

Vendor performance data   Data used in vendor evaluation projects, including such elements as **fulfillment rates** or times, rate of returns for approval plans, or number of claims. Many **ILS**s and other library systems can provide some of these data for the library.

Vendor-sponsored instructional program   A program that provides instruction and information for new library customers to learn about the vendor and its services, and for existing customers to learn about new vendor services and developments.

Vendor's host (or in-house) system   A computer system used internally by the vendor. Customers may have access to portions of the system via the **Internet**, allowing them to see general information and records related to their library. *See also* **computer-based services**.

WMS   **WorldShare Management Services** is OCLC's **ILS**, comprised of an integrated suite of cloud-based library management and discovery applications, offering librarians a comprehensive way to manage library workflows and access to library collections and services. *See* http://www.oclc.org/en/worldshare.html.

WorldShare Management Services   *See* **WMS**.

Z39.50 protocol   International Standard ISO 39.50 is a search-and-retrieval protocol by which one computer can query another computer and transfer resulting records. This protocol provides the framework for online public access catalog users to search other systems bringing a seamless interface among systems that would otherwise be incompatible. *See* http://www.loc.gov/z3950/agency/.

ABOUT THE EDITORS AND CONTRIBUTORS

SEVER BORDEIANU is the director of technical services, outreach librarian for philosophy/religion and foreign languages, and professor in the College of University Libraries & Learning Sciences at the University of New Mexico, Albuquerque, New Mexico. He also teaches undergraduate courses in the Organization, Information & Learning Sciences program. He previously worked at the University of Michigan and University of California, Irvine. He received his BA in philosophy and his MA in philosophy and German literature from the University of Mississippi. He received his MLIS from the University of Texas at Austin. He is the author of a book and over 30 articles, chapters, and columns and has given numerous presentations and webinars. His research and consulting interests include cataloging (serials and authority control), competitive procurement/RFP process, and collection development. He has served on several RFP committees.

STEPHEN BOSCH is the materials, budget, procurement, and licensing librarian at the University of Arizona, Tucson, Arizona. He received his BA in history and religion from Marietta College and his MA in Chinese history and his MLS from the University of Arizona. He has authored five books and over 30 articles, and book chapters. He has given numerous presentations and webinars on a variety of topics. He has chaired and served on many editorial and advisory boards and state and national committees and received the ALA-ALCTS Leadership in Library Acquisitions Award. His research and consulting interests include serials and books pricing, the economic models for scholarly communications, the changing landscape of the information industry, licensing, procurement, and acquisitions. Stephen has participated in various roles on many RFP/RFI committees.

LEA J. BRIGGS is the administrative and operations coordinator and assistant professor in the College of University Libraries and Learning Sciences at the University of New Mexico, Albuquerque, New Mexico. She also manages the LIBROS Consortium, a group of 17 academic libraries in New Mexico, and teaches undergraduate courses in the Organization, Information & Learning Sciences program. She received her BS in accounting from Northern State University, her MLS from Emporia State University, and her EdD in educational administration, specializing in adult and higher education, from the University of South Dakota. She has published several articles and given numerous presentations and webinars. She has served on state, regional, and national boards and committees and received the Librarian of the Year Award from the South Dakota Library Association. Her research and consulting interests include library spaces, management, services to distance students, the competitive procurement/RFP process, and strategic planning. She has co-chaired and served on several RFP committees.

EDWARD CASTILLO-PADILLA is the facility services manager at the College of University Libraries & Learning Sciences at the University of New Mexico. Prior to his current position, he was a manager in Public Services/Access Services. He attended the University of New Mexico and is the author of a chapter on disaster recovery. As facility services manager, his leadership helped the library recover from two major floods and a fire, earning him the Exemplary Employee Award. He also served as the library's functional expert on several RFP committees to select vendors for disaster recovery.

MARY CHEVREAU is the chief executive officer of the Kitchener Public Library in Kitchener, Ontario, Canada, where she provides the vision and leadership for programs and services for the Kitchener and surrounding communities. With a focus on print and digital literacy, and as a champion for arts and culture, she participates on boards, roundtables, and community initiatives to promote and strengthen the library's place as a core community hub. Through her leadership, the library is developing a reputation as a library innovator in Canada, with the first Wi-Fi lending program in the country, a 200+ musical instrument lending library, and a multiformat/media storytelling initiative through tattoo art entitled "Our Ink, Our Stories." She received her BA in music from Western University (formerly the University of Western Ontario) followed by an MLIS also from Western University. Prior to joining the library, she ran the North American Sales Division for Innovative Interfaces, a library management systems provider. During her tenure, she literally worked with hundreds of public libraries in North America, an experience that enables her to view the future of libraries through a unique lens.

JUSTIN D. CLARKE is the director of sales and marketing for HARRAS-SOWITZ Booksellers and Subscription Agents, where he previously served as product manager and regional sales manager. He holds a degree in German language and literature from Oberlin College. Prior to joining HARRAS-SOWITZ, he worked in technical services at Swarthmore College Library and was the SFX administrator for the TriCollege Consortium. He also worked in Collection Development at Temple University setting up foreign language approval plans. He speaks regularly at conferences on the vendor perspective of acquisitions, best practices, and activity in the information industry.

SUSANNE K. CLEMENT is the director of collections, outreach librarian for history, and associate professor in the College of University Libraries & Learning Sciences at the University of New Mexico, Albuquerque, New Mexico. She has more than 20 years of professional experience as a corporate solo librarian and as a faculty librarian with various administrative positions at University of Kansas, Utah State University, and University of New Mexico. She received her BA and MA in history from Illinois State University and her MLIS from Emporia State University. She has been an instructor for ALCTS for several years, teaching fundamentals of collection development and management, and has published in the areas of collection development, including a book, several book chapters, and more than 40 articles and conference proceedings. She is currently coeditor of *Collection Management*. She most recently cochaired an RFP committee for a serials vendor.

CATHERINE JANNIK DOWNEY is the department head of Access Services and Information Commons and associate professor in the Daniel J. Kaufman Library at Georgia Gwinnett College, Lawrenceville, Georgia. Her responsibilities include the archives and institutional repository. She received her AB in history and government from Sweet Briar College. She received her MLIS and MA in history from the University of Southern Mississippi. She is one of the founding organizers of the Access Services Conference. She has served on statewide committees, ALA-LITA committees, and as a reviewer for the *Southeastern Librarian*. She is the coauthor of two articles and has given numerous presentations on topics including institutional repositories, electronic theses and dissertations, RFID, and civil rights. She has served on two RFQ committees.

CHRISTOPHER HOLLY is a director of Software as a Service Innovation for EBSCO Information Services. Prior to joining EBSCO, he served as the executive director for Cooperative Computer Services (CCS), a 24-member public library consortium in northern Illinois. He received his BA in music with a minor in anthropology from the University of Virginia. He holds an MLIS degree from the University of Pittsburgh and an MBA degree from Loyola University Chicago. He has focused on improving systems and services for libraries for more than 15 years. Before leading CCS, he served in a variety of customer-centric roles at Ex Libris and then Innovative Interfaces, where he worked closely with academic, public, and special libraries.

LAURA KOHL is the principal cataloger and assistant professor in the College of University Libraries & Learning Sciences at the University of New Mexico, Albuquerque, New Mexico. She received her BA in history from the

University of New Mexico and her MLIS from the University of Pittsburgh where she specialized in Archival Science. She is the author of several articles and chapters on topics ranging from cataloging to workflow within libraries. Prior to working at University of New Mexico, she was a cataloger and archivist for the New Mexico History Museum in Santa Fe. She was the lead cataloger for the Historic Maps of New Mexico Project supported by the Council on Library and Information Resources and the Andrew W. Mellon Foundation, through their Cataloging Hidden Special Collections and Archives program. Her experience includes the cataloging of special collection material, PCC and NACO cataloging, archival processing and encoding, collection management, and library and archival preservation and binding.

KIRSTEN LEONARD is the executive director of the Private Academic Library Network of Indiana (PALNI) in Indianapolis, Indiana. Prior to joining PALNI, she was at Indiana University Kokomo as the assistant director of Institutional Research and Electronic Resources/Documents Librarian. As the CEO of PALNI, she oversees 11 staff and coordinators, strategic objectives from all functional areas, and needs of the PALNI libraries. By reducing duplication of effort, this deeper collaboration has allowed staff in PALNI libraries to focus, explore, and innovate to more effectively address user needs and provide better services. She holds an MLIS from Wayne State University and an MA from Case Western Reserve University. She is an advocate for library collaboration having served on the OCLC Global Council and the International Coalition of Library Consortia coordinating committee and serves on the board of the Academic Libraries of Indiana. She has conducted research on library web pages, published a chapter on electronic resource management, and was an author on the Indiana University's *White Paper on the Future of Cataloging*. She is a graduate of the Harvard Leadership Institute for Academic Librarians and is a recurring keynote speaker on deep collaboration to consortia and groups of academic libraries. She has led multiple Indiana University system-wide and consortia review processes and negotiations for library systems, services, and resources.

ANNE E. MCKEE is the program officer for resource sharing at the Greater Western Library Alliance (GWLA). She is the GWLA staff liaison to both the Collection Development and Resource Sharing/Document Delivery Committees. She received her BA in library science from Western Kentucky University and her MLS from Indiana University Bloomington as well as has done some graduate work in Folk Studies. She has had a very diverse career in librarianship, including head of serials at two academic libraries, a former sales representative for two subscription vendors, and now as a consortium officer for the past 18+ years. A former president of NASIG, Inc., she is a member of the *Serials Review* editorial board and has served on national/international committees and several library advisory boards and most recently was a working group member for the Charlotte Initiative: an Andrew W. Mellon funded research grant. She has given numerous national/international presentations and webinars as well as being the author/coauthor of several articles, sidebars, and a book chapter. Her primary research or consulting interest is in negotiation: teaching how to negotiate and the imperative of utilizing ethical negotiations. She has the unique perspective of having written or served on several RFP/RFI committees on three fronts: a consortium officer, a vendor representative, and an academic librarian.

ANDREW K. PACE is the executive director, Technical Research at OCLC. He leads a team of research scientists and engineers who track library and broader data science trends and is responsible for building a coordinated R&D strategy for OCLC Research. Previously, he directed the development of the WorldShare Platform, WorldShare Management Services, CONTENTdm, and several other library management applications. Prior to joining OCLC, he spent nine years at North Carolina State University Libraries as head of information technology. He has a BA in rhetoric and communication studies from the University of Virginia and earned his MLIS from the Catholic University of America. He is a past president of the Library Information Technology Association (LITA), a division of ALA, and is a current member of the ALA Council, and the ALA Executive Board for 2016–2019. He has served on numerous ALA committees and the NISO editorial board. He has published widely in trade magazines, scholarly journals, books, and is the author of *The Ultimate Digital Library* (2002), the first book on the relationships between libraries, vendors, and dot-coms. He has written several RFPs and has read and responded to more than he can count.

SHANNON D. PEARCE is the acquisitions librarian for the Austin Independent School District in Austin, Texas. She previously worked at Garza High School in Austin. She received her BA in English and theater from Graceland University, completed education coursework at Texas State University, and received her MSIS from the University of Texas at Austin. She is certified as a school librarian and English language arts teacher in the state of Texas. Her areas of interest include collection development, shared digital collections, and preventing summer reading loss. She has chaired, cochaired, and served on several RFP committees.

KYLE R. RIMKUS is the preservation librarian and assistant professor of Library Administration at the University of Illinois at Urbana-Champaign, where he is responsible for articulating and leading the implementation of a library-wide strategy for preserving and providing access to digital collections. Kyle received his BA in Germanic studies from the University of Illinois at Chicago and his MS in library and information science as well as his MA in French literature from the University of Illinois at Urbana-Champaign. He has published broadly on issues related to digital preservation and digital library management.

PATRICIA M. RODGERS is the director of the North American Library Services office for HARRASSOWITZ Booksellers and Subscription Agents. She received her BA from Clemson University and ML from the University of South Carolina. She previously worked at the Baugh Biomedical Library/ University of South Alabama as assistant director of technical services and finance. She has held positions in the Medical Library Association, the Southern Chapter of the Medical Library Association, Alabama Health Libraries Association, and NASIG. She authors the RFP responses for the North American customers for HARRASSOWITZ.

LEE SOCHAY is the head of acquisitions at the Michigan State University Libraries. He received his BS in electrical engineering from Michigan Technological University. He received his MLIS from Wayne State University. With 19 years of experience as a sales engineer in both writing RFPs and developing proposals, he was hired by the Michigan State University Libraries to develop the RFP for a discovery tool and implement the project with the successful bidder. As the head of acquisitions, he has implemented the RFP process for subscription management services.

CHRISTINE N. SRAHA manages the acquisitions unit in the College of University Libraries & Learning Sciences at the University of New Mexico, Albuquerque, New Mexico. She received her BA, with honors, in linguistics from the University of Kansas. She received her master of accounting degree, with honors, from the University of New Mexico. She recently served as the acquisitions functional expert on an RFP committee to select a serials vendor and previously was a member of the RFP committee that selected the library's new ILS.

KATINA STRAUCH, emerita assistant dean of technical services, at the Addlestone Library, College of Charleston, retired in September 2016 to devote herself full-time to running the Annual Charleston Library Conference, which she founded in 1980; to editing *Against the Grain*, which she founded in 1989; and to help with the Charleston Company (includes the *Charleston Advisor*, the *Charleston Report*, the *Fiesole Retreats*), which she cofounded with Becky Lenzini. She is also interested in pursuing other opportunities. She holds a BA in economics and an MLS, both from the University of North Carolina at Chapel Hill. She had a distinguished career in libraries, winning numerous awards and serving on the IMLS board. She has published widely. She has two children—Raymond, who is in the Army Corps of Engineers, and Ileana, an oncologist and hematologist—and five grandchildren. She has been married to her husband, Bruce, for over 40 years.

DANA D. VINKE is the principal librarian of operations at the Torrance Public Library in Torrance, California, where he oversees adult services, facilities, and technology. He has provided adult programming workshops for UCLA, the California Librarian Association Conference, and Infopeople. He received his BA in psychology from California State University, Long Beach, and his MLIS from the University of California, Los Angeles. He was the 2015 award recipient of the CLA Technology Professional Award. He serves on the Council for California Center for the Book Advisory Committee and the Long Beach City College Library Technician Advisory Committee. He has been the project manager on numerous RFP processes, including ILS, physical materials procurement, and digital materials.

FRANCES C. WILKINSON is the senior associate dean and professor in the College of University Libraries & Learning Sciences at the University of New Mexico, Albuquerque, New Mexico. She is also administrative director of, and teaches graduate course in, the Organization, Information & Learning Sciences program, which offers BS (STEM), MA, and PhD degrees. She received her BA, with distinction, in communication, MPA, and EdD in educational leadership from the University of New Mexico. She received her MLS from the University of Arizona. She is the author of seven books and over 50 articles, chapters, and columns and has given numerous presentations and webinars. She has served on editorial and advisory boards and state and national committees and received the ALA-ALCTS Leadership in Library Acquisitions Award. Her research and consulting interests include leadership, management, organizational development, competitive procurement/RFP process, disaster preparedness and recovery, acquisitions, and computer ergonomics. She has chaired or served on numerous RFP committees.

INDEX

Note: Page numbers followed by words "tab" and "fig" in italics indicate tables and figures, respectively.